THE
DOLLAR
MELTDOWN

THE
DOLLAR
MELTDOWN

Surviving the Coming Currency Crisis
with Gold, Oil, and Other
Unconventional Investments

Charles Goyette

Portfolio

PORTFOLIO
Published by the Penguin Group
Penguin Group (USA) Inc., 375 Hudson Street, New York, New York 10014, U.S.A.
Penguin Group (Canada), 90 Eglinton Avenue East, Suite 700, Toronto, Ontario, Canada M4P 2Y3
(a division of Pearson Penguin Canada Inc.)
Penguin Books Ltd, 80 Strand, London WC2R 0RL, England
Penguin Ireland, 25 St. Stephen's Green, Dublin 2, Ireland (a division of Penguin Books Ltd)
Penguin Books Australia Ltd, 250 Camberwell Road, Camberwell, Victoria 3124, Australia
(a division of Pearson Australia Group Pty Ltd)
Penguin Books India Pvt Ltd, 11 Community Centre, Panchsheel Park, New Delhi – 110 017, India
Penguin Group (NZ), 67 Apollo Drive, Rosedale, North Shore 0632, New Zealand
(a division of Pearson New Zealand Ltd)
Penguin Books (South Africa) (Pty) Ltd, 24 Sturdee Avenue, Rosebank,
Johannesburg 2196, South Africa

Penguin Books Ltd, Registered Offices: 80 Strand, London WC2R 0RL, England

First published in 2009 by Portfolio, a member of Penguin Group (USA) Inc.

1   3   5   7   9   10   8   6   4   2

Copyright © Charles Goyette, 2009
All rights reserved

PUBLISHER'S NOTE: This publication is designed to provide accurate and authoritative information in
regard to the subject matter covered. It is sold with the understanding that the publisher is not
engaged in rendering legal, accounting or other professional services. If you require legal advice or
other expert assistance, you should seek the services of a competent professional.

LIBRARY OF CONGRESS CATALOGING-IN-PUBLICATION DATA
Goyette, Charles.
The dollar meltdown : surviving the impending currency crisis with gold, oil,
and other unconventional investments / Charles Goyette.
p. cm.
Includes bibliographical references and index.
ISBN 978-1-59184-284-2
1. Commodity exchanges. 2. Commodity futures. 3. Investments. 4. Financial crises—United
States—History—21st century. I. Title.
HG6046.G69 2009
332.63—dc22   2009021866

Printed in the United States of America

To my wife, Ali, who makes everything she encounters better, including me; and to my sons Michael and Steven, who believe in Liberty.

Contents

SECTION I: WHERE WE ARE

1. The Day Jim in Scottsdale Figured It All Out—and How
   the Treasury Secretary Saved Him from the Stock Market Crash!   3

2. Bailouts: Banking Blunders and Boondoggles   11

3. Debt: First There Is a Mountain . . . Then There's a Bigger Mountain!   29

SECTION II: HOW WE GOT HERE

4. Gold: The Quality of Money   43

5. Inflation: The Quantity of Money   56

6. American Money: A Superior Sleight of Hand   71

SECTION III: WHAT HAPPENS NEXT

7. How It Comes Down: Likely Scenarios   87

8. Toppling the Dollar: Your New World Order Is Waiting!   107

9. The Authorities Are in Charge: Or So They Think!   121

SECTION IV: WHAT TO DO

10. What to Do: Overview   139

11. Investing in Gold: Glittering Opportunity   148

12. Silver: Who Says It's Second Place?   166

13. Oil: Still Making the World Go Around   177

14. Real Things: Can't Live Without 'Em   196

15. Bonds: A Crash Course   211

16. Alternative Currencies: Worth Mentioning   222

17. Last Thoughts   230

Information and Resources for Investors   233

Acknowledgments   237

Bibliography   239

Index   241

SECTION I

WHERE WE ARE

The Day Jim in Scottsdale Figured It All Out—and How the Treasury Secretary Saved Him from the Stock Market Crash!

It didn't have to be that specific day. It could have been weeks or months earlier or later. But something broke through for Jim on an ordinary day in the summer of 2008. I know because he called me on the air to let me know.

"Jim in Scottsdale, good morning," I said, punching up line four on my morning talk show in Phoenix.

"Charles, I have been listening to you talk about the government debt and the U.S. dollar for a couple of years now. At first when you talked about what you call the Washington Party—the mess the Republicans and Democrats have gotten us into—it used to make me mad. Because I thought my party was different and it was the other guys who were to blame. Anyway, I just wanted you to know I sold all my stock yesterday. I'm buying gold."

"Jim, you've had a breakthrough," I said. "What finally got to you?"

"Well, your reports on the real estate market got my attention," he said. "I can see some of the things you were talking about in my own neighborhood."

"Foreclosure rates are rising," I said, "and we're just getting started."

"Yeah, that got me thinking," he continued. "But it was the story you told about the treasury secretary in China that did it. Now I'm convinced. These people are out of their minds! So I sold $100,000 worth of stock. I want out of the stock market. And out of the dollar. Period. And I'm going to start buying gold!"

Jim in Scottsdale sure got the point of the story. It was about John W. Snow, the prior Bush secretary of the United States Treasury, in China a few years ago, instructing the Chinese to save less and borrow more! Americans saved nothing; the Chinese are among the biggest savers in the world. I told the story because it explained the philosophy responsible for turning America's economy upside down. And Snow's bizarro-world advice to the Chinese could be traced directly to the current chairman of the Federal Reserve System. So I brought it up and wondered aloud at the secretary's confusion. China's economy had been growing like crazy; ours not so much. Their economic strength was waxing; ours was waning. We, some of the world's richest people, had to borrow from them, some of the world's poorest, to keep our federal beast fed. And Mr. Snow thought the Chinese needed to take a lesson from us?

"They're just heeding the advice of that ancient Chinese sage Ben Franklin," I said. "It's difficult to translate from the original Chinese, but it goes something like this: A penny saved is a penny earned!"

But Mr. Snow had been listening to a different Ben, a Princeton economist named Ben Bernanke, who served as chairman of Bush's Council of Economic Advisers when he offered up his "they save too much" theory. This Ben, now the chairman of the Federal Reserve, and the rest of the Washington wizards know better than Ben Franklin. They would have the Chinese spend their way to prosperity. His advice for the Chinese is bad enough for them, but what about for us? Just who does Secretary Snow and Chairman Bernanke think will fund America's debt if the Chinese don't?

We're about to find out.

And so on a day in early June 2008, when the Dow closed at about 12,300, Jim sold his stock. It wasn't at the top when the Dow was at 14,000. It wasn't at even at 13,000 where it had been the month before. But Jim could see that ideas have consequences and that there were some pretty peculiar notions about money and wealth going around in Washington. Those ideas have already determined the fate of the U.S. dollar. It's not going to be pretty and Jim decided not to be victimized by the dollar meltdown.

The New York Times reported that Secretary Snow thought to lecture the Chinese during his visit on "better methods of analyzing credit risk and a greater willingness to make loans based on objective judgments of risks and opportunities." Perhaps the secretary's attention should not have wandered so far from home, because it would soon become apparent that credit risks more properly his concern were screaming to be analyzed. Saving nothing and spending more than we earned was about to get America in deep trouble. The mortgage bubble was growing. And even as Snow spoke, the dollar was beginning a thirty-three-month move that burned away 25 percent of its value against the euro and foreshadowed the meltdown to come.

Jim in Scottsdale didn't have to wake up to trouble ahead for the U.S. economy on that particular day. Often a good look at the metastasizing U.S. debt moves people to action. For example, Jim could have been paying attention a few years earlier when Congress raised the government's debt ceiling to $8.18 trillion. This is the way the event was reported in *The Washington Post* on November 19, 2004:

> With last night's passage of the debt ceiling increase, the government's borrowing limit has climbed by $2.23 trillion since President Bush took office: by $450 billion in 2002, by a record $984 billion in 2003 and by $800 billion this year. *Just the increase in the debt ceiling over the past three years is nearly 2 1/2 times the entire federal debt accumulated between 1776 and 1980.* (Emphasis added.)

Gold was $442 that day. Or Jim could have gotten the message sixteen months later. On March 16, 2006, the U.S. Senate voted to raise the debt ceiling again, this time to $9 trillion. Gold was $554.

But picking some other day that Jim might have started buying gold misses the point. Gold has a long way to go just to again equal its highs of a generation ago. In inflation-adjusted terms the current price would have to reach $2,500 an ounce or more! But at some point people's primary concern will be "How many ounces of gold do I have?" rather than "What is the dollar value of my gold?"

In deciding to act, Jim dodged the stock market train wreck. Nine months later the Dow was down about 45 percent from Jim's exit point;

the Standard & Poor's 500 index had fallen by 50 percent. If he hadn't gotten out, Jim's losses, depending on when he bought his stocks, would probably have been enormous. In the meantime, Jim has also gotten out of an irredeemable paper currency that has lost 96 percent of its purchasing power under the Federal Reserve System's mismanagement. He has established a position in the world's longest lasting form of money. And he has done so at a time when the conditions that will drive the dollar lower and gold much higher are accelerating, as you will discover in this book.

The future of the dollar has already been determined. It doesn't depend on whether Democrats or Republicans are in charge. About the same time that Jim realized the dollar was in big trouble, I agreed on the air with Senate majority leader Harry Reid that the fiscally reckless Republicans did need to be thrown out of office. But I also said that with his bunch in charge it would still be spend, Spend, SPEND! He ducked the issue. Said something about everybody in Washington needing to work together to get things done.

Get things done? Haven't these people done enough?

- In the months after the election of President Obama, Americans were losing jobs at the rate of 22,000 a day; from January 2007 through the first quarter of 2009, they'd lost 5.1 million jobs; 13.7 million Americans were out of work and 32.2 million Americans were on food stamps.
- America lost more than a quarter of its manufacturing jobs, 4.4 million altogether, in the eight Bush years.
- Americans' retirement plans have been smashed; pension funds are at risk; annuities and the insurance companies behind them are shaky; the government programs that were said to back them up do not have the money to do so.
- By February 2009 the U.S. government had committed $9.7 trillion to the bailouts, an amount Bloomberg News reported sufficient to pay off more than 90 percent of the nation's mortgages. In March Bloomberg upped its estimate of government loans, spending, and guarantees in

the programs to $12.8 trillion, more than all the existing U.S. national debt.

- One in eight American homes either were in foreclosure or had payments past due at the end of 2008; U.S. homes have lost $6.1 trillion in value in the last few years, $3.3 trillion in 2008 alone; almost 19 million homes in the United States sit vacant, unoccupied.

- $50 trillion in value disappeared from world financial markets—stocks, bonds, currencies—in 2008 alone; in a few short months after the bank bailouts got under way Americans lost $11 trillion in the stock markets.

- Republicans and Democrats have conspired to give us a military debacle based on false representations (including forged documents) that will cost $3 to $5 trillion or more.

- The parties have collaborated to produce record debt of $12 trillion; President Obama acknowledges the prospect of "trillion-dollar deficits for years to come." Trillion-dollar deficits? The 2009 deficit alone is looking more like $2 trillion, so half the budget will have to be borrowed. Meanwhile lurking right around the corner are monstrous unfunded federal liabilities (pension and medical promises made by the government upon which people rely, but for which no provision has been made to pay). The dollar, once "good as gold," has come close to resembling the peso, as it, along with gas and groceries, has been rocking up and down as though alternating between the fever of inflation and the chill of depression—never a good sign.

Haven't these people done enough?

Enough. Jim figured it out in 2008. But the gold market itself woke up in 2002. Maybe I can tell you why.

The day after the 2002 midterm elections, Republican senator Jon Kyl joined me on the air in my studio. The Republican advantage in the House had grown. It was the first time since FDR that the president's party gained in the off-year elections of his first term. And they retook the Senate. Kyl, chairman of the Senate Republican Policy Committee, was flush from victory and looking forward to being a part of the new Senate majority. I had other priorities:

"Can you look me in the eye and tell me that in two years the federal government will be smaller and cost less?" I asked.

Kyl was briefly disoriented. Deer-in-the-headlights look. "Well, it sure better be," he said after an uncomfortably long pause.

"You don't sound too confident about it," I replied. The national debt ceiling at the time was $6.4 trillion. Now it's $12.1 trillion.

Markets move on news and information and are said to be pretty good at discounting future events. By the spring of 2002, the gold market, in its prescience, decided the American empire, like the Russian, the British, and the Roman empires before it, was going to go for broke—literally. Florida senator Bob Graham was chairman of the Senate Intelligence Committee at the time. He later told me and my listeners that in February 2002 the commander of the Central Command, General Tommy Franks, confided to him that resources were being taken off the pursuit of Osama bin Laden in Afghanistan to prepare for Bush's elective war in Iraq. On March 16 in Jeddah, Vice President Cheney met with Saudi Arabia's heads of state. The word was out. With Bush and the neocons starting to promote a larger war in the Middle East, sober observers had figured out that Republicans and Democrats were going to bankrupt the country and destroy the dollar. On March 27, 2002, gold moved above $300 an ounce to stay.

After the Republican majority had made a mess of things for a few years, and sent gold to $625, Americans thought it was time to try the Democrats again and gave them a majority in both houses in the next midterm elections, on November 7, 2006.

But it was business as usual. A year later the Senate voted another $850 billion increase in the U.S. debt ceiling, increasing it to almost $10 trillion. Gold had begun the month at $672; that day it traded at about $740.

But there is much more to come. Gold is like a canary in a coal mine. Its price is a referendum on the quality and quantity of government money. It is signaling the meltdown of the dollar. Conventional investments have been the place to be in the recent past: stocks from 1982 to

2000; real estate boomed as the authorities engineered a loose credit environment to cushion the consequences of their prior bubble popping; the dot-com market. But gold's recent advances signal that we are in a period of major transition now. The American dollar's role as the world's reserve currency is inherently unstable and the signs of a breakdown are all around. Just as the monetary authorities have been unable to reinflate the high-tech bubble or the real estate bubble, when the dollar bubble is finally burst, no other paper currency will be able to take its place—at least for a generation or two when the costly lessons of irredeemable currency may have to be relearned in another era.

This book will help you learn those lessons—before the calamity. But it is not for the faint of heart or for those poisoned by a pointless loyalty to a particular party. It includes a straightforward, clear discussion of the mess the Republicans and Democrats have made of America's prospects and prosperity. And it makes clear that you have options, that you can protect yourself and profit even in this time of financial turbulence. If you are uncertain about today's economic environment, you will want to read the first sections carefully. Section I shows you where we are today. You'll get the whole story on America's debt, both visible and hidden. You'll learn how bailout bills and stimulus spending have dug us in an even deeper hole and what it all means for the future. Section II describes how we got into this mess. It is particularly helpful because you will learn to see old familiar patterns in some of the newest economic developments. This will help you judge the future by the past. It lays out the real fundamentals about money and shows you exactly how the monetary system in the United States today has been crippled so that you can avoid being victimized by it. Section III puts it all together: how the dollar meltdown happens, the most likely scenarios, the role of foreign creditors like China, and how the authorities will react to these problems of their own making. A currency crisis is not a pleasant event. The dollar meltdown will change America and you'll want to be ready for it when it comes. Section IV focuses on how you can survive the meltdown and even prosper. You'll get practical investment advice for the difficult crisis ahead. If you already understand the dollar meltdown, the importance of tangible assets like gold and silver, oil, and other natural resources in a currency crisis, and what the crisis

means for interest rates, this is where you will discover specific investment recommendations you can put to use right away.

While no one knows exactly how the future will unfold, the day or
the hour of individual events, the laws of economics have not been
repealed. America's debts will be accounted for. While elected officials
can act recklessly or wisely, in panic or judiciously, the prospects for
knowledgeable and responsible economic behavior on the part of the
governing classes is too small to merit long contemplation. Their propensity through time has been to rely instead on the deceit of inflation
or upon default and repudiation. But as each act of the drama unfolds,
you will be prepared to understand the choices the authorities are making, the consequences of each of those choices, and even the language
they use to confuse and divert attention from their responsibility.

For Jim in Scottsdale, the laughable absurdity of a senior government official's views finally caused him to act on what he had learned
over several years on my radio show. But large economic events have
now been set in motion and you don't have the leisure of several years
of daily conversation to learn what they are and how they will unfold.
You need to be awake and alert now, able to read the signs of the economic times. This book will prepare you at once to act in profitable
ways because you will understand the underlying issues as they present
themselves. And, as you will see in the next chapter, they've been presenting themselves at a furious pace lately. Indeed, if America's debt is a
powder keg about to blow, the fuse was lit with the rush of bailouts and
stimulus spending.

CHAPTER TWO

Bailouts

Banking Blunders and Boondoggles

The appearance of periodically recurring economic crises is the necessary consequence of repeatedly renewed attempts to reduce the "natural" rates of interest on the market by means of banking policy.

—Ludwig von Mises

. . . in our system of profit and loss, we cannot possibly think that the government should bail the banks out of bad loans they made, but allow them to keep the profits on the good ones.

—Milton Friedman

Nationalizing Finance

"You people move along. There's nothing to see here. The authorities are in charge. Keep moving!"

That was the spirit of a piece in *The New York Times*, "Here Are Some Answers to the Public's Questions About the Financial Crisis," the morning after President Bush signed the $700 billion bailout bill:

> **Q. If taxpayers finance this recovery plan, will Social Security and Medicare be affected?**
> A. There will be no effect on Social Security and Medicare, which are paid for through deductions from paychecks

and contributions from employers. Yes, Social Security and Medicare face some problems that will have to be addressed sooner or later, but to avoid a headache, you should think of those issues apart from the current financial crisis. And tune out oversimplified, alarmist language.

In a cavalier flourish of simplification, the writer repeatedly dismisses concerns about a growing "mountain of debt" and about federal speculation at the taxpayers' expense, while making light of concerns about the purchasing power of the dollar and the government's ability to fund its future promises. In one sentence he warns not to bother your pretty little head with such weighty stuff, while in the next he warns of oversimplification. And what of the bills coming due? You are advised to get "some perspective," because it is not we who will have to pay them, but little children who have been tucked snug in their beds. At this point one has to check the byline to see if Scarlett O'Hara is writing for the *Times:* "I can't think about that right now. If I do, I'll go crazy. I'll think about that tomorrow."

Although risking being tagged "alarmist," one could have seen in the early events of the year a foreshadowing of what became clearly visible later as the Panic of 2008. It was January when Bank of America bought the nation's largest mortgage lender, troubled Countrywide Financial.

In March, investment bank Bear Stearns, having suffered the collapse of its subprime mortgage hedge funds, was taken over by JPMorgan in a deal engineered with a $29 billion advance from the Federal Reserve.

When a midsummer run started on IndyMac Bank, a California thrift deep in the mortgage loan business, police had to be called in to maintain order at a branch in Encino. After depositors withdrew $1.3 billion in just days, IndyMac was taken over by the FDIC.

But even the most headache-averse journalist's attention should have been transfixed by a twenty-seven day dervish dance of interventionism and expenditures that began in September with the seizure of the nation's two largest mortgage finance companies. It was four whirling weeks that amounted to the nationalization of American finance.

The frenzy got under way in earnest on a Sunday, September 7, 2008, as the Bush administration took over Fannie Mae and Freddie Mac and committed $200 billion of taxpayer money to the bailout. By the end of the week Fed officials were meeting frantically with the heads of Goldman Sachs, JPMorgan Chase, Morgan Stanley, Citigroup, and Merrill Lynch to try to find a way out of a deepening mess. Sunday, September 14, shortly after midnight, Lehman Brothers announced it had filed for bankruptcy protection. Next insurance giant AIG asked the Federal Reserve for a $40 billion bailout, the first in a snowballing series of handouts for the company that before long reached $170 billion. That's a cost of about $2,000 for a family of four. At the same time, Bank of America agreed to take over Merrill Lynch, which had staggering losses in mortgage-backed securities, for $50 billion.

The problems with AIG, the largest U.S. insurer, and Merrill Lynch, the largest retail stock brokerage firm, should have served as a cold slap in the face for Americans. The giants of finance that represented themselves as skillful managers of the markets, advisers on all things financial, and trusted planners for their clients' security and retirement, were stunningly inept at managing their own affairs. It was plain that the lions of Wall Street didn't know what they were doing. And not only were they advising you on your portfolio, but it was from their ranks that Washington's financial wizards were drawn. The consequences for individual investors and the economic health of the country are almost too painful to contemplate.

The financial markets reeled as they absorbed all the news. Gold had its biggest one-day move in history on Wednesday, September 17, roaring up $70 in the market, up a total of $84 in after-market trading; Reserve Primary Fund, the nation's oldest money market firm, "broke the buck," its share value falling below the $1.00 money market fund standard, thanks to losses from its holdings of Lehman securities; that day the Commerce Department reported housing starts hit a seventeen-year low in August, down 33 percent from a year earlier.

In the midst of events, Treasury Secretary Henry Paulson and Ben Bernanke met with President Bush. It was Thursday, September 18. *The New York Times* reported months later that Bush wondered aloud that day, "How did we get here?" One wonders whether those in the room

were the best people to ask. None of them had been among those raising alarms as the market distortions were put in place. As good a question would have been, "Why are we doing this?" The explanations the
public got were that the authorities' whir of activity would save the
"financial system." How the extension of more credit would ameliorate
a crisis created by excess credit wasn't explained. Also missing from the
authorities' explanations were examples of financial bubbles, once having popped, being successfully reinflated. No amount of interventionism has been able to reinflate the Japanese real estate and stock market
bubbles that burst twenty years ago. Nor was there any clarity offered to
explain why financial institutions that were incapable of sound operations should be preserved. The benefits to stimulus recipients were clear,
but a holistic approach demands examination of not just benefits, but
costs as well. The impact of the burgeoning debt on America's creditworthiness and on the value of the dollar are among those costs.

Timothy Geithner, soon to be named President Obama's new treasury secretary, was the president of the Federal Reserve Bank of New
York at the time. He had solemnly explained the prior April that but for
the Fed's bailout, the failure of Bear Stearns would have led to falling
stock prices and downward pressure on real estate prices. Such a failure,
said Geithner, would have led to "a greater probability of widespread
insolvencies, severe and protracted damage to the financial system and,
ultimately, to the economy as a whole." This, of course, is precisely what
happened after the bailout.

Even as Bush was meeting with Bernanke and Paulson and wondering what happened, the Federal Reserve came up with $280 billion to
provide liquidity to the markets. By seven o'clock in the evening, the
secretary and the chairman were meeting with congressional leaders to
discuss what eventually became the $700 billion taxpayer-funded bail-
out. The next morning, Friday, September 19, Paulson announced the
establishment of a U.S. guarantee program for the money market fund
industry, funded with $50 billion from the Exchange Stabilization
Fund, a government fund used for currency manipulation. On Saturday, September 20, an overnighted bailout bill was in the hands of lawmakers. It was a simple, three-page, $700 billion package which raised
the debt ceiling to $11.315 trillion. And it included a little self-referential,

Constitution-upending twist that maintained that decisions by the secretary under that act "may not be reviewed by any court of law or any administrative agency." "This is a big package, because it was a big problem," said President Bush. He could have broken the cost down, but no doubt some speechwriter thought better of it: about $2,300 for every man, woman, and child in America.

On Monday, September 22, oil prices had their biggest one-day move in history, as crude jumped more than $25 a barrel. But all eyes were trained on banks that were on the brink of toppling. On Thursday night, federal officials seized Washington Mutual, the nation's largest savings and loan, after a $16.4 billion run on the bank. Five months earlier at WaMu's annual meeting some of the bank's stockholders caught a whiff of the plunder that was passing for management of major financial institutions. Why, they wondered, were mortgage losses being withheld from the calculation of senior management bonuses? WaMu became the largest bank failure in U.S. history. Wachovia Bank, the nation's fourth largest, toppled next. A takeover of Wachovia by Citigroup was announced on Sunday, September 28. Citigroup agreed to be responsible for $42 billion in mortgage losses while the FDIC would absorb any losses above that. The announcement proved to be premature. As it turned out, Citigroup was in no position to take over anything. It received a $25 billion bailout of its own in October, followed by $20 billion more and massive federal loan guarantees in November. Wells Fargo ended up with Wachovia in a $15.1 billion deal.

As the fourth week of the financial fury got under way, there was a short-lived rebellion in the House of Representatives. In a vote on Monday, September 29, the House rejected the bailout by a vote of 228–205; the Dow Industrials fell 777 points, a move of almost 7 percent. Tuesday, September 30, was the last day of the U.S. government's budget year, fiscal 2008. It proved to be the largest annual deficit in history. The $455 billion shortfall represented a 280 percent increase over the year before. A 12.5 percent jump in Pentagon spending, to $595 billion, and $18.2 billion to cover FDIC-insured deposits contributed to the deficit.

Meanwhile, the counter on the National Debt Clock whirled past $10 trillion. The famous thirteen-digit clock installed in Times Square in 1989 couldn't properly accommodate the higher numbers when the national debt broke into fourteen-digit territory on September 30. The clock operators, apparently expecting more of the same kind of reckless government we've been getting, plan to install a fifteen-digit clock.

The Senate passed the bailout bill by a margin of 74–25 on Wednesday, October 1. Two days later enough arms had been twisted and enough sweeteners had been thrown into the pot for 91 Republicans and 172 Democrats to join forces to pass the bailout bill, 263 to 171. Of the larded and porked-up bill he signed in haste that day, Bush said, "We have shown the world that the United States will stabilize our financial markets and maintain a leading role in the global economy." Meanwhile the Commerce Department reported 159,000 more jobs lost in September.

The Bailout

The Emergency Economic Stabilization Act of 2008 created the $700 billion bailout (plus $100 billion in add-ons) Troubled Assets Relief Program (TARP), a wealth transfer scheme so brazen as to leave one breathless. Another Fed bubble had popped; losses in the real estate mortgage meltdown were real; they had already taken place. The only real question was who would be made to eat those losses: the investment banking community that earned untold millions in fees each year for their dazzling financial footwork, or Americans with no complicity in the debacle and their offspring, young and yet-to-be-born, who would go through their entire adulthood burdened by heavy debts.

The loss transfer scheme met with more than a cold shoulder from the public. It met with outright hostility. One New Jersey congressman said his calls were running 50-50: 50 percent "no," and 50 percent "Hell no!"

The bailout also generated the derision it deserved. One blog posting described it succinctly: "Taking money from people who made good investments and giving it to people who made bad investments in the hope that the people who made bad investments will make good investments in the future and the people who made good investments will keep making them even though they will have less money to do so."

The lame-duck president let Secretary Paulson call the tune, while he tap-danced through a couple of White House performances: ". . . without immediate action by Congress, America could slip into a financial panic." (His first treasury secretary, Paul O'Neill, said of the president at the time, "I don't think he understands or knows much about any of this and it shows.") Paulson, the former Goldman Sachs CEO, was determined to reliquefy Wall Street even at the risk of the treasury's solvency. The bailout was sold to the governing classes under the guise of reinflating the mortgage market, an act of self-evident futility. If the last bubble could be reinflated, people would still be coughing up millions for dot-com business plans scrawled on cocktail napkins and the NASDAQ index would be over 5,000. Unlike their counterparts in the Senate, members of the House, closest to the people and all up for reelection in a month, resisted the bailout at first go-around, but the pork fest of more giveaways, the heavy arm twisting, and talk of opponents being blamed for the next Great Depression prevailed. One representative, Brad Sherman, D-CA, claimed on the House floor that members were told without the bailout there would be martial law in America. And so the Paulson plan passed, a mechanism to transfer the losses from institutions that in the expectation of gain willingly undertook the risk of loss to those who had no opportunity for gain or willingness to undertake loss.

If the idea seems antithetical to the American way, it is. Philosophical consistency is not to be expected from politicians, but shouldn't shame for supporting the giveaway have spread rampantly among Republicans? After all, the 2008 Republican platform had just been passed at the beginning of September. It addressed the mortgage meltdown in these terms: "We do not support government bailouts of private institutions. Government interference in the markets exacerbates problems in the marketplace and causes the free market to take longer to correct itself." And what about modern-day conservatives who some years before opposed Hillary-care, insisting that socialized medicine is a mistake for the body politic? How then had socialized investment banking become overnight a prescription for economic health? When foreign heads of state, from Iran's President Musaddiq, who was toppled for it in 1953, to Putin in Russia or Chávez in Venezuela, nationalize their country's oil, they become enemies of the American state. But when American leaders nationalize finance, the people are told it's for the good of all concerned. Before long South American Marxists including Hugo Chávez were taking great delight in calling "Comrade Bush" a fellow traveler.

The early costs of the frenzy of "rescues" were astonishing. A week into October, Bernanke claimed the Fed had already committed $800 billion in loans to banks and other activities, and that was before $200 billion for Freddie and Fannie and before the $700 billion bailout. The bailout gave new life to the expression "Legislate in haste, repent at leisure." It only took a couple of months to notice that the bailout produced none of the promised results in mortgage values. The Treasury handed out the first tranche of the TARP money, $350 billion with virtually no accountability for how the money would be spent. Early in 2009 the Congressional Oversight Panel was able to conclude that the Treasury had paid $78 billion more than market value for the first $254 billion it spent.

While all eyes were on the bailout debate, September 30, like some eerie fiscal planetary conjunction, went unnoticed, a silent harbinger of America's economic future. While fiscal year 2008 ended that day, rolling up an all-time-high deficit of $455 billion, the explicit national debt actually increased by more than a trillion dollars for the year, breaking through an astronomical $10 trillion. Meanwhile, all but eclipsed by the debate over the bailout bill, President Bush signed another stopgap spending bill that day. This one was for $634 billion, including $5 billion in earmarks, $25 billion in low-interest loans to automakers (yes, even foreign ones!), and a 6 percent bump in Pentagon spending. By the time he signed the bailout bill three days later, it had been a $1.34 trillion week. As part of the bailout, commanding the sun and the moon of economic reckoning to stand still, Congress raised the national debt ceiling to $11.315 trillion. (Four months later it would raise the debt limit again, this time to $12.1 trillion.)

The Paulson plan was represented as an attempt to undo the harm of mortgage market excesses by again inflating mortgage assets on the balance sheets of Wall Street players. It was a strange, homeopathic remedy, a "hair of the dog" approach for a problem that was caused by excess credit engineered by the Federal Reserve to begin with. Rather than letting housing prices that had inflated beyond sustainability deflate, instead of letting a market of buyers and sellers arrive at some equilibrium, at values that reflected the actual conditions of supply and demand, the plan called for more of the asset inflation that led to the bust. Only this time it was to be done with taxpayer money. The idea of pumping more air into a tire that had already had a blowout was ridiculous on its face, and the populists were right in suspecting that it was Wall Street welfare, a case of the politically connected of American finance passing the Old Maid of loss to the people.

Informed observers, the Cassandras who had seen the bubble forming and tried to raise the alarm when it would still do some good, were, of course, not consulted about the plan. Five years to the month before the Fannie and Freddie bubble popped, Congressman Ron Paul introduced a measure that would have avoided the calamity. His September 2003 remarks in the House Financial Services Committee on the dangers of government-sponsored enterprises (GSEs) like Fannie and Freddie are nothing less than a shockingly precise preview of exactly what came to pass:

> This explicit promise by the Treasury to bail out GSEs in times of economic difficulty helps the GSEs attract investors who are willing to settle for lower yields than they would demand in the absence of the subsidy. Thus, the line of credit distorts the allocation of capital. More importantly, the line of credit is a promise on behalf of the government to engage in a huge unconstitutional and immoral income transfer from working Americans to holders of GSE debt. . . .
>
> Ironically, by transferring the risk of a widespread mortgage default, the government increases the likelihood of a painful crash in the housing market. . . .
>
> Despite the long-term damage to the economy inflicted by the government's interference in the housing market, the government's policy of diverting capital to other uses creates a short-term boom in housing. Like all artificially-created bubbles, the boom in housing prices cannot last forever.

When housing prices fall, homeowners will experience diffi-
culty as their equity is wiped out. Furthermore, the holders
of the mortgage debt will also have a loss. These losses will
be greater than they would have otherwise been had government policy not actively encouraged over-investment in
housing.

Perhaps the Federal Reserve can stave off the day of reckoning by purchasing GSE debt and pumping liquidity into
the housing market, but this cannot hold off the inevitable
drop in the housing market forever. In fact, postponing the
necessary, but painful market corrections will only deepen
the inevitable fall. The more people invested in the market,
the greater the effects across the economy when the bubble
bursts.

In viewing the Paulson plan, the Cassandras must have wondered
how often the same discredited economic nostrums need to be refuted.
But the administration didn't turn to Ron Paul for advice. Nor did it
consult the scholars at the Ludwig von Mises Institute, who had warned
about the government-sponsored expansion of bank credit and money
and its inevitable cycle of bubbles and busts. Instead Bush turned to
Henry Paulson and his team from Goldman Sachs, despite the fact that
under Paulson's leadership as CEO, Goldman Sachs had been among
the industry's leaders in the issuance of subprime and other
mortgage-backed securities, rotten paper that was downgraded scores
of times by Standard & Poor's and Moody's Investors Service. And Bush
followed the counsel of Fed chairman Ben Bernanke, who was on board
and at the helm as the Fed frothed up the real estate and mortgage
bubbles to begin with.

Insufficient Regulation?

It has assumed the status of a mantra: The governing classes and their
unofficial public relations staff—the nation's media and commentators—
would have it that the housing bubble and credit bust were the result of

insufficient regulation. That is like saying that the *Titanic* sank because of an insufficiency of ice. Indeed, the entire miserable episode was the creation of regulation. When other regulatory bodies do damage, the effects may be limited. The Federal Milk Marketing Order interferes with milk prices and costs consumers unfairly, but does little else. But the harm the Federal Reserve does is inescapable; it reaches everywhere, damaging every nook and cranny of the economy. Regulating the nation's supply of money and credit, the Fed was the primary engine of the mortgage debacle. It was full steam ahead as it cut interest rates an astonishing thirteen consecutive times between January 2001 and May 2003, pushing the Fed funds rate all the way down from 6.5 percent to 1 percent, where it was left for a year! Of course Bernanke voted with then-Fed chairman Alan Greenspan on the cuts. In fact, in the 11–1 vote of the Fed's Open Market Committee to drop rates to 1 percent, the lone dissenter actually wanted a bigger cut. At 1 percent interest, the real rate of interest, that is, the nominal rate minus inflation, was below zero.

The effects of the contrived low rates were several. First, with the real rate of interest negative, creditor institutions and other lenders predictably began scrambling for opportunities to earn positive real rates of return. They looked to the mortgage market. Next, Americans began sensing that their money was being debauched at a rate higher than the rate of return. Why, then, save at all? Why not spend or "invest" in homes? Why not, under the circumstances, borrow as much as possible? And that was most easily done in real estate.

Since real interest rates were below zero, it could be said the Fed was letting people borrow money for free—borrow today and pay back less value down the road! It is the kind of economic wonderland that cultivated some real hucksters. For research on my radio show during the middle of the boom, I called on a mortgage broker, one highly visible in Phoenix for the easy-money promise of his advertising. Not having purchased a home in some time, I was surprised at what little documentation I would have to produce to secure a substantial loan. But I was more astonished when he tried to steer me to an enticing adjustable rate loan with little down and a short window of low initial rates.

"Why would I do that?" I asked. "These are the lowest rates since my parents were young. Why expose myself to higher rates down the road?"

"Don't worry about that," he assured me. "Reagan put this thing in there so that interest rates will never go back up again!"

I couldn't believe what I was hearing. "Reagan put *what* thing in *where*?" I demanded.

Of course it was too complicated for him to explain, but I could "trust him" on it. So if somebody was giving away free money, why should it be a surprise that a crowd of something-for-nothing sharps and parasites showed up? Try giving away free booze and see if you don't draw more than a few drunks.

To expand the market beyond the most creditworthy borrowers, mortgages of every hue and stripe were created. There were variable rate mortgages, negative amortization mortgages, teaser rate mortgages, no document loans, interest only loans, no-down-payment loans, and more. Then Greenspan urged still more speed. He gave a widely noted speech suggesting adjustable rate mortgages might be preferable to fixed rates. This was truly astonishing! With interest rates already the lowest they had been since the 1950s, was he suggesting that the outlook for variable rate mortgages was a lifetime of being reset still lower? Greenspan even encouraged the development of more alternatives to fixed rate mortgages.

Just as "insufficient regulation" had become a mantra of the commentariat and talking heads, "failure of the market" became a catechism. But if they couldn't detect the Fed, the Regulator of Regulators, stoking the engines of cheap credit and the hand of the maestro himself, Greenspan, directing the affair, it should be no surprise they couldn't detect the role of regulatory interference in lending standards. In normal circumstances no lender is eager to loan money without assurance of repayment or interest premiums to offset the risk of an occasional default. Creditors are quite capable and often very sophisticated in self-regulating against risk. Those who aren't soon disappear. If an individual lending institution capsizes, it is the natural culling of imprudent or reckless businesses. But when a whole flotilla of such institutions sink at once, it is reasonable to look for the regulatory reefs upon which they have been wrecked. Like pirates whose fake light-houses drew hapless ships to plunder, political pirates distort otherwise self-regulating economic activities with laws and regulations aimed at winning favor among specific beneficiaries. By the time their false signals produce casualties, they have slipped away in the darkness, taking their booty of donations and interest group support, but with no responsibility for the destruction they themselves have caused.

And so it was at the hands of political regulators that credit standards were lowered and loan denials fell sharply. Informed observers, or at least informed observers not in thrall to the state, could see it from the beginning. A *New York Times* headline on September 30, 1999, foreshadowed the coming cataclysm. It read "FANNIE MAE EASES CREDIT TO AID MORTGAGE LENDING." The story described a pilot program that the agency hoped to make nationwide, one that would make mortgages available "to individuals whose credit is generally not good enough to qualify for conventional loans." It reported that Fannie Mae was under "increasing pressure" to make loans available to low- and moderate-income borrowers. Of course it presaged problems. Even then the story cited Peter Wallison, an American Enterprise Institute fellow, saying the program had the makings of the savings and loan debacle all over again. "If they fail, the government will have to step up and bail them out the way it stepped up and bailed out the thrift industry."

The steps of increasing regulatory intervention involved congressional pressure for Fannie Mae and Freddie Mac to loosen lending standards, accompanied by goals set by the Department of Housing and Urban Development for the agencies to significantly increase their financing of moderate- and low-income housing. An October 2008 article in *The Wall Street Journal*, "How Government Stoked the Mania" by Dr. Russell Roberts, identified those specific targets for loans below an area's median income as 42 percent in 1996, escalating to 52 percent in 2002.

What HUD did with Fannie Mae and Freddie Mac, the Community Reinvestment Act did with other lenders. Roberts wrote that "the CRA was 'strengthened' in 1995, causing an increase of 80 percent in the numbers of bank loans going to low- and moderate-income families." Between the Fed's credit creation and the mandates of political regulators, a disaster was in the making. Real estate lending was racing ahead at breakneck speeds. Trillions of dollars in new loans were made. But it couldn't last. After a year of 1 percent interest rates the Fed began to raise them again, up seventeen times to 5.25 percent by June 2006. In 1996, 9 percent of loan originations were subprime; ten years later, when the bubble burst, 20 percent were subprime.

Blunderers to the Rescue!

Amid the wreckage and debris, it seems not to have occurred to any of the usual suspects in the media to ask why we should buy a "rescue" map from those who charted the course to calamity. The new map was more of the same. Bernanke and Paulson advised attempting to perpetuate the unsustainable valuations of the bubble. Incredibly, Bernanke even told the Senate it was his intent that the government should use bailout appropriations to pay more for troubled assets than need be. He would have taxpayers pay at some mythical price as though the markets had recovered.

At the core of the Paulson-Bernanke plan was a futile resistance to falling prices. It was uncomfortably reminiscent of the Great Depression of the 1930s, when what should have been a short excess-adjusting recession was dragged out into more than a decade of depression, in part by the insistence that artificial price levels be enforced. A madness resulted during the Roosevelt administration in the presence of widespread hunger and deprivation among people who desperately needed low prices, when crops were plowed under and "piggy sows" and sucklings were ordered to be slaughtered. In that respect, the New Deal wasn't so new after all; Hoover too had set his administration at odds with natural price levels. By insisting on artificially high wage rates, he was rewarded with the highest unemployment rates in American history.

With each new initiative, we can shake our heads in astonishment and wonder if the governing classes are capable of learning from the past. Among the solutions that Congress voted in the $700 billion bailout bill was an increase in federal deposit insurance, from $100,000 to

$250,000 per depositor per bank through 2009 and presumably to be extended thereafter. This is another case that screams of the complicity of regulators in our economic predicament. There is no cost to any legislator in voting for this higher insurance; he passes no new tax hike or revenue measure, nor does he take the money from an existing program. It's just an act of Congress and a stroke of the president's pen.

Perhaps the Washington water is responsible for the widespread memory deficit disorder. Lawmakers there don't seem to remember what happened the last time they raised FDIC insurance. A middle-of-the-night conference committee provision was slipped into legislation in 1980 raising deposit insurance from $40,000 to $100,000. The risk for federally insured depositors to that amount was the same regardless of the institution's practices. And to keep their customers, solvent and conservatively run institutions had to match rates paid by the highest flyers and biggest risk-takers of the industry. Savings and loans, advertising for depositors during the period, took out full-page newspaper ads promoting their high rates of interest. They did not advertise the soundness of their lending practices to attract depositors. They did not advertise reports by an independent bank rating agency about their solvency, or the safe banking practices some private insurer might have demanded of them. They simply advertised their certificate of deposit rates along with a little Federal Savings and Loan Insurance logo. Then as now, there was no cost to the politicians in raising the deposit insurance limits.

But in the real world, all these governmental economic activities—insuring bank deposits, providing guarantees to Fannie Mae and Freddie Mac, bailing investment bankers out of their follies—all these things have a cost. The costs are evaded by the reckless and feckless politicians, but are very real to the taxpayers. When the savings and loans failed, it was the people who were forced to cough up $125 billion to cover the insured losses. Plus interest on the thirty- and forty-year bonds that had to be issued to cover the losses.

In the current environment, one investor told me that because he spread his $100,000 deposits around at a variety of insured banks, by the end of the summer of 2008 he had already been through three FDIC takeovers for the year. The call from the regulators had become routine. And when asked whether he would like to withdraw his deposit at each institution, he was absolutely indifferent to their solvency or future commercial prospects, prudently run institutions having no more attraction than reckless ones. All that mattered was maintaining the rate of return for the life of the deposit. This impact of guarantees on consumer behavior is counterproductive, as is the unseen cost of the government's drawing investment dollars from competing uses that may be more productive, but have no such government guarantee to offer.

At any level of guarantee, FDIC insurance is a Washington artifice exactly like one of the greatest frauds of them all: the Social Security Trust Fund. In both cases, the money does not exist. There is no Social Security Trust Fund, because there is no money. It has been spent. Similarly, there is no FDIC Insurance Fund. It has been spent. The constant use by the government of terms like "insurance," "reserves," "funds," and "trust" is employed to deceive the people. There is no reserve, no insurance, no fund, and no trust.

A former chairman of the FDIC shattered any illusions about the "fund." William Isaac was chairman during the Reagan administration. Since the institution's financial statement showed a fund during his tenure, a U.S. Treasury balance of $11 billion, he wrote that he thought he'd take a look at the money. He called Treasury Secretary Donald Regan:

ISAAC: Don, I'd like to come over to look at the money.

REGAN: What money?

ISAAC: You know . . . the $11 billion the FDIC has in the vault at Treasury.

REGAN: Uh, well, you see, Bill, ah, that's a bit of a problem.

ISAAC: I know you're busy. I don't need to do it right away.

REGAN: Well . . . it's not a question of timing . . . I don't know quite how to put this, but we don't have the money.

ISAAC: Right . . . ha ha.

REGAN: No, really. The banks have been paying money to the FDIC, the FDIC has been turning the money over to the Treasury, and the Treasury has been spending it on missiles, school lunches, water projects, and the like. The money's gone.

ISAAC: But it says right here on this financial statement that we have over $11 billion at the Treasury.

REGAN: In a sense, you do. You see, we owe that money to the FDIC, and we pay interest on it.

ISAAC: I know this might sound pretty far-fetched, but what would happen if we should need a few billion to handle a bank failure?

REGAN: That's easy—we'd go right out and borrow it. You'd have the money in no time . . . same day service most days.

ISAAC: Let me see if I've got this straight. The money the banks thought they were storing up for the past half century—sort of saving it for a rainy day—is gone. If a storm begins brewing and we need the money, Treasury will have to borrow it. Is that about it?

REGAN: Yep.

ISAAC: Just one more thing, while I've got you. Why do we bother pretending there's a fund?

REGAN: I'm sorry, Bill, but the president's on the other line. I'll have to get back to you on that.

Isaac's rich irony injects some needed humor into our predicament. Besides, who hasn't enjoyed the three-card monte show on the street corner? Or been entertained by the carnival pitchman separating the hayseeds from their money? How could we watch without chuckling as Hank Paulson lurched from one plan to the next, explaining one day that injecting capital directly into banks is a bad idea and that it didn't work for the Japanese, while the next day announcing that Treasury will buy $250 billion in bank preferred stocks? Or when Obama treasury secretary Geithner announced his bailout plan to great fanfare, but didn't really know what it was?

But it's far too dark to laugh for long. When Bush said, "These measures are not intended to take over the free market, but to preserve it," doesn't it bring to mind similar disclaimers from days gone by? In the madness of Vietnam, there was the officer who said, "It was necessary to destroy the village in order to save it." Or in the assault on the Branch

Davidians in Waco, where the children had to be killed so that they could be saved.

That it was maddeningly self-contradictory was nothing new. At the beginning of the year Bush thought giving families $600 or $1,200 tax rebates would be good for the economy, even if the money had to be borrowed and added to the already staggering debt load. But if giving them $600 per family was a stimulant, why didn't Bush mention that a bailout costing every American $2,300 would be a depressant?

We watch them all scurrying busily about, trying to paper over real losses, robbing millions of American Peters to subsidize a few hundred banking Pauls; thinking all the hustle and bustle of their activities will make them seem capable. But all the while they flail about in the darkness of their economic ignorance, believing there is only one side of the balance sheet, the assets of recipients, while ignoring the liabilities they pile on the taxpayers.

There is an old Zen saying that it's better to be doing nothing than to be busy doing nothing. With every new stimulus plan and bailout, each day's new initiative, every loan guarantee, each new spending bill; with every accounting fraud and "injection of liquidity into the banking system"; with each unbalanced budget, record deficit, and debt ceiling increase, the governing classes, Republican and Democrat alike, are destroying the dollar and with it our prosperity. A look at the debt they have accumulated on our behalf, both visible and hidden from view, describes the extent of the damage and reveals our inescapable future.

CHAPTER THREE

Debt

First There Is a Mountain . . . Then There's a Bigger Mountain!

I place economy among the first and most important republican virtues, and public debt as the greatest of dangers to be feared.

—Thomas Jefferson

Christmas is a time when kids tell Santa what they want and adults pay for it. Deficits are when adults tell the government what they want and their kids pay for it.

—Richard Lamm, former governor of Colorado

We Owe It to Ourselves

Elected officials say some of the most astonishing things. As I began writing this section someone sent me a video of a senior member of Congress, California Democrat Pete Stark, insisting some years ago that the national debt is a measure of the country's wealth:

INTERVIEWER: So the more you owe, the more you're worth?
CONGRESSMAN STARK: In federal accounting. . . . In the national scheme of things that's quite right.

The national debt was less than $6 trillion at the time of the interview; it's $12 trillion now. So are we twice as wealthy? Then why have consumer prices climbed 40 percent since? For decades politicians

dismissed those warning about mounting federal debt with the inge-
nious explanation that after all, "we owe it to ourselves!" One can only
imagine the act was perfected from the back of the snake-oil wagon on
the carnival circuit:

> POLITICAL HUCKSTER: Step right up here, kid! I'll tell you what I'm
> going to do. But first you need to loan me a hundred
> dollars!
>
> HAYSEED VOTER: But will I get my money back?
>
> POLITICAL HUCKSTER: Sure! Lend me a hundred bucks, but only give
> me fifty of it now. That way you'll owe me fifty bucks, and I'll
> owe you fifty bucks, and we'll be even!

Step right up indeed! But, hucksterism aside, "we" actually don't owe
it to "ourselves," any more than I can be said to owe money to myself. If
we owe it to ourselves, why is a family of four paying about $6,000 per
year in interest on the national debt? In fact the government owes
money it has borrowed to specific people. These are people who have
payrolls to meet and retirement needs upon which they depend. It owes
people with bank deposits, savings accounts, Treasury bills and bonds,
and it even owes little children with U.S. savings bonds. All of these
have future educational, health care, retirement, and other plans for
their money. When the government borrows money for some perceived
good or vote-buying scheme today, it burdens future taxpayers with the
cost. They must spend their capital, their future well-being, on consumption for which they had no say. The debt grows from year to year
with no expectation that it will ever be paid off. There is only the expectation that payment for today's consumption can be rolled forward
interminably. No one who buys a government bond today expects that
it will be paid at maturity except by the issuance of another bond
tomorrow.

In fact, this facile dismissal—"we owe it to ourselves"—could have
been made about America's escalating mortgage debt before the house
of cards collapsed. In any event, it can't be said we owe the national debt
to ourselves any longer. We are increasingly dependent on foreigners

whose holdings are now more than 25 percent of our national debt, double what it was twenty years ago. On average, a family of four is paying more than $130 per month just in interest to foreign holders of American debt.

Meanwhile "We owe it to ourselves" is being supplanted by a new talking point. It is a rhetorical dismissal that says that we've had a higher ratio of debt to gross domestic product in the past; that as a share of the GDP, the national debt really isn't that large. Besides, we are told, we can grow our way out of it. Which is the same thing you may have been told about your adjustable rate mortgage: don't worry, your equity will grow and you will be able to sell or refinance before the higher rates kick in.

There are several things that must be said in response to the claim that our debt is manageable because as a percentage of our entire economy it is not as high as it has been in the past. The gross federal debt is 80 percent of GDP. That's the highest it's been since the 1950s. But that percentage of debt was much more manageable then because fifty years ago America was a creditor nation; now America is a debtor nation. Fifty years ago America maintained a trade surplus; now our trade deficit, having grown for a generation, is immense. Fifty years ago America was the world's manufacturing hegemon; now America's manufacturing base is being lost to the world. Fifty years ago Americans were savers. Now the Chinese have shown us what it means to defer consumption and save.

America's Hidden Debt

But all of that is to strain at a gnat while swallowing a camel. In truth, the nature of the U.S. debt is so enormously understated that it amounts to accounting fraud. There is the official "on the books" debt of the U.S. government. This is the part of the debt that is acknowledged by government, politicians, and the media alike. When you discover that U.S. government debt surpassed $10 trillion on September 30, 2008, and is now racing to $12 trillion, it is only this official part of the debt that is being reported. When you hear that the national debt ceiling was increased seven times during the Bush presidency, or that with President Obama's $787 billion stimulus plan the national debt ceiling was raised to $12.1 trillion—you may think that is all quite a bit and quite enough. It may seem staggering that your personal share of the national debt is about $36,000. That's $144,000 for a family of four. That may seem substantial.

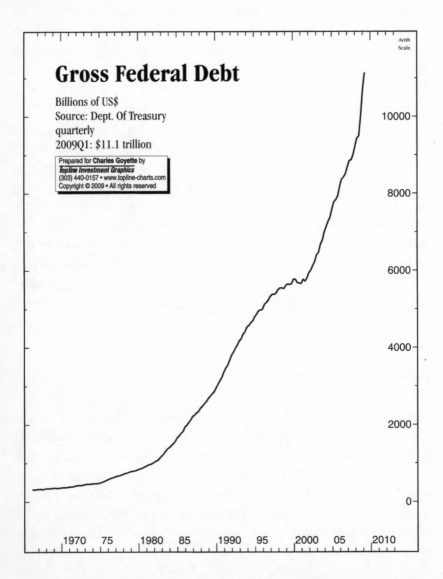

"But wait," as they say in the infomercials, "there's more!" The debt is not really just $12 trillion! By any commonsensical definition of the term "debt," something owed, the real debt is larger. If you have paid into Social Security for a lifetime and you believe your promised benefits are a debt of the government; if you believe that the government should make good on promises of veterans' health care; if your bank has been paying insurance premiums to the FDIC and you expect that in the event of a run on the banks loss coverage is a debt of the government; if you have been paying the government for medical coverage which you will expect to be there when the need arises; if you believe that government "guarantees," tossed around like confetti lately, are real promises upon which institutions and individuals should rely; then you will agree that the government's debt is much larger than the $12 trillion on the books. All of these expectations represent unfunded liabilities: promises the government has made, but for which no provision to pay has been made. Just as the bulk of the iceberg is below the waterline, the visible "national debt" is only the tip of the government liabilities. And just as so many major American financial institutions cracked up on submerged credit derivatives, America's hidden debt—the amount of money that would have to be set aside and earn interest to meet promises already made—a staggering sum, $59 trillion—is there, right below the waterline, unseen, hidden government debt that has America on a collision course with bankruptcy.

In hopes of averting a calamity, David Walker spent years warning the country about America's hidden debt. Walker was the comptroller general of the United States, the head of the Government Accountability Office for ten years, until he resigned in 2008 so that he could speak about the problem without limitation. Walker calls the problem of hidden federal debt "a super subprime crisis."

Two weeks before he announced his resignation, Walker joined me on the air in Phoenix. With 2008 being an election year, I told him that I didn't see anything fundamentally different in the character of those running for office from those who spent this nation into our current predicament. "The system is broken. Our current system, both in the legislative and executive branch, is badly broken," he said. "The first three words in the Constitution, 'We the People,' must come alive. The

people are responsible and accountable for what does and does not happen in Washington. We've had too many people who have not been
informed and not been involved. And that's how we got where we are
today." Walker's answer at least helped to dispel the idea that leadership
and direction can be expected from the political class.

The problem is so big that even the normal empty promises about
balancing the annual budget are inadequate. In fact even if the budget
was balanced, says Walker, the unfunded liability problem would still
continue to grow by $2 trillion to $3 trillion a year.

"One of the things you find when you're in Washington long enough
is that there are certain words that don't mean the same thing as in
Webster's dictionary. One of those is 'trust funds.' There are no trust
funds! A trust fund to you and me is a separate and distinct legal entity
with fiduciary responsibilities and liabilities, with real assets that are
earning returns to meet obligations. You know what's in the trust funds
of United States Social Security and Medicare? Debt! We're funding our
promises with our own debt!"

What does $59 trillion in hidden debt mean to you? Your share is
$193,442. For a family of four it's $773,770. That's a lot of debt, especially since the median household income in America is only $50,000.

But wait! There's more!

The president of the Federal Reserve Bank of Dallas, Richard Fisher,
shocked the alert segment of the financial world in a May 2008 speech
when he described the growth of the federal debt as "a frightful storm"
that, if unattended, "will be unimaginably more devastating to our economic prosperity than the subprime debacle. . . ." Beginning with Social
Security, Fisher walked through the long-term outlook for entitlements,
which, he said, if unchanged, "is nothing short of catastrophic."

> The amount of money the Social Security system would need
> today to cover all unfunded liabilities from now on—what
> fiscal economists call the "infinite horizon discounted value"
> of what has already been promised recipients but has no
> funding mechanism currently in place—is $13.6 trillion, an
> amount slightly less than the annual gross domestic product
> of the United States. . . .

The good news is this Social Security shortfall might be manageable. While the issues regarding Social Security reform are complex, it is at least possible to imagine how Congress might find, within a $14 trillion economy, ways to wrestle with a $13 trillion unfunded liability. The bad news is that Social Security is the lesser of our entitlement worries. It is but the tip of the unfunded liability iceberg. The much bigger concern is Medicare. . . .

Please sit tight while I walk you through the math of Medicare. As you may know, the program comes in three parts: Medicare Part A, which covers hospital stays; Medicare B, which covers doctor visits; and Medicare D, the drug benefit that went into effect just 29 months ago. The infinite-horizon present discounted value of the unfunded liability for Medicare A is $34.4 trillion. The unfunded liability of Medicare B is an additional $34 trillion. The shortfall for Medicare D adds another $17.2 trillion. The total? If you wanted to cover the unfunded liability of all three programs today, you would be stuck with an $85.6 trillion bill. That is more than six times as large as the bill for Social Security. It is more than six times the annual output of the entire U.S. economy. . . .

Add together the unfunded liabilities from Medicare and Social Security, and it comes to $99.2 trillion over the infinite horizon. . . .

The "infinite horizon" model Fisher uses envisions $99.2 trillion being set aside today *just to cover the shortfall in these programs*; that is, over and above the existing payroll taxes, fees, and deductibles that must all still remain in place. Fisher calculates that your share is $330,000. For a family of four it's $1.3 million!

Of course it's an insurmountable cost and therefore impossible of solution. What about meeting the hidden debt through income taxes, personal and corporate, on a pay-as-you-go basis? That, says Fisher, would take a permanent 68 percent increase in income tax receipts. What that would mean in terms of actual tax rates is left unsaid, but it takes little imagination to realize that such increases would depress economic activity to the degree that the desired revenue would retreat from the tax collector's grasp, like the fruit that forever receded from the reach of Tantalus in Hades.

Perhaps the hidden debt can be met with spending cuts, leaving revenue unchanged. That, too, is an impossibility, because such cuts would demand almost all discretionary spending, says Fisher. "So all we would have to do to fully fund our nation's entitlement programs would be to cut discretionary spending by 97 percent. But hold on. That discretionary spending includes defense and national security, education, the environment, and many other areas, not just those controversial earmarks that make the evening news. All of them would have to be cut—almost eliminated, really—to tackle this problem through discretionary spending."

Whether by impossible spending cuts, crushing levels of taxation, or the lump sum provisions of money nobody has, America's debts at any level—$12 trillion, $59 trillion, or $99.3 trillion—won't be paid. They will simply be rolled over again and again until America's creditors are unwilling to loan any longer. The nation is in the same position as someone who has taken a cash advance from his Visa card to meet his mortgage payment, and then has taken out a new MasterCard credit line to pay his Visa bill. Credit card debt juggling may appear to work in the short run, but it is a road to financial ruin. And just as compound interest is said to be the investor's best friend, it is the debtor's worst nightmare, as debt growth becomes exponential.

The American Piñata

How did we get into this hole? Neither Republicans nor Democrats should be allowed to blame it on their opposites. Modern voters cannot be allowed to think it all dates back generations to the New Deal or even to the Great Society. Just a few years old now, the hidden debt in Bush's prescription drug plan already eclipses that of Social Security.

Medicare Part D was born of Republicans and Democrats' attempting to outbid one another for the affection of senior voters. Despite the financial hole the nation was in, the political classes kept digging.

Enacting a prescription drug bill might be thought a strange platform for small-government conservatives since it represented the largest expansion of entitlements since the 1960s, but determined to win the senior constituency, the Bush administration offered up a plan big enough to trump recent Democratic plans. To quell a revolt from a few reluctant House conservatives, it couldn't exceed a budget resolution already agreed to with a ceiling of $400 billion over its first ten years. All such projections should be viewed with suspicion to begin with. In 1990, twenty-five years after its enactment, the original Medicare program was projected to cost $9 billion; the actual cost that year was $67 billion.

The new Bush drug bill was brought to the floor for final passage in the middle of the night on November 22, 2003. Securing its passage involved a long night of heavy-handed politics: unilateral voting rule changes, arm-twisting, and even charges of threats having been made and bribes offered.

Shortly after Bush signed the bill that emerged as the nation slept, the White House offered a new cost projection for the $400 billion measure: $534 billion. The higher estimates had been known to the White House for months. Medicare's chief actuary testified before the House Ways and Means Committee that he had given higher estimates to the White House in June, months before the vote. Richard S. Foster also disclosed that his job had been threatened by administration officials if he revealed the actual projections for the drug bill to members of Congress, forecasts running as high as $600 billion that would have prevented its passage. Foster said his boss, Medicare administrator Thomas A. Scully, a Bush appointee, had repeatedly warned him he would be fired, a claim that was corroborated by an e-mail that eventually turned up from one of Scully's aides warning Foster that the projections were only to be shared with Scully and that "the consequences for insubordination are extremely severe."

The pharmaceutical industry got revenue it wanted from the new law, by one estimate an additional $13 billon in the first year; as much as $100 billion over the first eight years. And George W. Bush got the votes he wanted and another four years in office. But then, shortly after his reelection, the White House released new numbers. The $400 billion measure would now cost not $534 billion, but $720 billion. During the period that Congress was misled about the costs of the bill, Scully was lining up his next career move. Ten days after Bush signed the bill into law, Scully joined a lobbying firm and registered to represent Aventis, Abbott Laboratories, and Praecis Pharmaceuticals.

Weeks after Bush signed the bill, talks got under way about a position in the pharmaceutical lobby for Republican representative Billy Tauzin, described as the principal author of the bill and its lead sponsor. Before his term expired, it was announced that he would be the new president of the Pharmaceutical Research and Manufacturers of America, the drug companies' major lobbying organization, at a reported salary of $2.5 million a year. The *New York Times* reporter for the December 16, 2004, story on Tauzin's move must have had a sense of irony. He wrote, "Drug makers said that the job was not a reward for Mr. Tauzin's work on the Medicare bill, which followed the industry's specifications in many respects."

America's national government has moved way beyond a political spoils system. A spoils system leaves the host alive so that a politician's occasional ne'er-do-well brother-in-law can be put on the payroll. America has become a piñata: everybody gets a crack at it. Presidents and other elected officials pass the big stick around as a reward to those who help keep them in charge of the piñata party. The American media plays the role of the party's mariachi band, keeping festive spirits high. And the people in their demographic and interest groups all line up to take a whack at the goodies. America has become a piñata.

But the piñata does not survive the party. It is bashed to bits.

The story of the Bush drug bill deserves telling not because it is egregious. It broke no new ground of venality. On the contrary, it illustrates politics as usual in the age of the American piñata. Without shame the Republicans and Democrats alike have made politics nothing more than the process by which the goodies are divided. The Bush drug bill is important to us only because it is so large, a bigger part of our hidden debt than Social Security itself. Walker, the former comptroller general, says it is "probably the most fiscally irresponsible piece of legislation since the 1960s," while Fisher, the Dallas Fed president, says it adds $17.2 trillion to our unfunded liabilities.

Of course, the debt doesn't stop at $12 trillion, $59 trillion, or $99.2 trillion. In response to the mortgage crack-up, there have been more debt guarantees, new so-called moral obligations, additional insured deposits, and even stimulus packages yet to come. There is little to be gained by keeping a running total, since the end point has already been reached.

It goes without saying that government spending is growing faster than government revenue. But government debt is growing faster than the gross domestic product. Interest expense on the national debt for FY 2008 of $451 billion is within just a few billion dollars of the $455 billion deficit. But that doesn't tell half the story. Because of the budgetary fiction that allows for war spending that doesn't show up in the budget and that little trick of taking the Social Security surplus and leaving an IOU in its place—fostering the illusion that the money is being saved even as it is really being spent—the U.S. debt actually increased by $1 trillion over the fiscal year.

Is it rational to act as though this growing mountain of debt will have no impact on the value of the dollar? By now almost everyone, especially those who have been through the hard knocks of foreclosure, has learned that prudent people need to be concerned about borrowing and their ability to pay their creditors back. But there is no such constraint on the government. Whatever interest rate it must pay to keep borrowing and spending, whatever the cost of operating, it will pay. Even a poor credit rating will not stop it; it will simply offer ever higher interest returns to induce buyers to take the risk of its poor credit. Rising interest rates make the cost of financing the government's already unsustainable debts higher as well. Soon the frenzy of borrowing and spending is swallowed in a black hole of economic collapse.

After the mortgage panic, can anyone other than a congressman really believe that "the more we owe, the more we're worth"? Maybe that confusion is to be expected from the governing classes and their lapdog press, such as the news writer who insists that the government's bailout spending will have "no effect on Social Security and Medicare." When his drug bill added the biggest burden to the hidden debt since the Great Society, Bush said, "This week Congress made significant progress toward improving the lives of America's senior citizens." Really, Mr. President? Because America's senior citizens, and everyone else on a fixed income, will be among the hardest hit by the dollar meltdown.

At least David Walker understands that failure to solve the problem of hidden debt means a depreciating dollar and a lower standard of living. "Young people in particular will end up paying double or more in taxes what the current generation pays if they don't become more involved," he said.

Americans may be oblivious, but there are people watching our debt and the dollar very nervously. If you look carefully, you will see that they are beginning to squirm and are growing increasingly anxious. Because not everyone believes that wealth is just more zeroes on a piece of paper or that money can be created out of thin air.

SECTION II

HOW
WE
GOT
HERE

CHAPTER FOUR

Gold

The Quality of Money

For 2,500 years the global electorate has identified gold as the most reliable standard of value—which means that gold, a specific amount of gold, is the best possible unit of account, the best proxy for all goods, services and financial assets that are involved in the banking system and exchange economy.

—Jude Wanniski

Good money is coined freedom.

—Swiss proverb

In the Beginning

The words we use are rich with history. Our word "salary" comes from the Latin word for salt. Roman soldiers were sometimes paid in salt, prized for its life-sustaining capacity. Still, the individual soldier couldn't consume endless quantities of salt himself; it was a commodity that could be traded. We refer to this former role as money when we say that someone is "worth his salt."

Another word involving money, "pecuniary," comes from a root word for cattle. Cattle remain representations of wealth in parts of the world today and continue to be used as a means of exchange. Bread's ancient monetary role can still be noted in words like "bread" and "dough," when used to represent money.

But over the years people have discovered that as money, commodities such as salt, cattle, and bread have real drawbacks. To serve efficiently money must be both desirable and relatively scarce. Salt, cattle, and bread have met those conditions, although salt would serve as a poor form of money in places where it was readily available. But there are other qualities of good money that these lack.

Money needs to be fungible, that is, one unit must be capable of being substituted for another without meaningful change in value. One grain of salt is pretty much like another. In some communities and among some neighbors, one loaf of bread can be exchanged for another. Cattle are less fungible, differing widely in kind and quality. If you agree to sell the tribal chief your daughter for ten head of cattle, you may feel different when he shows up at your hut with a small herd of old, tubercular cows.

Money functions best if it is divisible. One may settle a small bill by dividing up a portion of salt or bread, but the value of a milk cow drops sharply when halved or quartered.

Another important attribute of money is durability. Salt, properly stored, is durable. Not so bread which, when labeled "day old," is sold at a discount. Like bread, cattle lose value after a certain age. And as ranchers have from time to time experienced, the cost of raising and maintaining cattle can even exceed their market value.

Over time mankind has discovered that gold meets all the requirements of an effective money. Gold is relatively scarce, universally desirable, fungible, divisible, and durable. In fact gold (and silver, although for purposes of illustration our attention in this chapter is on gold) functions so well as money, some believe it was actually created for that purpose. Perhaps it was.

Gold is certainly scarce. Gathered together in one place, all the gold in the world, all the gold in coins, in teeth, in jewelry, and in works of art, all the gold buried in backyards, in banks, and in government vaults could be consolidated into a cube a mere twenty-two yards on a side.

Gold is universally desirable. It is recognized and prized everywhere around the globe and has been for centuries. While salt's desirability as a medium of exchange declines in places where it is mined or reclaimed, the desirability of gold has nothing to do with location or geography. It is valued as highly in the gold mining areas of South Africa as it is in the financial centers of Europe or the remote jungles of South America. In fact gold's desirability is so universal that it would be easier to specify those who don't recognize its unique allure and function. Prominent among those are certain politicians and economists whose influence has been out of proportion to their insight. Of them we shall have more to say later.

Gold is fungible. It is an atomic element, just one of slightly more than 100 basic forms of matter, with an atomic weight of 79 on the periodic table of elements. Each ounce of gold, refined to its pure form, is exactly like every other ounce of gold, despite its age, where it was mined, or how it was processed. In short, gold is gold is gold.

Gold is divisible. It is so divisible and easily worked that it has been prized by artisans and craftsmen, ancient and modern. Gold leads all metals in malleability and ductility (followed as you would expect by its sister precious metal, silver). Gold is so malleable that it can be hammered into a leaf or sheet of foil three millionths of an inch thick—so thin that such a leaf is actually translucent, transmitting a greenish light. Although gold is a phenomenally heavy metal, with a cubic foot of it weighing more than half a ton, it can be processed so thin that people can actually eat it! Perhaps you've sampled it yourself atop pastries in fine restaurants, which gives new meaning to the term "a rich dessert." Some even extol gold's property as a nutritive supplement. Gold is so ductile that a single ounce can be stretched into a wire thirty-five miles long. No value is lost when gold is divided, nor need it remain divided.

Gold is virtually imperishable. Gold is the most stable, the least chemically active of all the metals. It does not rust, tarnish, or corrode. Gold coins lost on the ocean bottom and recovered after centuries are as bright and shiny as the day they were minted. Gold is as prized for its permanence as it is for its bright luster.

Golden Civilizations

Because of its attributes gold has been chosen in free economies to serve as money. No government had to make a law; no tyrant, dictator, king, sultan, or sheikh had to issue a decree for gold to be chosen as money. It did not have to be forced on a reluctant population by a central planner, regulator, fascist, socialist, or bureaucrat. Gold has served as money both in the absence of rulers and states and despite their best efforts to outlaw it. As a matter of fact, in every case in which a government has decided its citizens are better off not owning any gold, it has never been because the so-called "barbarous relic" was without value. The government has simply wanted all the gold for itself. A closer look will reveal that where gold serves as money there is no need for rulers, leaders, tyrants, planners, governments, or states to direct the monetary system at all. That should elicit a sigh of relief from anyone who has observed the serial calamities all of the aforementioned have created in their inevitable manipulation of money to their own advantage and to the detriment of the people.

An economy based on reliable precious metal money goes hand in hand with a healthy civilization. The citizens of ancient Athens were among the first to adopt an honest precious metal currency. The result was history's first strong commercial power. By the fifth century B.C. Greece was the leading importer of the world's raw materials and the leading exporter of the world's finished goods. While no one could belittle the material blessings of this prosperity, there were other blessings as well. That century Athens gave us some of the finest art, literature, and philosophy the world has ever known. It was the century of the Parthenon and of the playwrights Euripides and Sophocles. It was the age of Herodotus, known as the father of history, and it was the time of Socrates. "I thank God," said Plato, "that I was born Greek not barbarian, freeman and not slave, man and not woman; but above all that I was born in the age of Socrates." Such sentiments would not be considered politically correct today, but they reveal that even Athenians recognized theirs was an uncommon era. And a remarkable time it was, remembered twenty-five centuries later as a high point in human culture's slow evolution. But while Athens was creating a special place for itself in history, its cruder neighbor Sparta was lagging behind. Even through the classical age of Greece, the fifth century, Spartans used primitive iron bars as their instrument of barter. No wonder Sparta never flowered like Athens! The metaphorically sensitive will note that iron is associated with Ares (Mars to the Romans), the Greek god of warfare and bloodlust, as well as with the rust-hued planet. In Sparta a statue of Ares in chains was meant to represent the city-state's unbreakable linkage to the martial spirit. Athens was presided over by a different spirit for which the city-state was named: Athena, the goddess of wisdom. It was in Athens that Socrates demonstrated that argument, rather than a mere clash of opinions or dispute, could be an act of progressive refinement, not unlike the refinement of silver. We should not be surprised that silver was thought to represent truth, and that the word "argue" comes to us from the same root as the Latin word for silver. That word, *argentum*, is also familiar to us from the chemical symbol for silver, Ag, and even from the name of the country that was thought in the seventeenth century to be the "Land of Silver," Tierra Argentina.

Reliable gold coinage contributed to another civilization's having flourished for eight hundred years. During the period that Europe was plunged into the Dark Ages and commerce could still depend on bartering cattle, the Near and Middle East were enjoying untold prosperity. Constantine, the founder of the Byzantine Empire and the first Christian head of the Roman Empire, introduced a coin of about one-sixth ounce of gold. This coin, the golden bezant, was minted for eight centuries without alteration except to improve its purity and uniformity. Several hundred thousand bezant were eventually minted as the coin became a recognized store of value and standard accounting unit for trade from China to the Atlantic Ocean. So popular and dependable was the bezant that it helped make the Byzantine Empire the commercial center of the world, with the consequent material blessings flowing to its citizens. No civilization since has equaled the stability and honesty of the money the Byzantine Empire gave the world. But like all good things, it would not last forever, and eventually Byzantium's rulers began to debase the money, diluting its gold content by surreptitiously adding ever more base metals to the coinage. As the integrity of the coin declined, so did the empire. Today the shame brought on by the debasement of this once prestigious coinage lives on in our language when we describe a plot or scheme as being "byzantine," referring to its deviousness and underhandedness.

Finally, after the long Dark Ages, a golden day dawned again for Western civilization when in 1252 the city of Florence reintroduced European gold coinage. The gold florin was minted for almost three hundred years with a standardized gold content. Predictably during this time the city became a hotbed of activity: both as a leading center of commerce and as a patron home to creative greats such as Leonardo da Vinci and Michelangelo. Philosophers and scholars from east and west met in Florence, where the important work of Plato was rediscovered, a rebirth of idealism that helped fuel the Italian Renaissance. The precondition for all this creative enterprise of art and thought was a thriving commercial and financial center, made possible by an honest precious metal currency.

Close to our own time gold's record in human affairs continues to shine. Britain was on the gold standard for nearly two hundred years, from 1717 until 1914. It was a prosperous period for Britain, during which the country gave birth to the Industrial Revolution and the tiny island nation established outposts around the globe: Africa, India, the Far East, Australia, the South Pacific, and North and South America. One fourth of the earth and its people were ruled by the British Empire. But as the Romans discovered and Americans will learn to their great sorrow, empires are unsustainable edifices. The British finally abandoned the discipline of the gold standard in 1914 to fight the First World War. That war, like America's first Gulf War, was never allowed to end. Predictably, then, it flared up again in the Second World War. While the British were victorious in both, by the time the fires were finally put out, the empire upon which the sun truly never set collapsed in the smoldering ruins of bankruptcy.

The importance of precious metals in a nation's destiny was a lesson not lost on some bold British subjects. When the United States broke away from the mighty empire and declared independence, economic issues were central to the decision. The founders of the new republic knew enough about the importance of gold and silver to mandate their use in the Constitution, giving the Congress the power to coin—not print—money. Similarly, the several states were forbidden by Article 1, Section 10, to make "anything but gold and silver coin a tender in the payment of debts." These were wise provisions born of experience. The failures of the unbacked, irredeemable paper currencies of first the colonies, and then the Continental Congress ("Not worth a Continental!") were fresh in their memories. And unlike today's governing classes, the generation of the founders was learned and well read in the precedents we have described in this chapter.

This is not a smug defense of commercialism and material values to which our higher cultural and spiritual aspirations must be subordinated. It does not suggest that the genius of Athens and the inspiration of the Renaissance were nothing but the product of an economic dogma or the result of the good tastes of bankers. But honest money in the form of gold is really very much like honesty elsewhere in our personal and social relations. That one's word be "good as gold" is self-evidently desirable in cultivating the mutual interdependence of a complex and sophisticated culture, while honest money has been a liberating prerequisite for the division of labor in which people are free to flourish in their own individual preferences. Since we have already had recourse to the wisdom of the founders, let us leave the point about the foundational importance of sound money to other human pursuits with the words of John Adams, who understood that refined civilizations are built on such hierarchies:

> I must study politics and war that my sons may have liberty to study mathematics and philosophy. My sons ought to study mathematics and philosophy, geography, natural history, naval architecture, navigation, commerce, and agriculture, in order to give their children a right to study painting, poetry, music, architecture, statuary, tapestry, and porcelain.

With the foundation of freedom and honest money in place, the achievements of America began to multiply. Commerce thrived and the people prospered, while the rest of the world benefited from the spillover of America's consequent wealth, industriousness, inventiveness, and creative genius.

The historical case for gold and silver money can hardly be overstated. Such money combines the twin virtues of quality and quantity:

just as its quality is objective, independent of the stability or honesty of the issuing party, so too is its quantity relatively fixed, not susceptible to sudden change by fiat. Where precious metals serve as currency, good things happen. Conversely, when gold and silver have been abandoned, serious economic and political consequences result. Nations or peoples that are net accumulators of gold rise; those that dishoard fall. This rule does not bode well for the United States. The U.S. nation-state once held 652 million ounces of gold. Government has squandered 60 percent of this. Today, the nation is left with only 261.5 million ounces of gold. That is, if the representations that are made by the government and the Federal Reserve are to be believed.

America Abandons Gold

Gold and silver were essential to the founders' plan for America. They certainly knew the difference between printing money and coining it, and yet, while the Constitution has not been amended in that regard, we have become a nation of printing press and electronic entry money, backed by debt. So what has happened that gold and silver are nowhere to be found in the American monetary system?

Gold and silver were first forsaken during the Civil War. Wars are costly undertakings; the War Between the States was no exception. Drained of its precious metals reserves, the banking system stopped settling its obligations in gold. Congress then authorized the issuance of the "greenback," another irredeemable printing press currency. By the end of the war, $450 million of this paper money had been issued. The United States was off the gold standard from 1862 until 1879. By the end of that period, though, the government had built up its stock of gold and was able to redeem the outstanding greenbacks. The country was back on the gold standard, where it belonged and where it stayed for more than half a century.

Honest money was dealt another serious blow when a presidential executive order in 1933 and the Gold Reserve Act of 1934 forbade gold ownership by American citizens. It was somehow imprudent, indeed criminal, for Americans to own gold themselves, but this apparently dangerous element was safe in the hands of the government. It is hard for some to imagine today the mentality that must have pertained at the time on the part of those who complied with orders to turn their real money over to the bureaucracy. But others were reading the signs of the times, and the amount of gold coins in circulation and gold in bank vaults mysteriously began declining steeply months ahead of President Franklin D. Roosevelt's confiscation. While millions of Americans were willing to risk felony charges to hold on to their gold, almost 22 percent of the gold coins in circulation were turned in to the government at the going rate of $20.67 per ounce. But once the gold was in the government's hands, the price was suddenly raised to $35 per ounce. The dollar was devalued by 69.3 percent and the American people were thereby instantly swindled out of $3 billion.

It is instructive to linger on this episode. Americans at the time were just as apt to carry an actual twenty-dollar gold piece in their pocket as a twenty-dollar "bill," a gold certificate. For convenience, one might well carry the paper money, but in and of itself it had no more value than any other piece of paper. Its value lay in the fact that this gold certificate was, after all, simply a claim check, a warehouse receipt for the real money, the gold, for which it could be exchanged at any time. Embellished by ornately engraved scrollwork to enhance the illusion of credibility, the twenty-dollar bills actually bore the inscription, "This certifies that there has been deposited in the Treasury of the United States of America twenty dollars in gold coin payable to the bearer on demand."

The repudiation of this promise was breathtaking in its audacity, but it was conducted in a very precise manner. Since the U.S. $20 gold pieces contained a little less than an ounce of gold, actually .9675 troy ounces, gold was nationalized at the price of $20.67 an ounce, so that each $20 gold coin could be exchanged—and would be exchanged under penalty of law—for a new $20 bill. Today, seventy-five years after the fact and with an indifference that would shame a petty thief, the Treasury's Web site offers this response to the hapless who believe the Treasury's promise to pay in gold:

QUESTION: I have some old gold certificates and would like to trade them in for gold. What should I do?

ANSWER: Gold certificates were withdrawn from circulation along with all gold coins and gold bullion as required by the Gold Reserve Act of 1934. Gold certificates circulated until December 28, 1933. That is when the President ordered private owners of gold certificates to deliver their notes to the Treasurer of the United States by midnight on January 17, 1934. It was then illegal to hold gold certificates. . . .

Under 31 U.S.C. 5118(b) as amended, "The United States Government may not pay out any gold coin. A person lawfully holding United States coins and currency may present the coins for currency . . . for exchange (dollar for dollar) for other United States coins and currency (other than gold and silver coins) that . . ." citizens may lawfully own. Although gold certificates are no longer produced and are not redeemable in gold, they still maintain their legal tender status. You may redeem the notes you have through the Treasury Department or any financial institution. The redemption, however, will be at the face value on the note. These notes may, however, have a "premium" value to coin and currency collectors or dealers.

So much for engraved promises on paper, although for consolation we are told they may have some value to collectors of oddities! While some Americans were willing to risk fines of $10,000 and ten years in prison to defy their government's gold grab (a "temporary" measure, a "respite" to prevent hoarding), no new gold coins for circulation were minted after 1933. Still, there was silver. Silver coins continued to circulate and some of the paper currencies, silver certificates, were redeemable, although the promise to pay the bearer in "silver dollars" was replaced in 1934 with the suspiciously vague promise to pay in silver. Of course, that too would come to an end. The issuance of silver certificates ceased in 1963; next the government repudiated its promise to redeem them for silver on June 24, 1968. But it was not unexpected. A few years earlier President Lyndon B. Johnson had issued an executive order halting the minting of silver coins altogether. Johnson claimed that silver had become too valuable to be used as money. This should have raised some alarm among those who thought that money was supposed to be valuable. With the exception of some half-dollars minted with a sharply reduced silver content until 1970, the government halted silver coinage in 1964. Thereafter it issued base-metal coins with no precious metal content at all. Even so, it went to a great deal of trouble to foster the illusion that the new coins were still silver or at least of substantial value. Gold and silver coins are often milled, that is, they have reeded or serrated edges. If the "king was in his counting house, counting out his money," as the nursery rhyme told, he was quite possibly actually engaged in an act of theft, filing off edges of the precious metals of the coins that passed his way. Milling the coins' edges made this fraud detectable. Although no one would have an interest in filing off the edges and collecting the base metal of the new U.S. coins, the Treasury continued the practice of milling the new coins for appearance's sake. Furthermore, while the dimes, quarters, and half-dollars are made from a copper coin blank, the mint goes to the added expense of cladding these in copper-nickel because the alloy has a silver appearance. And thus is the illusion made complete!

One may wonder why all this was necessary. After all, President Johnson had made assurances to us that the new coins would trade side-by-side with the silver ones forever. Johnson had never learned the principle identified twenty-five hundred years ago and known today as Gresham's law: bad money drives out good. People will tend to hold on to and save good money such as real silver coins, while spending and passing along the bad money. To illustrate the point of Gresham's law, you will have noted that you can get change in paper dollars for any transaction, but the clerk at 7-Eleven has never given you change in silver dollars. Instead of trading side-by-side forever as the president had claimed, the real silver coins began to disappear from circulation at once.

Despite the disappearance of gold and silver coins from the domestic monetary scene, as far as foreigners were concerned the dollar still had some ties to gold. Since the end of World War Two the dollar has been the accepted reserve currency of the world, initially because of its promised convertibility to gold. The London Gold Pool was established in 1961 to maintain the fiction of dollar convertibility at the rate of $35 to the ounce. To keep the price stable, the pool was supposed to sell gold when the price rose above that benchmark and buy when it fell. Like all convoluted monetary schemes, it wasn't to be trusted. Hadn't the United

States repudiated the gold claims and bonds of its own citizens? Hadn't the government reneged on its promises to pay its own people in silver? Apparently foreigners didn't think they would fare any better. They wanted real gold for their paper dollars.

Chief among those recognizing the dishonorable management of the dollar was French president Charles de Gaulle. Despite his Cassandra-like warning to President Kennedy that involvement in Vietnam would trap him in "a bottomless military and political swamp," the French have been on the receiving end of a great deal of antipathy in American popular opinion. Much of this was on display during the lead-up to Bush's debacle in Iraq. For their trouble in again warning America off the new foreign adventure, the French were met with contempt. President Jacques Chirac wanted the debate over an Iraq war to be both serious and calm. When President Bush warned Iraq a month before the war that "the game is over," Chirac wisely advised, "It's not a game, and it's not over." For their trouble, the French were met with ridicule. Members of Congress instructed their restaurants to rename French fries "freedom fries"; know-nothing talk show hosts broadcast stunts pouring French wine down toilets; late-night comedians talked of "cheese-eating surrender monkeys." German reluctance to support Bush's war was like that of the French. But what had the French done to be singled out for special contempt? The answer: de Gaulle. Among his indiscretions, early on he had asked America to honor its promises of dollar convertibility to gold. Seeing monetary chicanery afoot, that America was paying its debts by simply printing more dollars as desired, in 1958 de Gaulle instructed the Banque de France to accelerate the conversion of its dollar reserves into gold. He had France's debts from World War Two paid off by 1963 and two years later sent the French navy to pick up $150 million of French gold held in U.S. Federal Reserve vaults in New York. Refusing to let the French be financially victimized, he called for a new monetary system "on an indisputable monetary base that does not carry the mark of any particular country. . . . Yes, gold, which does not change in nature, which is made indifferently into bars, ingots and coins, which does not have any nationality, which is considered, in all places and at all times, the immutable and fiduciary value par excellence."

In all these things, de Gaulle was acting prudently. American authorities were effectively floating bad checks; de Gaulle was presenting those checks for collection on an account with insufficient funds. Honorable people, discovering they have written bad checks, strive to make it right. But chest-thumping Americans, following the cue of the governing classes responsible for the fraud, chose instead to vilify the victims of their economic deceit and thus were planted the seeds of the American enmity toward the French. The war-making classes would cultivate that enmity carefully during the buildup to Iraq.

In truth, the French had just shown up early for the run that was forming on America's gold bank. In a short period between November 1967 and March 1968 the United States lost $3.2 billion from its gold holdings. Private buyers took up four hundred tons of gold from the London pool on a single day in March. At that point the United States' bluff had been called: the dollar was no longer good as gold. The London Gold Pool ceased operations on March 14, 1968. From that day forward foreigners holding U.S. dollars—which they had accepted as claim checks for gold in the first place—had to stand in line to get gold from the Treasury. And stand in line they did. By the summer of 1971 the foreign demand to exchange dollars for gold was beyond containment. President Richard Nixon slammed shut the gold window entirely on August 15, 1971. The act amounted to a confession that the dollar's "good as gold days" were over.

Having abandoned its constitutional golden heritage, the American monetary system was no longer restrained. The authorities were freed to create dollars as they saw fit. But the experience of other currencies severed from the discipline of gold demonstrates that while a gold-based monetary system confers its special blessings, its abandonment is accompanied by its own peculiar affliction: inflation.

CHAPTER FIVE

Inflation

The Quantity of Money

With the exception only of the period of the gold standard, practically all governments of history have used their exclusive power to issue money to defraud and plunder the people.

—F. A. Hayek

Paper money eventually returns to its intrinsic value—zero.

—Voltaire

Money's Mysterious Malady

A quick survey of pronouncements by government officials over the past generation would convince anyone that inflation is a strange and occult malady. It has been characterized as "the nation's number one problem," and "the cruelest tax of all." Haven't we been told endlessly that "we are winning the war on inflation," or that "this administration has gotten a handle on inflation"? President Bush responded to rapidly rising gas and grocery prices with a show of concern ("people have got to understand that here in the White House we are concerned"). All the hand-wringing notwithstanding, inflation never goes away; sometimes we have more, sometimes less, but inflation persists. It's like the cough a chain smoker can't shake. In fact most Americans have never lived through a single year that wasn't inflationary. Most have experienced at least four years of double-digit inflation, while older baby boomers and those near retirement age have seen annual inflation inch up to double-digit levels as many as half a dozen times.

What is inflation? How is it created? Where does it come from? What is its impact? Why does it "run away"? And can it "run away" again? For answers to these and all our questions, one might think to turn to Ben Bernanke, chairman of the Board of Governors of the Federal Reserve. Bernanke has expressed himself with the kind of clarity we have come to expect from Fed chairmen. At the International Monetary Conference in Barcelona in June 2008, Bernanke commented on current market conditions, saying, "Inflation has remained high, reflecting continued sharp increases in the prices of globally traded commodities." In other words, prices are going up because prices are going up. This is the stuff of those stand-up entertainers who delight in the comic use of tautologies. News accounts don't report whether conference attendees, the heads of many of the world's largest financial institutions, burst out laughing. But the gag must have played well because Bernanke went on to milk it again. "A rough stabilization of commodity prices, even at high levels, would result in a relative rapid moderation of inflation." When prices stop going up, so will inflation.

The governing classes have gotten away with such hilarity for a long time now. President Gerald Ford went on television during his administration to advise the people that the best way to deal with inflation was to be sure to lick their dinner plates clean. With grocery prices climbing out of sight in the middle of 2008, Britain's Gordon Brown dusted that approach off again. Like a nagging home economics teacher, the prime minister instructed British subjects to take more care storing fruit and vegetables to reduce waste. But thirty-four years earlier President Ford had taken his campaign to the limit of credulity, urging Americans to be sure to send for their WIN ("Whip Inflation Now") buttons! Years later, in his autobiography, Alan Greenspan, eventually to become Federal Reserve chairman, but at the time the chairman of Ford's Council of Economic Advisers, described thinking how "unbelievably stupid" the WIN program was. Nice of him to speak out a generation too late. The next president, Jimmy Carter, thought to appoint a "chief inflation fighter." Given the comedy that surrounds the subject, one may be forgiven for assuming the new appointee's job was to go around the country servicing America's unlicked dinner plates! But Professor Alfred Kahn had a better act of his own that he tried out on national television in November 1978. Appearing on NBC's *Meet the Press*, Kahn was asked by economics correspondent Irving R. Levine how he intended to take on inflation:

> MR. LEVINE: In order to cure any illness, one has to diagnose the cause. What do you see as the principal cause of inflation?
>
> PROFESSOR KAHN: I'm going to evade that question, because I don't know what the principal cause of inflation is. The essence of what the President has proposed is a multi-faceted attack. I think that the problem of inflation is so deep-rooted in western society, can be attributed to such broad social causes, that I think for example the inflation we are experiencing in the United States today is in some important way related to the fact that I see people throw papers on the sidewalk of Pennsylvania Avenue when I walk to the subway. And it distresses me enormously. Or I see them walk on the grass. It has something to do with a sense of being members of a single society rather than, and as I have put it, and forgive me for repeating, 200 to 225 million people at perpetual war with one another.

All this is good material for finalists on *Last Comic Standing;* not so good for a troubled economy. Did the chairman really think the prices are going up because prices are going up? Did the chief inflation fighter actually believe that it's all about broad social causes like stepping on the grass? Is it conceivable that these specialists of monetary, treasury, and banking functions really don't know the truth so foundational to their own activities? Or do they really know the truth and for reasons of their own prefer to propagate a smokescreen of deceit to provide cover for the activities of their patrons? Which is worse, that they are ignorant and in charge of our economic environment or that they are liars and in charge of our economic environment? Perhaps it doesn't matter.

Inflation is quite simply an increase in the money supply—or the supply of money and credit. Inflation is well understood; it is always and everywhere a monetary phenomenon. Inflation (*an increase in the supply of money and credit*) causes prices to rise. Rising prices are not inflation, they are a result of inflation. An increase in prices across the economy is a result of an increase in the money supply. Any definition that says inflation is rising prices mistakes cause for effect and is symptomatic of the confusion or deceit in public policy that has undermined our economic health.

A simple example will make clear why the inflation of the money supply causes prices to rise. Suppose for a moment that this book you are holding is a rare first edition. You and your fellow book enthusiasts have come together in an auction to bid for this prized volume. Imagine that you have each come to the auction carrying $1,000 with which to bid. Now there is only the single book—which is why it is rare. As the auctioneer entertains bids, we soon find that the price of the book can be bid as high as $1,000. But suddenly the door in the back of the room bursts open and in comes a monetary official, carrying a satchel filled with freshly printed money. He goes through the room looking for deserving faces, those who will vote for his party or are deserving in some other way, to whom he slips an additional $100 bill. As the auction continues we soon see the book bid up to $1,100 dollars. There is still only one book because the bureaucrat did not produce another. But he did increase the supply of money in the room, which resulted in a price increase. We have just witnessed inflation.

Our economy is much like a giant auction. People bid for the available goods and services according to their individual means and preferences. Just as in our book auction there is but one book, the goods and services in our economy are limited. The bureaucrat at the auction does not add to those goods and services or produce any other real wealth. Just as the increased money supply in the auction provides for the price of the book to rise, an increase in the supply of money and credit allows for prices of available goods and services to be bid higher. Imagine that in the deep of night, some Washington wizard waved his wand and doubled the amount of money each person has. No new wealth would result; prices would adjust accordingly. It's not hard to see that prices would double while the purchasing power of the currency would be cut in half. To eliminate inflation then, you need not lick your plate clean, show concern in the White House, pick up the trash on Pennsylvania Avenue, declare war, or wear a button. The responsible party must stop inflating the supply of money and credit.

For generations paper money has provided governments with a quick and convenient means of increasing the supply of money. As far back as the thirteenth century the adventurer Marco Polo marveled at the act of "alchemy" by which the great Kublai Khan "causeth the bark of trees, made into something like paper, to pass for money over all his country."

> All these pieces of paper are issued with as much solemnity and authority as if they were of pure gold or silver; and on every piece a variety of officials, whose duty it is, have to write their names, and to put their seals. And when all is prepared duly, the chief officer deputed by the Kaan smears the Seal entrusted to him with vermilion, and impresses it on the paper, so that the form of the Seal remains stamped upon it in red; the Money is then authentic. Any one forging it would be punished with death. And the Kaan causes every year to be made such a vast quantity of this money, which costs him nothing, that it must equal in amount all the treasure in the world.

Gold and silver impose a discipline on governments, even plenipotentiary ones like the Great Khan's. A government cannot by decree, legislation, or edict double the amount of gold in the treasury, while paper currency can be produced at very little cost. A gold money supply can only be increased by the expenditure of human time, effort, and ingenuity, much to the consternation of governments that prefer paper money, whether of mulberry bark or linen stock, because it verges on being costless. There have been occasional but not prolonged gold inflations. On being shipped back to Spain, the huge quantities of gold the conquistadores had plundered in the New World caused successive waves of inflation to sweep across Europe. But as the discovery of a new continent is hardly a repeatable phenomenon, true gold inflations have been the exception while paper money inflations have been the rule.

Before the advent of paper money, inflation usually took the form of coinage debasement. If the reigning monarch was a spendthrift, or had gotten involved in an unpopular war for which he was reluctant to tax the people directly, he had to find a new way to come up with some money. Typically such a ruler had reserved to himself the sole preroga-tive of minting the realm's gold and silver coins. For example, he would direct the mint to file off one one-hundredth part of each gold coin as it came through the counting house, or realloy each coin with one one-hundredth part less gold. By the time 10,000 coins had come through the treasury he had accumulated enough gold to create 101 new coins, all of which were his to spend. Our monarch had not created any real wealth—any goods or services. He had simply resorted to fraud, deceiving those in the economy into believing there was sud-denly more wealth about. Recalling our auction example with the amount of goods and services unchanged, the ruler's newly minted gold coins will bid up prices so that the new coins have taken on value to the exact degree that the 10,000 coins that had passed through the mint lost value. Holders of those 10,000 gold coins will find higher prices. Their currency has lost some of its value; it has been devalued to pay for the belligerency and extravagance of the monarch.

The emperor Nero, the proverbial fiddler in the ashes of a burning Rome, was not surprisingly responsible for just such a coinage debase-ment. Both Julius Caesar and his grandnephew Augustus Caesar had attempted to maintain the integrity of the money. But just forty years after Augustus, Nero reduced the weight of the gold and silver coins by more than 10 percent. It was all downhill from there. Before long once-mighty Rome was minting base metal coins with a thin wash of silver, designed to fool the people into believing it was real money. (Now you know where the U.S. Treasury got the idea!) Needless to say, Rome was losing its dominance in the affairs of men. The barbarians were at the door. Attila the Hun demanded and got a ton of gold a year from Rome, a bribe to keep his hordes from sacking the city.

While Rome declined, the Byzantine Empire ascended, employing the honest gold coinage described in chapter 4. But after eight hundred years, that coinage too was debased and the Byzantine Empire began to fall. As is usually the case, the emperor Alexius Comnenus began the debasement to pay for his extravagance and corruption. Meanwhile throughout the Middle Ages, European heads of state made the debasement and devaluation of coinage their special pastime. It was a primitive method of inflation, but it worked as long as they had the force of the kingdom to coerce their subjects into accepting this devalued money, much as legal tender laws today represent the force of government compelling private individuals to accept fraudulent government money "for all debts, public and private." King James II of England coined debased money of copper, lead, and even pewter. The Irish called these coins *uim bog*, meaning "soft metal." They knew such coins had little intrinsic value. Their disdain for this debased coinage is believed to survive today in our word "humbug."

The inflation process jumped to a new level of sophistication in seventeenth-century England. People had become accustomed to taking their gold to the local goldsmith, paying him a fee to look after their metal. The goldsmith issued a paper claim check for the deposited gold, promising to deliver the gold to the owner upon demand. Before long people discovered it was easier to exchange these paper receipts in transactions than it was to make a special trip to the goldsmith, withdraw their gold, and complete their transaction. Soon the exchange of these demand deposit slips became commonplace. They were readily accepted because the receipt holder could take his receipt to the goldsmith and redeem it with ease for the actual gold it represented.

Before long the goldsmiths noticed that relatively few of the receipt holders came to claim their gold at any one time. The convenience of the paper gold receipt was so great that seldom did anyone demand the underlying metal. Some goldsmiths seized upon the opportunity to create more receipts for gold than they actually had on hand. It was no more than a counterfeiting scheme of course, and if caught, a goldsmith could lose his head. It was then that the goldsmiths hit upon a novel idea. Rather than create these receipts for gold they didn't have, adding to their own wealth, they would issue these receipts to others as loans. That would arouse less suspicion. These goldsmiths turned bankers would profit from the arrangement by the interest they charged. Once the system got rolling they profited tremendously. For example, a goldsmith/banker who had a thousand ounces of gold on deposit would print up receipts for four times that much. Instead of receiving interest on the thousand ounces he actually had available to lend, he got interest on all four thousand ounces. Fractional reserve banking had been invented; the reserves maintained were a mere fraction of what had been loaned out. The practice had an unfortunate side effect: it was inflationary. The banker had created new money that entered the economy, bidding up the price of goods and services many times over.

There was, however, a pitfall in this scheme. From time to time rumors would circulate about the insolvency of these neophyte bankers and occasionally a run would develop. Customers would beat down the doors, demanding the gold their paper receipts promised was being held in safekeeping for them. If the gold wasn't there, the goldsmith was in serious trouble.

These early bankers soon learned to seek the protection of the king. It was like a marriage made in heaven. The banker could acquire large sums of money that could be lent to the sovereign at a favorable rate of interest. He in turn would lend the force of law to the banker's "money." It became legal tender, which means subjects were required to accept the currency under threat of law "for all debts, public and private." Of course this creation of paper money was highly inflationary, but the inflation was in the best interest of both the banker and the king. The inflation process was the very source of the banker's livelihood. He earned interest on the inflated quantity of money he loaned. It mattered little to him if this money continually lost value. He was taking his percentage on money he would not otherwise be able to loan. For his part, the king found a ready source of capital for his adventures. He could tax his subjects to pay the banker back, but he could have what he wanted today, deferring payment until tomorrow. And as the king was typically the largest debtor around, inflation served him well. The currency units he paid the banker back with were less dear than the units he had borrowed. As usual the only losers in the scheme were the subjects. These people found that what money they had was worth less and less. Their money lost value in the economy to the extent that the new money bid prices higher.

The Reign of Terror Inflation

Are you as smart as a French peasant? So goes the saying in the gold business. And indeed French peasants had a national history that once encouraged them to keep some gold and silver coins on hand to isolate themselves from government inflations. One of the world's most dramatic and devastating inflations took place in Revolutionary France during the period from 1790 to 1796. The Reign of Terror revolutionaries made it their first order of business to issue paper money without any gold or silver backing. The first issue of these *assignats* was based upon church property that had been confiscated. But even when the underlying land was sold, the government let the paper money continue to circulate. One wave of paper money led to the next. Predictably gold, silver, and even copper coins began to disappear from circulation.

This French inflation was accompanied by all the other disastrous economic policies imaginable: wage and price controls, currency repudiations, and the wholesale redistribution of wealth and disregard of property rights. Penalties for violating the economic edicts of the government's central planners were severe, including generous applications of the guillotine. In his landmark report on the French inflation, Andrew Dickson White relates the extremes to which the government went in trying to repeal rational economic behavior:

> To spread terror, the Criminal Tribunal at Strassburg was ordered to destroy the dwelling of anyone found guilty of selling goods above the price set by law. The farmer often found that he could not raise his products at anything like the price required by the new law, and when he tried to hold back his crops or cattle, alleging that he could not afford to sell them at the prices fixed by law, they were frequently taken from him by force and he was fortunate if paid even in the depreciated fiat money— fortunate, indeed, if he finally escaped with his life. . . .
>
> [The government] decreed that any person selling gold or silver coin, or making any difference in any transaction

between paper and specie [gold and silver] should be imprisoned in irons for six years; that anyone who refused to accept a payment in *assignats*, or accepted *assignats* at a discount should pay a fine of three thousand francs; and that anyone committing this crime a second time should pay a fine of six thousand francs and suffer imprisonment twenty years in irons. Later on the 8th of September, 1793, the penalty for such offenses was made death, with confiscation of the criminal's property, and a reward was offered to any person informing the authorities regarding any such criminal transaction. To reach the climax of ferocity, the convention decreed, in May 1794, that the death penalty should be inflicted on any person convicted of "having asked, before a bargain was concluded, in what money payment was to be made."

The issue of paper money continued at a frantic pace. The mobs demanded laws "making paper money as good as gold." The government, eager to buy their affections, passed ever more severe measures. But it was as unable to turn paper into gold as the alchemists had been unable to turn lead into gold. The only things transmuted in France were prevailing conditions into greater poverty. White reports that from 1790 to 1795 a measure of flour had risen from 2 francs to 225; a pair of shoes from 5 francs to 200; a pound of soap had risen 44 times in price; a pound of sugar 70 times. Even so, the wages and rewards of the productive plummeted, while gamblers and speculators profited. In less than six years the Revolutionary Government of France had issued 45 billion francs of paper money. One franc of gold was worth 600 francs of paper. And out of the ashes of the economically destroyed France arose the dictator Napoléon and his seventeen years of war, empire, and bankruptcy.

Germany's Fiery Inflation

Wars must be allowed to end. World War Two ended; Germany and Japan emerged as American allies. The Vietnam War ended and today Americans vacation there; our trading relationships are extensive. The shrimp you have for dinner tonight may well have been farmed for you in Vietnam. Conversely, the first Gulf War with Iraq was not allowed to end. Although the United States quickly achieved its objective of ending Iraq's occupation of Kuwait, American bombs continued to fall on Iraq for twelve years. Inevitably new warfare with Iraq eventually ensued, costlier and more deadly for all concerned. But the textbook example of a war that was not allowed to end is World War One. It was a war that historians are still at pains to explain. At least twenty million people—mostly civilians—were killed. Tragically, before long most of the same parties were at war again. World War Two, the most expensive war in history, spelled widespread deprivation, suffering, and carnage, after which seventy million humans—again mostly civilians—lay dead.

Germany had been accustomed to paying for its wars by looting the vanquished. As the loser in the Great War, Germany was more susceptible to being looted than to looting. And looted it was. Despite President Woodrow Wilson's promises of magnanimity, the Allies proved to be vindictive in victory. Although Germany had laid down its arms with the armistice of November 11, 1918, the victors imposed a blockade on Germany that closed the ports to food shipments for the civilian population and went so far as to prevent German fishing in the Baltic Sea. The "starvation blockade" persisted for eight months after the armistice and resulted in widespread famine and death in the civilian population.

This cruelty foreshadowed the terms of the peace in which the Allies' appetite for revenge and plunder went unchecked. The ruinous reparations imposed on Germany under the Treaty of Versailles were initially 269 billion gold marks. That's about $2.8 trillion at recent gold prices. The British even forced a provision for Germans to pay the pensions of all the Allied soldiers. While the reparations total was later reset to 132 billion gold marks, the burden was punitive.

The victors were incidentally quite clear in demanding that war reparations by Germany be paid in gold:

> **Article 262.**
> Any monetary obligation due by Germany arising out of the present Treaty and expressed in terms of gold marks shall be payable at the option of the creditors in pounds sterling pay-

able in London; gold dollars of the United States of America payable in New York; gold francs payable in Paris; or gold lire payable in Rome.

The Allies wanted gold; the German people got paper. The German central bank turned it out at a blazing pace: billions, trillions, quadrillions of paper marks. Men working in German factories would rush to the gates at pay time and hand their wages to their wives, who rushed to spend the paper money as quickly as possible because it lost value by the hour. People literally carried bushel baskets of almost worthless currency to do their shopping. The story is told of one fellow pushing a wheelbarrow full of money to do some shopping. On the way he decided to stop at a tavern for a quick beer, and carefully parked his wheelbarrow outside. When he finished his drink he came out to find his money still there—but his wheelbarrow had been stolen! It would be funny were it not for the underlying human tragedy. Thousands of industrious, hardworking German families found that their insurance policies, their pensions, their life savings wouldn't buy a cup of coffee. They were wiped out.

In 1918 at the end of the war there were just over 22 billion marks in existence. By November 1923 there were over 518 quintillion marks in circulation. Even the hellish pace of two thousand printing presses had not been able to keep the paper money coming fast enough. In fact the Germans had to resort to printing on only one side of the bill. It improved their efficiency greatly. (Some years ago U.S. senator William Proxmire introduced a bill to have one side of the dollar printed by the offset method, instead of the higher quality intaglio process currently in use. The object of his bill was to enable the Bureau of Engraving and Printing to increase its paper money printing efficiency by 30 percent.) At the beginning of the war the deutsche mark had been worth about 24 cents. By late 1923 a pound of meat cost three 3.2 trillion marks. The price of an egg had gone from a quarter of a mark at the end of the war to 80 billion marks in November 1923. The economy was left in shambles. Out of the ashes of the destroyed German economy and the smoldering resentment of the people arose the National Socialist Workers Party, the Nazis, and the advent of Adolf Hitler.

While the Treaty of Versailles looms large in the narrative of the German inflation, by the end of the war in 1918, and months before the treaty was drafted, the German central bank, the Reichsbank, and the Ministry of Finance had already begun flooding the economy with credit and money. Earlier in this chapter we asked whether the monetary and government officials really don't understand inflation, or whether they are simply cynical enough not to care as they destroy an economy. The question could well be posed again about the textbook case the German experience provides. Did educated and sophisticated German central bankers and monetary officials really not know what they were doing when they ran the printing presses day and night, or when they saw that shops had to close at lunchtime each day just to re-price their inventories? Did they think the destruction of the German middle class would be a good thing? That chaos and the alienation of people throughout Germany would be without consequences? Were there some who believed the aftermath of the inflation would provide an environment for a desirable political and cultural change? That a big dose of national socialism was a prescription for a healthy and wholesome country? Perhaps some did. Perhaps the public faces of the German government were simply uninformed and incurious stooges such as we have seen among our own government officials. But not all the responsible parties could plead ignorance. Historian Paul Johnson writes that no one in the German financial and business establishment "cared a damn" for the currency:

> They speculated and hedged against it, shipped capital abroad and, in the case of the industrialists, invested in fixed capital as fast as they could by borrowing paper money.
> . . . The big gainers, apart from the government itself, were the landowners, who redeemed all their mortgages, and the industrialists, who repaid their debts in worthless paper and became the absolute owners of all their fixed capital. It was one of the biggest and crudest transfers of wealth in history. The responsibilities were clear; the beneficiaries of the fraud were easily identifiable.

Of course governments are the primary beneficiary of inflation as they seek to sustain themselves whether through welfare or warfare. But the complicity of the banking and financial sector, specifically those in bed with the government in the implementation of the inflation, cannot be overlooked. As in Germany, these enablers of inflation have political connections and inside knowledge of the changes in monetary policies, as well as first access to the newly created money before its value has been diluted, spending and investing it at lower prices before the new money has been equally disseminated throughout the economy, causing prices to rise. Those who receive the money last, by such means as lagging wage hikes or in benefits indexed to consumer price increases that have already taken place, are hurt most.

The German experience remains helpful in assessing prospects for future government policies, even in the United States. No matter how destructive a blow-off runaway inflation is, there are those with near-term incentives to encourage it without regard to the long-term consequences. First among those are the government and the governing classes, followed by those in the banking and financial sector who are positioned to exploit such policies. Those financial institutions, large insurance companies, and banks have a clear moral obligation to use their considerable political clout to resist the destruction of the value of the deposits, insurance policies, and pension plans their clients have been paying for over a lifetime. But they did not do so in Germany, and they have not done so in the United States. Meanwhile, chief among the victims of inflation are those who save, such as bank depositors, those who buy bonds, and fixed income investors, retirees, and pension plan owners. In other words, all the virtues of thrift and savings that contribute to a healthy and prosperous economy are penalized.

Nightmare in Zimbabwe

Finally in this section a word about the recent mind-boggling runaway inflation in Zimbabwe. It is a tragic tale of bloodshed and ruin. Zimbabwe, formerly the British colony Rhodesia, was once a food exporter. Now after decades of Afro-socialism, it cannot produce enough food to feed itself. Life expectancy has collapsed as well. Even the country's wildlife is being decimated in the press for food.

Inflation in Zimbabwe ran about 32 percent a year ten years ago, but can now only be said to be in a factor of untold millions of percent a year; the country's official numbers showed the annual inflation rate hit 231 million percent in the summer of 2008. One week the central bank announced a new 100 billion dollar note (that's with eleven zeroes); the next it announced plans to lop ten zeroes off the next issuance of paper money. Several weeks later those announcements were followed by the release of the new one million Zimbabwe dollar bill. That was followed by the issuance of a new 50 billion dollar note. These currency capers might be more amusing were they not an eerie harbinger of our own possible future. And after all, the real experience of living through such madness is nightmarish: unemployment is 80 percent, while a third of the population are refugees in their own country. Here's a typical observation about life in Zimbabwe from the London *Times* in 2008:

> Moses Chikomba does not care much about politics. He does not care whether the land is owned by blacks or whites. All he cares about is that his $50 billion monthly salary will buy him just two bars of soap. In three days it will buy only one.
>
> "What does the future hold for us?" he asks, clutching the near-worthless notes with their eye-popping strings of zeros.

"We are all billionaires who can afford to buy nothing," he said; another commented, "We are wondering what comes after trillion?" Just as shining a spotlight on a thief run amok makes conditions tough for other petty thieves and pilferers, the transparency of it all has finally become an embarrassment to other inflating governments. Germany's foreign minister even ordered the German company that provided Zimbabwe with the fine banknote stock for its legalized counterfeiting to stop deliveries. The *Los Angeles Times* marked the event with a headline that betrays the news media's confusion about all things economic: "LACK OF BANK NOTE PAPER THREATENS ZIMBABWE ECONOMY."

But that won't stop the fraud. Robert Mugabe, Zimbabwe's president, has to keep the paper money flowing to pay off the militias and thugs who keep him in office. The lesson that arms us for the future is this: ultimately the survival of the government and the governing classes (at least in the reckoning of those in charge) trumps the resilience of the economy and the well-being of the people.

CHAPTER SIX

American Money

A Superior Sleight of Hand

Government finance and the nation's medium of exchange have in the future to be two separate things.

—Ludwig von Mises

The real secret of magic lies in the performance.

—David Copperfield

Inflation in the United States

We have come a long way from the days of old when kings clipped coins as they came through the counting houses, or debased the coinage by diluting its precious metals content with base metals. It is true that this time-worn debauchery of the coinage is still honored today in the clad sandwich coins of the U.S. Mint. But paper money, the offspring of warehouse receipts, provides a more efficient means of counterfeiting. Economist Ludwig von Mises once observed that government is the only agency in the world that can take a valuable commodity like paper, slap some ink on it, and make it totally worthless. While we speak of printing press money, and while you can visit the Bureau of Engraving and Printing in Washington, D.C., and see that the presses do turn it out at an impressive rate, the mere printing of currency is much too transparent for modern times. American inflation is the product of a more sophisticated sleight of hand made possible by the

Federal Reserve System. Alchemists of antiquity, who spent their entire lives trying but were never able to "goldify the lead," would have been in awe at the way modern central bankers "monetize the debt." This process of turning debt into money is truly an act of central banking wizardry.

The government runs deficits by spending more money than it has. The government's debts are then used as collateral for the creation of new money. It works something like this: Suppose I ask you to lend me $1,000. You might reply: "How will I know the loan is secure? What will you give me for collateral?" "Don't worry," I say reassuringly, "I've charged quite a bit on my MasterCard, and I owe Visa a lot of money as well. Let me give you the receipts from my purchases to hold as collateral." It is astonishing to think you would hold evidence of my debt as collateral for money you have given me, but this is in effect what the Federal Reserve and the Treasury do. The greater the government's debt, the more money the Fed can create.

This system of creating money is so incredible it seems as though it were designed to hide the inflation process from the public. Certainly not more than one in a thousand understands the operation. The federal government runs a deficit and must borrow money by selling bonds to cover the difference between what it receives in taxes and what it spends. The Federal Reserve is empowered by law to enter the market to buy these government debt securities, usually U.S. Treasury bonds, from the handful of dealers it uses. In purchasing these Treasury debt instruments, the Federal Reserve pays by making a deposit in the dealer's account at its bank. Now this money with which the Fed purchases these bonds did not exist until just that moment. It was created out of thin air! Of course this creation of new money increases the total supply of money in the nation, thereby devaluing all the money that existed before.

Now the plot thickens. America's banks, regulated by the Federal Reserve, are fractional reserve banks. Recall our first fractional reserve banker/goldsmiths who lent out receipts for more gold than they actually had on deposit—until they got caught, that is. Similarly, fractional reserve banks are allowed to maintain on hand only a fraction of the deposits that have been made with them as a reserve against withdrawals.

This relies on the assumption that not all the banks' depositors will come in at once to make withdrawals. The bank can then earn interest income by loaning customer deposits in excess of the amount required to be held in reserve. The Federal Reserve affects credit conditions by adjusting the reserves the banks must keep on deposit with the Fed. By lowering the reserve requirement, it allows banks to loan more money; by raising the fraction of its deposits that must be held in reserve, it causes banks to loan less.

Fractional reserve banking multiplies many times over the money increase of the Federal Reserve's debt monetization. If the recipient of this newly created money on account in its bank withdraws it from the account, the inflation process ends in the amount of the new money created by the Fed. But suppose the recipient leaves the computer credit of new money in its account. The deposit, representing money created out of thin air by the Fed to begin with, is now in a commercial bank. The bank presents this deposit to the Federal Reserve for payment. At this point the bank has increased its reserves with the Fed and, as a fractional reserve bank, it is entitled to lend out several times more money than the amount of the deposit. If the Fed allows the banks to loan as much as ten times its reserves, the creation of a billion dollars by debt monetization means the money supply can be increased by as much as ten billion dollars in the fractional reserve system. Now this is power inflation! Debasing coins or running currency printing presses is mere child's play.

The Federal Reserve claims its activities are in pursuit of influencing interest rates. The federal funds rate, what banks pay one another to borrow money overnight to maintain their required reserves with the Fed, is "targeted" by the Fed. The Fed doesn't set this rate, but engages in the activities we have described, buying and selling securities and adjusting bank reserve requirements, until the banks are borrowing at that rate, as though it is ideal. But there is nothing ideal about the rate. In fact, the Fed's aim is not controlled by the target; the target is moved to accommodate the Fed's aim. If the Fed chooses to shoot for increased credit in the economy, it will move the target lower. If it chooses to tighten credit, it will move the target higher.

Let us imagine that the Federal Reserve wants to "stimulate the economy." In pursuit of that objective, it will inflate the money supply, in the process lowering interest rates. The Federal Reserve will buy large amounts of government bonds, moving interest rates lower (for the time being). That makes credit cheaper, inducing more borrowing by the private sector at these lower rates, increasing economic activity and employment.

Sometimes the Federal Reserve wants to "cool an overheated economy." Such terminology is more sleight of hand, meant to mislead. Are they saying that the employment rate is too high, that too many people have jobs and are making too much money? What they really mean, but don't dare say, is that the results of their last round of inflation are starting to get out of hand. Prices are moving up fast and, like Frankenstein's monster turning on its creator, the Fed's inflation will eventually make interest rates go still higher to offset the depreciation of the currency. In this case the Fed's aim is to "disinflate," to undo some of the damage it has done by now lowering the inflation rate for a time. But note, the Fed never wishes to deflate. It always intends to inflate, only to a lesser or greater degree. In such a circumstance, the Fed can sell government securities, now disinflating the money supply, hoping to slow down rising prices, but raising interest rates in the process. The analogy with Frankenstein's monster is apt, as the Fed lurches from one policy to the next, heedless of the destruction it leaves in its trail.

The effect of rising interest rates is the opposite of what the Fed intended when it first set out to "stimulate the economy" and interest rates moved lower. But in the face of the Fed's inflation, credit eventually becomes more expensive, slowing borrowing by the private sector at these higher rates, decreasing economic activity and increasing unemployment. Higher interest rates also increase the cost of financing the government's debts. Taking a larger share of tax revenues for debt service means less discretionary spending—vote buying—for the politicians. Is there another government action that would lead to lower interest rates? It could spend less, and have to borrow less. The absence of the U.S. government and its voracious appetite in the credit markets would mean lower interest rates.

To recapitulate, inflation in the United States is a result of the Federal

Reserve turning government debt into money. That money multiplies again and again as it is lent out several times over by fractional reserve banks operating under the regulation and control of the Federal Reserve.

The Federal Reserve System

The Federal Reserve is central to America's most devastating bubbles and busts, and is responsible for almost a hundred years of criminal-scale dollar destruction. While a thorough treatment of the Fed is beyond the scope of this book, some of the most common criticisms have merit and demand attention:

1. The Federal Reserve System is unconstitutional. Preeminently, the enumerated powers granted the federal government do not include the establishment of a central or national bank. In addition, federal revenue must only be raised by means of bills originating in the House of Representatives, not in the marbled halls of the Federal Reserve. Federal Reserve activities that fund the government's debt by currency manipulation are not without cost; trillions of dollars have been embezzled from Americans by this device. By debt monetization, government acquires money to spend without debate, legislation, or vote, by commensurately devaluing the currency held by the people. No wonder critics say this amounts to nothing less than taxation without representation.

The Constitution also delegates to Congress, and only to Congress, the power to coin money and regulate its value. Obviously Federal Reserve Notes are neither coin nor are redeemable in coin. Furthermore, powers and authority divided among the branches of government by the Constitution cannot be transferred to one another. Imagine how preposterous it would be for Congress to attempt to shirk the authority the people's representatives have to set tax rates, and delegate those functions to the executive branch or to a private company. But the authority Congress has over money and its value has been delegated to a private institution without constitutional authority.

2. A central bank such as the Federal Reserve represents the politicization of money. Karl Marx believed this to be indispensable to his objectives. In his *Communist Manifesto*, Marx listed ten points necessary in the creation of a Communist state. Point five demands:

> Centralization of credit in the hands of the State, by means of a national bank with State capital and an exclusive monopoly.

Politicized money feeds the dreams of the politically ambitious, seeing correctly in the central bank a means to their ends that does not involve the consent of the governed. It is a powerful device for steering a country along any chosen course and as such is incompatible with the very idea of self-government and a free people.

3. From its shadowy beginnings until today, the Federal Reserve has been cloaked in secrecy. This secrecy conceals its hidden beneficiaries, and obscures the costs paid by the people. Foreshadowing the mortgage meltdown fifteen years later, Fed chairman Alan Greenspan drove interest rates down sharply in the early 1990s, with an eye to providing cheap liquidity to the banking sector. It was good for the likes of Merrill Lynch, JPMorgan, and Chase Manhattan, which saw their depressed stock prices take off, but it had a costly impact on Americans. Driving rates to 3 percent by the time he was finished, Greenspan fundamentally altered the investment outlook and risk-taking proclivities of retired people and baby boomers alike, as they sought to make up in the stock market for the certificate of deposit and fixed income returns that had disappeared. Ultimately Americans lost $6 trillion in that Greenspan stock market bubble. But while the profits of the banks from market distortions are privatized, banking system losses, as we are witnessing, are socialized. More alarming is the role of the central bank in

funding wars not popular enough to be sustained by direct taxation. This function has been on display since the Federal Reserve Act of 1913 was first passed. Economist Murray Rothbard pointed out that the new act, which took effect in November 1914, coincided with the outbreak of World War I, so its inflationary capacity was put to the test right away:

> . . . it is generally agreed that it was only the new system that permitted the U.S. to enter the war and to finance both its own war effort, and massive loans to the allies; roughly, the Fed doubled the money supply of the U.S. during the war and prices doubled in consequence. For those who believe that U.S. entry into World War I was one of the most disastrous events for the U.S. and for Europe in the twentieth century, the facilitating of U.S. entry into the war is scarcely a major point in favor of the Federal Reserve.

4. The shadowy nature of the Federal Reserve extends to its ownership and auditing. It is certainly the duck-billed platypus of institutions: part private at times; part government at others. The Fed's public relations material calls it "an independent entity within the government, having both public purposes and private aspects," and that it "is not owned by anyone." Even so, privately owned member banks must own stock in the regional Federal Reserve banks. That stock pays the bankers an automatic 6 percent annually.

Its apologists are quick to insist that the Federal Reserve is audited and point to General Accounting Office audits and to audits of regional Federal Reserve banks. It is certainly fine that mechanical functions like check clearing operations are audited, but where the real action is, it's a different story. The GAO is specifically forbidden from auditing the Fed's dealings with foreign government and other central banks as well as prohibited from examining Open Market Committee transactions, the Fed's primary instrument in the growth of money and credit. The severity of America's economic problems may soon put an end to this Fed secrecy. By the spring of 2009, a bill by Congressman Ron Paul,

H.R. 1207, "The Federal Reserve Transparency Act," which would provide for the Fed to be audited by the end of 2010, had picked up dozens of cosponsors (from both parties) in the House and been introduced in the Senate.

"Shadowy" is the word to describe another operation in which the chairman of the Federal Reserve is a key member, along with the treasury secretary and the heads of the Securities and Exchange and the Commodity Futures Trading commissions. The President's Working Group on Financial Markets, the so-called Plunge Protection Team, was created by presidential executive order after the short-lived October 1987 stock market crash. Reportedly it was active in supporting the markets after the 9/11 attacks, and again several times since then. Recently it is said to have convened in the Oval Office of the White House on March 17, 2008. Its mission is thought to be to include using regulatory authority, arm-twisting, and policy means to influence stock prices. But the real arrows in its quiver are the resources of the Treasury and the Fed to buy stock market indexes and other financial instruments to prop up financial markets. The problems inherent in these shadowy operations are many; basic among them are favoritism and distortions in the marketplaces, the confusion resulting from deceptive and unsustainable price signals in the markets, and the impact of these distortions on other markets that compete for investment dollars. If the Plunge Protection Team was supporting stock prices in early 2008, it was doing so while price/earnings ratios on stock indexes were closer to bull-market highs than to bear-market lows. Simply put, resources earned by, and taken from, Americans to begin with would have been used to provide them with misinformation about valuations in the economy and to lure them into investments they would not otherwise make. If this is what this secretive cabal has done, it bears grave responsibility for the tragic stock market losses Americans have suffered.

But is this what the Federal Reserve chairman, the secretary of the treasury, and the rest of the President's Working Group on Financial Markets are actually doing? Few know, and those who do aren't talking. One embarrassing public display reveals just how successfully this market manipulation is concealed. It was in January 2008, in the heat of the race for the presidency, on a nationally televised Republican candidates' debate on MSNBC. The unemployment rate was rising and the defaults from the subprime mortgage meltdown were spreading. The British press reported that "a mood of deep alarm has taken hold in the upper echelons" of the Bush administration, which had just convened the Plunge Protection Team for an Oval Office meeting. Under the circumstances, Ron Paul asked Senator John McCain what he, as president, would do with the Working Group on Financial Markets. Would he keep the group? What would its role be? Would he have its activities brought into the sunlight of public disclosure? What followed was one minute and thirteen seconds of befuddled response more suited to a confused teenage beauty pageant contestant than the eventual presidential nominee of his party. Senator McCain, with twenty-five years in the House and Senate voting on crucial economic issues, did not have a whisper of a clue what the Working Group is!

For a moment let us take a look at past issues of constitutionality and even beyond the shadowy and secretive nature of the Federal Reserve and the conviction of our founders that power should not be allowed to pool and concentrate in the manner that a central bank provides. Let us take a benign view of the Federal Reserve on all those issues and focus solely on its mission. What we discover is that this mission, managing the nation's financial conditions by orchestrating money, interest, and credit conditions, cannot possibly be accomplished.

The world's central banks today are, like our Federal Reserve, remnants of the nineteenth century, an age that celebrated the engineer. It was an era that saw manual labor–based production begin to give way to machine-based production; the introduction of the railroad and oil refining; the development of steel and the telephone; and other engineering marvels like the Suez Canal and the transatlantic cable. The accomplishments of engineering deserved to be celebrated. The problem—one that persists today—occurs when the psychosocial sciences like economics attempt to ape the means and methods of the physical and natural sciences. When this syndrome of the age in economics is accompanied by the coercive power of the state, the result is a reduction of human beings to measurable units of production, statistical units deemed problematic in their variation and insignificant in their individuality, mere workers and consumers that could be ordered about or managed as aggregates, a consequence that has been very harmful indeed.

This engineering conceit in central banking imagines the economy to be some great machine: with the opening of a valve here, the calibration of a meter there, and the pull of a lever, the economy can be set in motion at an optimal rate. Boards, bodies, and bureaucrats, having ample aggregates and supplementary statistics, would know just which levels of supply and demand should pertain at any moment, and with the levers of money supply and the fine-tuning of interest rates, they could speed up or slow down the economy like an assembly line. With perfect knowledge these technocrats could allocate resources and labor in the most efficient means possible, much like managing the power output of a hydroelectric dam or maximizing the speed of a steam locomotive. One need only remember the fabled Goldilocks economy of previous Federal Reserve chairman Alan Greenspan, the Maestro: "It was not too hot and not too cold, but just right!" Of course, Greenspan also admits he didn't "get it" about the housing bubble until very late, in 2005 and 2006, despite home mortgage debt growing from $1.8 trillion to $8 trillion during his tenure. Nor did he foresee the stock market bubble before it popped in 2000. And he somehow missed the recession of the early 1990s. Greenspan's successor, Ben Bernanke, didn't get it either. As chairman of the President's Council of Economic Advisers in October 2005, he told Congress that he wasn't concerned about a housing bubble. A year and a half later, in March 2006, deep into the mortgage meltdown, he testified as Fed chairman that problems in the subprime market were "contained." Yet by the fall of 2008, the U.S. Treasury was pumping money seemingly without limit into Freddie Mac and Fannie Mae, two congressional creations that were responsible for 42 percent of U.S. home loans.

Criticism of Fed chairmen, whether Alan Greenspan or Ben Bernanke, would not be justified on the grounds that they do not have perfect knowledge. No one does. But their craft is predicated on the assumption that they can allocate resources more knowingly and set interest rates with a wisdom superior to the realities of supply and demand.

Perhaps a story set in the near future can relate the hopelessness of the Fed's pretenses and even something of the damage they have done to America's prosperity. Apparently embarrassed by almost a hundred years of failures and perhaps even a bit worried that the citizens are beginning to wise up to them, the members of the Federal Reserve Board finally decide to try something new. They acquire one of the newest-generation supercomputers, the latest Silicon Valley has to offer, truly a leading-edge machine with almost godlike powers of computation. It is networked to everything and can access any bit of digital information available anywhere. If it is known to mankind, at last the Fed will be able to crunch it all and make wise decisions based on complete information and perfect calculation.

And so they gather around the machine, programmed, online, and ready to go, and nervously type in their first question: "What is optimal money supply?"

The machine hums and processes for almost an hour as formulas, digits, and data dance across the face of the monitor. At last the numbers slow down, the screen clears, and the board members press forward to read the answer as it slowly appears before them:

It reads: "87.3127 trillion Chinese yuan."

The implication of the story is painful. The U.S. dollar's preeminence in the world is not what it was—and why should it be? Ninety-six cents of the value of every dollar has vanished on the Fed's watch, and we've seen the worst depression and the worst bank failures in the nation's history, massive malfunctions in the credit markets, bubbles and busts, all under the great money and credit engineers of the central bank. It's been a costly affair, the infatuations of nineteenth-century intellectuals notwithstanding.

The economy is not a machine, and it cannot be centrally managed. Nobel Prize recipient F. A. Hayek called this belief that central planners could have information about widely dispersed economic conditions and needs and that they could be administered through a central point "the fatal conceit," which ignores crucial information communicated in the free movement of prices. Prices convey information instantly from near and far about supply and demand—and do so before the central bankers get their pants on in the morning. Before the meeting adjourns and the press release goes out, the Federal Reserve's latest decision on ideal interest rates for the economy is wrong—there will be discrepancies between the central bank's rate and the constantly changing real rate of interest—the Fed thereby conveying harmful misinformation. After all, interest rates are the price of renting money—and prices change all the time. This is not to say that no one relying on market prices ever makes a mistake. But profits and losses from those activities provide feedback upon which subsequent decisions can be based. This vital feedback mechanism is missing in centrally planned economies. When was the last time a Fed official lost his job, had to give back his salary, incurred huge personal loses, or paid penalties for being wrong?

The By-products of Inflation

If the sheer amount of wealth confiscated from Americans by the Federal Reserve isn't bad enough, the Fed's sins are compounded by the corruption of our political system, the illicit transfer of wealth it makes possible, and the wars that it enables. But inflation brings other economic ills in its wake. Among them is one we have alluded to by example. But the problem of malinvestment is so destructive that it deserves the spotlight of our attention. Malinvestment occurs in every level of the economy from individuals to the largest corporations. Malinvestment is a result of artificial credit conditions diverting resources along unsustainable paths. When the currency is not a stable unit of accounting, when the central bank creates credit conditions by monetary manipulation, people and businesses make decisions in ways they otherwise would not. The housing boom and bust is a painful lesson in the causes and consequences of malinvestment.

Just as the false signals of artificial credit cause malinvestment, so too does the uncertainty of an inflationary environment cause an increase in speculation and gambling. Speculators serve an indispensable function in providing liquidity to the markets and in voluntarily assuming risks producers and consumers prefer to forgo. If the producer of a commodity like silver needs to lock in a price to sell some of next year's production, so that he can plan and make commitments for future business costs, he may not find an actual industrial user for the amount of production he has to sell and the dates he has in mind. But in our sophisticated markets, speculators can be found willing to undertake the risk of price movements in an unknown future. Their willingness to absorb these risks results in a more liquid marketplace for both producers and users of commodities. But inflation distorts markets, multiplying the risks and uncertainties of every commercial undertaking. The market begins to demand more speculators, that is, more people to absorb these ever increasing monetary risks. As once productive people move their money and efforts to speculation, productivity drops. In an unstable economic environment, investments once prudent become gambles. Futures markets diversify into products once not volatile enough to require futures speculation. Options become the object of investments instead of the underlying product. The short-term speculative side of the marketplace grows all out of proportion to the long-term investment side. When unnatural levels of risk must be hedged, derivatives are king.

While gambling becomes a commonplace, economic deceit grows more widespread. The shrewd prey on the naïve. People enter into agreements in hopes of paying their obligations in terms of radically altered real values. Contracts may be abided by in letter, but not in spirit. Inflation, it has been said, is like a country where nobody speaks the truth.

This impairment of productivity by inflation-driven speculation is just one reason for the investor to consider withdrawing from the market's conventional investments. The argument for investor capital to "go on strike" is more persuasive in view of the impact inflation has on savings and capital formation. When money loses purchasing power over time, there is only one rational economic response: spend it. The aphorism of Ben Franklin is stood on its head—a penny saved is a penny wasted. The effect of this is a precipitous decline in the savings rate. Capital is deferred consumption; it is production that is not spent. Think of a farmer who must save a part of his harvest to seed next year's crops. But Americans have learned the lesson of a lifetime of easy credit and continuous inflation; they have been meager savers. In fact, in 2005, for the first time since the Great Depression, the U.S. saving rate actually went negative. Not only were Americans not saving any of their earnings, they actually began eating their seed corn, spending what savings they did have. Only with the shock of the market collapse have Americans begun to save again. But as the inflation rate rises, the saving rate will decline. It is hard to have capitalism when there is no net new savings.

But there is still a more serious consequence of money losing value over time. When inflation makes savings unrewarding, the future will arrive unprepared for. Social Security has been sweetly seductive in its assurances for the future. But as shocking as the realization that Americans are beginning to have that the retirement money they sent to Washington for a lifetime is not there, that the money has been spent—even beyond that shocking reality, no one has yet adequately calculated the impact Social Security has had on the behavior of Americans, diminishing their propensity to save for themselves. What present consumption might have been deferred and what mountains of capital might Americans have created in providing for the future for themselves? Unanswerable is what magic such massive capital investment might have created in terms of long-term wealth, prosperity, and opportunity for Americans and for humankind. Such rewards are unknown, but what one can be sure of is that those who have not provided for their future, for old age, for sickness and death, for economic displacements, natural catastrophes, and cultural change are liable, even eager, to become serfs of an all-powerful state. As Dostoyevsky's Grand Inquisitor said, "In the end they will lay their freedom at our feet, and say to us: 'Make us your slaves, but feed us.'"

WHAT HAPPENS NEXT

CHAPTER SEVEN

How It Comes Down

Likely Scenarios

Don't ask me where we're going to find the money. I'm going to get it where Paulson found it.

—Charles Rangel, House Ways and
Means Committee Chairman

Today was Presidents' Day. Congress commemorated George Washington's throwing a dollar across the Potomac by throwing $780 billion down a rat hole.

—Jay Leno, *The Tonight Show*

The Dollar/Debt Express

It may be that the Federal Reserve will be so discredited by its malfeasance that famed investor Jim Rogers will be proven right, and the central bank will cease to exist in a few years. In the meantime, the Dollar/Debt Express is a runaway train; a wreck lies dead ahead. The track is fixed, in place. It is far too late to throttle back the racing locomotive. A collision with economic reality is right around the bend; the destruction will be enormous.

This track of destruction consists of two rails: fiscal policy and monetary policy. Fiscal policy, the budgetary behavior of the government, represents the incentive or the will to inflate the money supply. Monetary policy is the Federal Reserve and its activities; it is the currency printing press that can be flipped on at a moment's notice and is thus the means of inflating the money supply.

The will and the means to inflate have conspired during our lifetimes to give us sustained, unrelenting inflation, rising to double-digit rates at several interludes. Presidents Johnson, Nixon, and their Congresses could have paid for their Southeast Asian war and their Great Society spending sprees through taxation. But that would have confronted the voters with the choice of continuing the warfare/welfare state. Fearing the outcome, the inflation alternative was an irresistible convenience. But what was once a convenience for those seeking to perpetuate their power in the nation-state is now a necessity. There is no other way. Obligations on the immediate horizon cannot be met on a pay-as-you-go basis. Shifting demographics are exposing the government's inability to meet medical and retirement promises. The money coming in does not keep pace with the money going out. The debt is beginning to compound. Can the problem be taxed away? The promises on which President Obama campaigned are largely redistributive. In fact the tax credits he has promised would result in checks from the IRS to people who pay no taxes to begin with, so any palatable tax increases will be offset by promised giveaways. Tax rates are already at a level of diminishing returns. Attempting to close the debt gap would demand such massive collections that new taxes would be no more useful than killing the goose that laid the golden egg. The end of the cold war has created a new world with three billion new capitalists and new venues for investment that are both safe and often more productive than in the bureaucratic state that America has become. Needless wars have added trillions to our debt and damaged America's brand name around the world, creating new economic alliances elsewhere around the globe. The hegemony of American manufacturing is over; the work is being outsourced. Meanwhile the prospects that the debt can be rolled over indefinitely are diminishing daily. America's foreign bank creditors, noting the foreclosures, short sales, and bankruptcies in America's real estate market, are already wondering if they have made no-qualifying, no-document loans to an unqualified borrower.

The laws of economics have not been repealed. The debt will be settled by one means or another. If it cannot be repaid, it will be repudiated. This is akin to "jingle mail," homeowners' leaving their keys in the mailbox and walking away from mortgages they cannot pay. But in this case the borrower is the government. This is not to suggest an all-at-once debt repudiation, a general default on all U.S. government obligations. Such a declaration of bankruptcy would be a game-ender. The high priests of government would bring their temple crashing down upon themselves.

There are some obligations that will be repudiated instantly. Eligibility ages for health benefits and retirement will be changed, an effective act of repudiation. (Imagine a private insurance company that owes its insured annuity payments beginning at age sixty-five unilaterally deciding not to pay until age sixty-seven. Jails are made for such acts.) But for the most part promises to pay will be defaulted upon by payment in currency that depreciates more slowly at first, then accelerating.

Hypocrisy is the tribute vice pays to virtue. Of course inflation is theft, like a fabric shop measuring the customer's order of silk with a yardstick of only thirty-two inches length this year and twenty-eight next, or the butcher pressing his thumb down on the scale. And who is left holding the bag? People depending on government promises; people who have paid taxes all their lives believing they were paying for retirement or health "insurance"; people who have loaned the government money by buying its debt instruments; individuals personally and in their retirement plans; institutional investors in Treasury bills and bonds, foreign and domestic alike; and anyone holding U.S. government dollars.

The authorities believe they can keep the institutions of government intact and continue their hold on power with the slow-motion debt repudiations of inflation. They have the means to inflate and the will to do so. Are there other centers of influence from which resistance to inflation can be expected? Local governments, which are closer to the people? Banks? Insurance companies looking after the long-term value of their customers' deposits and investments? On the contrary, from many of these corners inflation is welcomed. While our discussion of debt levels has been limited to federal debt, the national government has other constituencies hoping that their unsustainable debt can be inflated away as well. Total credit market debt—household debt including consumer credit and mortgages, bank loans, state and local government debt, commercial paper and more—is $51 trillion, over 350 percent of GDP. Over the last century the ratio has averaged 155 percent. This is a debt ratio that has turned straight up to unsustainable levels. Institutions struggling with debt of their own that is otherwise irredeemable can become silent supporters of highly inflationary policies, despite the long-term damage the currency destruction does to both business conditions and the culture. But saying some inflation is desirable is like saying a few termites are a good thing since they aerate a house nicely, providing for a gentle breeze in the summer.

Means and will plus a lack of resistance: these are the factors that make the case for inflation conclusive. Is there anything able to thwart the fiscal and monetary authorities even as they stoke the engines of the runaway Dollar/Debt Express?

Deflation

The popping of the real estate bubble, the largest leveraged asset bubble in financial history, saw trillions of dollars in presumed wealth disappear. It was followed by trillions in stock market losses, and like good money after bad, trillions more in bailout pledges added to the debt burden of American households. The resulting loss of wealth led immediately to lower consumption and investment in the economy. The effects of the credit contraction spread in no time at all, becoming visible in business closings and bankruptcies. If inflation is a monetary phenomenon defined as an increase in the supply of money and credit, the collapse of the asset price bubble had all the makings of its opposite, a decrease in the supply of money and credit: deflation.

It is easy to understand why deflation causes economists to cringe and politicians to shudder. As wealth or even the presumption of wealth, a result in the current instance of a supposed high level of home equity, begins to disappear, a cascading contraction in spending results; retail sales fall, offset by reduced retail employment. Household incomes drop, which in turn results in still lower spending that spills over into more unemployment as demand for goods and services is still further reduced. As debtors fail, their creditors in turn begin to be unable to pay their creditors until eventually the entire financial world is sucked into the spinning black hole of credit and wealth destruction.

It must be said, or at least it should be said in economics, that there are two sides of the equation. In an environment of deflation, in which the purchasing power of money rises, consumers defer spending and reduce their levels of debt. In the aftermath of inflation-induced malinvestment, prices begin behaving in a way that rewards savings, which is just what the economy needs. And as there are two sides to the equation, lower prices are good for many, such as would-be home buyers who had been priced out by the prior frenzy. Prices for consumer goods fall; bargains abound. Lower gasoline prices can save some families hundreds of dollars a month. Still deflation is the great bane of fiscal and monetary authorities. They prefer to assert their judgment about what prices should be, rather than let real prices, reflecting real conditions of supply and demand, prevail. In an attempt to halt the correction of prior excesses, the mutual agreement of buyers and sellers in a noncoercive market is frustrated, unsustainable financial decisions are made, and the agony of the adjustment is unnecessarily prolonged. There seem to be two reasons that the governing classes are willing to plunge the nation hopelessly deeper in debt to oppose deflation. First, there is a widespread belief that economic growth cannot occur in a period of sustained deflation. This view is incorrect. The United States has experienced robust growth in prolonged periods of deflation. Second, and most telling, the authorities see deflation as a challenge to their control of the economy. They are convinced that inflation is manageable, that it can be tweaked up or down at their whim. Deflation does not respond to their micromanagement in the same way. This powerlessness drives them to put the solvency of the nation at risk to "fight" deflation. Of course their prior management of credit and monetary conditions is the cause of the deflation. Just as the best way to avoid a Sunday morning hangover is temperance on Saturday night, so too is sound monetary practice the best preventative of a collapse.

Deflationary fears are heard in every downturn and recession. At first opposing forces seem to be at work, inflationary and deflationary. Long after housing prices had begun to fall, the commodities bull still ran, crashing through record high gold and oil prices. Eventually, though, as the credit collapse worsened throughout 2008, both sold off hard, gold 30 percent off its March highs of just over $1,000 to the low $700s by October, while oil fell 75 percent from its July highs of $147 to $34 late in the year. The alarm of deflationists, as they invoke the specter of the Great Depression or detect haunting similarities to Japan's endless slump, is used to justify massive intervention in the economy, bailouts, and stimulus programs. It is true that every inflation ends in a deflation just as every bubble bursts, so the arguments about deflation are serious and need to be met head-on to see if they are applicable, finally, this time.

Deflationists make the argument that in a period of a widening credit collapse, the monetary authorities discover that while they can make monetary reserves available in the banking system and contrive low interest rates to make borrowing attractive, borrowers may not be willing to take out loans at any price. If a business has declining sales, shall it borrow for more inventory, paying interest on the borrowed money while the inventory sits on a shelf unused? If a manufacturer already has excess capacity, at what price is it willing to borrow to expand? Will a sales enterprise borrow money to staff up new markets if its potential customers are filing for bankruptcy protection? Borrowing can become prohibitively expensive even at zero percent interest as dollars borrowed this year must be paid back in next year's dollars that are more dear. Consumers quit consuming when they discover that the dollar they don't spend today buys more tomorrow. The situation is often likened to trying to "push on a string." The Federal Reserve can monetize debt, purchase government bonds, and make reserves available to the banking system. But it can't force businesses to borrow. If no one borrows, there is no stimulative effect in the economy.

Deflation is a subject of special interest to many economists including Ben Bernanke, the current Federal Reserve chairman, who has written extensively about it. In a widely noted speech in 2002, Bernanke sought to answer the "pushing on a string" case for deflation, saying that the Fed and the government have sufficient means to ensure that any such interlude would be mild and brief. Bernanke provides a parable to illustrate the power of the printing press:

Today an ounce of gold sells for $300, more or less. Now suppose that a modern alchemist solves his subject's oldest problem by finding a way to produce unlimited amounts of new gold at essentially no cost. Moreover, his invention is widely publicized and scientifically verified, and he announces his intention to begin massive production of gold within days. What would happen to the price of gold? Presumably, the potentially unlimited supply of cheap gold would cause the market price of gold to plummet. Indeed, if the market for gold is to any degree efficient, the price of gold would collapse immediately after the announcement of the invention, before the alchemist had produced and marketed a single ounce of yellow metal.

What has this got to do with monetary policy? Like gold, U.S. dollars have value only to the extent that they are strictly limited in supply. But the U.S. government has a technology, called a printing press (or, today, its electronic equivalent), that allows it to produce as many U.S. dollars as it wishes at essentially no cost. By increasing the number of U.S. dollars in circulation, or even by credibly threatening to do so, the U.S. government can also reduce the value of a dollar in terms of goods and services, which is equivalent to raising the prices in dollars of those goods and services. We conclude that, under a paper-money system, a determined government can always generate higher spending and hence positive inflation.

In his parable, Bernanke is quite shameless about the use of the printing press. He illustrates the means by which dollars are devalued through inflation. He makes clear that if the Fed is determined it has arrows in its quiver, means to inflate, that it did not have in the 1930s. For example, the Fed's inflationary capacity is not limited by the stock of U.S. government debt. It can now monetize (buy) foreign government debt. Already the Fed is buying short-term corporate debt in the commercial paper market. It can even buy mortgages. Bernanke discusses several other means of countering deflation and concludes that the monetary and fiscal authorities "would be far from helpless in the face of deflation. . . ." Still this does not quite answer the "pushing on a string" argument of deflationists. What can the Fed do to be sure of generating public spending with its monetary policies? The answer: whatever it takes. The Fed will use any tool at its disposal to stop a threat of deflation. It will create new tools and assume heretofore unseen authority if need be. It is in this spirit that the Fed chairman won his nickname, "Helicopter Ben." Anticipating Obama's tax cuts, Bernanke suggested that a broad-based tax cut financed by inflation would almost certainly be effective. It would be the equivalent of shoveling money out of helicopter doors. This begs the question of how eager people will be to part with valuable goods when they see cheap paper money raining down from hovering helicopters. But the clear outline of many of the activities being undertaken by the Fed and the Treasury in their bailout activities to date can be seen in Bernanke's 2002 speech on deflation. It is a plan he suggested in 2003 as well to the Japanese, whom he criticized for not having taken the extraordinary steps available to a central bank to achieve the intended inflation. If borrowers won't borrow then instead of a credit inflation, you may expect a currency inflation to overcome the forces of deflation, and you will hear the helicopters revving up. But before that is necessary, you can be sure that even reluctant businesses and borrowers will begin taking out loans in the face of the Fed's assurances that they will be able to pay those loans back in cheaper dollars. Just as free-money, negative real interest rates helped create the housing bubble, Bernanke's suggestion of "credibly threatening" to increase the number of dollars and reducing their value represents more free money and another bubble, this time a dollar bubble. Whatever it takes.

As the scope of the credit collapse began to become undeniable, the Fed began aggressively pushing interest rates back down. Beginning in September 2007, the Fed lowered the Fed funds rate from 5.25 percent to 1 percent by October 2008, the lowest rate in more than five years. In December it pushed the rate down again, to a historically unprecedented range of zero to 0.25 percent. The authorities' posture on the crisis became clear: deflation has been taken off the table with the bailouts. Asset meltdowns were banned by government edict. After months of bailouts and guarantees, Bernanke dug his heels in again in January 2009, saying still more than guarantees and bailouts could be necessary. One week before Obama's inauguration, Bernanke used a speech in London to signal that fiscal measures and stimulus packages would be accompanied by other means. The Fed still has "powerful tools," he said, that it will use "aggressively" on growth and prices. The adjusted monetary base provides evidence of the Fed's seriousness beginning at the time of the bailouts. A narrow measurement of money supply, the monetary base reflects the Fed's "open market" operations. It consists of currency and commercial bank reserves with the Fed, so-called high-powered money that is the basis for lending many times over in the fractional reserve banking system. It provides a clear look at Fed policy.

Beginning in September 2008 the monetary base exploded. In just months, by the end of March 2009, the monetary base had grown at an annual compounded rate of 199 percent. This massive growth represents an aggressive monetary policy. Like a race car revving up at the starting line, nothing happens—until the clutch is popped. Then it takes off in a cloud of smoke and burning rubber. Similarly, a resumption in commercial bank lending will release this "powerful tool" of bank reserves, a powerful engine of monetary expansion and dollar destruction.

Whatever it takes.

Stagflation

Is there a state that mediates between depressed economic conditions and intense market liquidity operations; between high unemployment and new money creation; a state that includes trillions of dollars having disappeared in bankruptcies and foreclosures and yet sees increasing consumer prices as a result of monetary inflation? There is a term for such a state: stagflation. As the name implies, stagflation is a period of economic stagnation accompanied by inflation.

In deference to common usage, we will use the term *stagflation* to describe the period before us now, but it may not be entirely accurate.

While it includes inflation, the stagnation it describes means weak growth or no movement at all. The current outlook is for something much more turbulent, a period of volatility in economic conditions, both ups and downs, with seeming recoveries that only prove to be false starts; a rush of activity from federal jobs programs, resulting in the people being made poorer by the consequent dollar destruction. Just as hopes would rise in the Great Depression at signs of renewed growth and lower unemployment, they would be dashed by the costs of the accompanying economic intervention. Stagflation does not adequately describe a recession that is accompanied by rising prices, an inflationary recession. For many people involved in the economic debate it is an article of faith, a Keynesian dogma, that inflation ends the recession. It is this dogma that prevails among the governing classes. In service of the creed, the Fed contrives ever lower interest rates in search of "stimulation," which only frustrate the economy's need for savings and forestalls a recovery. An inflationary recession with its contracting economy is more destructive than inflation in a weak growth economy, but they are both debilitating. This condition that we will call stagflation is like having a fever and the chills at the same time, and is a sign that the body economic is shuddering from the relentless compulsions of meddlers.

The 1970s are remembered as a decade of stagflation. Stocks fell about 15 percent in 1973, more than 25 percent in 1974. Unemployment hit 9 percent, while the official inflation rate climbed to 12.2 percent in 1974 and 13.3 percent in 1979. It was a period of confused monetary policy. Businesses encountered Nixon's disastrous wage and price controls, which fixed the prices at which they could sell, while they also had to contend with huge increases in borrowing costs. And then came the oil shocks. OPEC warned repeatedly that a change in the value of the dollar would result in higher nominal oil prices, so when Nixon suspended dollar convertibility to gold in 1971, oil prices were bound to climb. They quadrupled from $3 per barrel in 1972 to $12 in 1974. They spiked again beginning in the late 1970s until they hit $35 in 1981.

Periods of stagflation are particularly painful because of the proliferation of mixed economic messages. During the stagnation decade the Fed funds rate was all over the map, from 3.5 percent in 1971 up to 11 percent in 1973; from 13 percent in 1974 back down to 4.75 by 1976;

only to head back up to 10 percent in 1978, then to 15.5 percent in 1979, and finally to 20 percent in 1980. Rates changed constantly during the decade—twenty-two times in 1973 alone, twenty-three times in 1978. It was like shaken-business syndrome. The changes were so frequent and violent it is no wonder many small and new businesses couldn't survive. The volatility can be attributed to a desire to micromanage economic conditions and control the exchange rates of a fiat currency. It almost makes current Fed policy look stable—for now—averaging a mere half-dozen or so rate changes a year.

We have already seen evidence of the flailing about by officialdom that will characterize the period ahead. By the time they collect information from the far-flung corners of the real economy, it is obsolete. They can never be ahead of the market. In July 2008, officials were concerned with the highest rate of price increases in seventeen years. But by October the Fed funds rate was cut in half because of falling prices. One thinks of treasury secretary Paulson's staggering from one iteration of the $700 billion plan that bears his name to the next. And the former Fed chairman had to flip-flop as he sought absolution in congressional testimony in October 2008. Alan Greenspan knew that all would be forgiven if only he could blame the collapse on the market and an insufficiency of regulation. The bubble impresario duly proclaimed himself "in a state of shocked disbelief," and discovered the whole episode demands "additional regulatory changes." This from the regulator in chief? Greenspan blamed a "once in a century credit tsunami." But who was the earth-mover for a good part of that century responsible for shifting the tectonic plates of interest rates?

It is appropriate that central bank monetary management should be likened to the bouts of drug and alcohol addicts. Just as in the early stages a little inflation seems to have some pleasurable consequences, so may the first-time user enjoy a novel high. As with a hangover, the periods of withdrawal from cheap, artificial credit conditions are painful. Rather than letting the toxic effects get metabolized, the addict takes another fix; for the alcoholic, the hangover is answered with another drink. For chronic addicts the old doses eventually lose the desired effects. Money and credit inflations will inevitably make prices rise, but the rush of business activity fails to materialize the way it did before.

Larger and larger doses of monetary easing are required. The result is that price increases can accelerate along with interest rates, but wages don't keep up. When you read about some celebrity dying of an overdose it's usually the same sort of thing: bigger and bigger doses to get the same high they got when they first started. In the economy monetary easing generates higher inflation in response to which lenders demand higher interest rates with premiums over the rate of inflation; higher rates slow down the recovery so that more easing is required, which unfortunately means higher interest rates. And so it goes.

Sometimes the monetary authorities see the results of the inflation they have created and in a fit of responsibility want to tighten before things get out of control. William McChesney Martin, Fed chairman in the 1950s and 1960s, serves as an example. In a remark that affirms our parallels with alcohol consumption, Martin said that the job of the Fed is "to take away the punch bowl just as the party gets going." But a little tightening slows things down, and politicians respond to the screams of unemployed voters for loose money. Just as Bush the elder blamed the Fed for the downturn that led to his defeat by a Clinton campaign that had made "It's the economy, stupid!" its watchword, Richard Nixon blamed his loss to John F. Kennedy in 1960 on tight money at the hands of Martin. Well before Nixon's own bid for reelection in 1972 he appointed Arthur Burns as Fed chairman. Burns was more conciliatory and presided over the wild gyrations of rates in the 1970s. Political pressure intersects with outdated economic reports, which are then sifted by officials with imperfect knowledge. It is especially in a period of turbulence that officials, pressured to "do something," send confusing signals by interfering in real markets and real-world conditions of supply and demand. Under the circumstances of stagflation, monetary officials act like soccer players: "If it moves, kick it. If it doesn't move, kick it 'til it does!"

While the authorities in the current environment can conspire to kick up the money supply until prices raise their heads, it will be some time before they will get the chastened American consumer back to the status quo ante. Those who lost jobs in the bankruptcies, like those who lost money in overpriced real estate, like those who saw their retirements go up in smoke as the stock market went down in ashes, all will be more cautious at least for a time—and are not likely to spend their first new paychecks on nifty consumer gadgets. It will take some time before people with no savings start buying the expensive electronic gadgets they used to snap up at Sharper Image or sharp new automobiles with snappy custom wheels. They will spend on essentials and pay down debt, at least as long as the memories of the collapse are fresh in their minds. This new chastened attitude informs our investment recommendations, in which you will find no high-priced restaurant chains with eye-popping wine menus and cork-popping champagne prices. No big-box consumer electronics retailers or high-end fashion sellers. Mostly just plain sensible things like real money (gold and silver), real energy (oil), and real things real people need (food).

The inflationary recession or stagflation model is particularly important at this juncture, where the downturn in all its severity meets the breathtaking stimulus expenditures. The situation is not unlike something seen by many parents: their little children, wired on candy and soft drinks, jumping on the sofas and bouncing off the walls in their hyperactivity, until they crash—hard—dead to the world, and sleep right through dinner. They get an immediate lift and pay for it later. The stimulus is like a college student drinking double-shot espressos late at night as he crams for finals, only to fall asleep at four in the morning and miss his nine A.M. exam. His wired state came at a cost that was paid later and foiled his intentions. The stimulus package doesn't give the economy anything it hasn't taken. This is what Nobel laureate economist Milton Friedman meant when he used the adage that there is no such thing as a free lunch. The initial buzz of activity from hundreds of billions of dollars of projects will be celebrated by the usual suspects in the media, generating hopes of new economic strength and a recovery at hand. But a holistic view of the economy will note the costs of the stimulus as well. For being largely unobserved, such costs are no less real and drain economic vitality to a degree actually greater than the expenditures. This appears to be the most likely path for the economy in the near term, a continuation of depressed economic conditions accompanied by a rapidly depreciating dollar.

The Crack-up Boom

As I pointed out earlier, most Americans have never lived through a single year that wasn't inflationary. While most have experienced at least four years of double-digit inflation, older baby boomers and those near retirement age have lived through as many as a half dozen double-digit inflation years. Because there have not been any double-digit inflation years in the United States since 1981, basic questions about hyperinflation have not been sufficiently examined. Here are three. First, can hyperinflation actually become a problem in a country of educated and sophisticated people, or is runaway inflation the stuff of African dictatorships and banana republics, impossible in the industrial world since the days of black and white newsreels? Next, instead of just a source of watercooler grousing about rising prices, at what point does inflation become such a broad-based concern that it is stopped? And finally, at what point does inflation become hyperinflation?

Perhaps the experience of Israel will provide an answer to the first question, if hyperinflation is possible in a literate and modern society in which there should be no illusions about its cause. Although the Israeli economy had grown powerfully for decades and the country's rank among developing nations improved as well, the Israeli monetary authorities met the challenges of the 1970s with massive inflation. From 13 percent in 1971 to an average rate of 40 percent in the mid-1970s, inflation climbed precipitously as the money supply grew to accommodate fiscal deficits. The inflation rate soared past 100 percent in 1979, which should qualify as hyperinflation by anybody's standard. But it kept going: close to 200 percent in 1983, and then to 445 percent in 1984. The joke was told in Israel that even when the price of a trip by bus or taxi was the same, it was better to take the taxi. Unlike the bus where you pay upon boarding, you don't pay for the taxi until the end of the trip, at which time the currency is already worth a lot less.

Americans seem to be willing to tolerate inflation as a low-grade swindle at a couple of percent a year, but our second question is never met head-on by the monetary authorities: how much do they think they can get away with? At what point do the people rise as one and demand an end to the embezzlement? Chairman Bernanke makes occasional remarks about the "wage-price spiral, in which wages and prices chased each other ever upward. . . ." So that's it? Prices chase wages, while wages chase prices until, like characters in a cartoon, they both fall over exhausted? The Keynesian economists, champions of budget deficits, spend a great deal of time in animated discussions of things like "cost-push inflation." None of this is very helpful. The answer is that inflationary policies can continue to persist indefinitely because opposition to them is a house divided. Inflation needs to be opposed on moral grounds from the beginning because it is theft at any level. Three percent inflation is the same as someone drilling into your safe deposit box every year and helping himself to 3 percent of your savings. Theft does not become acceptable if it is limited to just a couple of percent. Beginning with the failure to oppose inflation as theft from the beginning, different constituencies develop to perpetuate it. If it is only 3 percent from you, that may not be enough to make it worth your while to devote an enormous amount of time and resources to stop the theft. But for those who become dependent on inflation as its beneficiaries, its continuation is worth a great deal of effort and expenditure indeed. Policies are promoted, donations are made to politicians, chairs at think tanks are endowed, and enabling economists are subsidized and spotlighted, all in furtherance of inflationary policies. For the initial recipients of the newly created money, who spend it before the monetary creation has been assimilated in higher prices throughout the economy, inflation appears to be a good thing. For debtors who can pay debts in depreciated dollars, inflation below a certain level appears to be desirable. For recipients of government contracts who profit from deficit spending on things the people are unwilling to be taxed overtly for, it is their sustenance. It is helpful chiefly to governments themselves, the biggest debtors of all. A 4 percent inflation rate depreciates a government's $12 trillion debt by $480 billion a year.

But for the individual politician it can be a different story. Inflation reaches unsustainable rates for politicians only when it costs them their jobs. Just as the Republicans' losses in the economic turmoil of 2008 made them start chattering about their supposed commitment to fiscal responsibility, the Democrats' gains under a Republican president of forty-nine seats in the House and three in the Senate in the double-digit inflation environment of 1974 should have been a warning to the next president, Jimmy Carter, who was tossed out after the inflation spike of 1979–80. Inflation becomes intolerable for businesses and in civic life when the burden of indexing and accounting makes enterprise not worth the effort. Anomalies begin to pile up. A business spends more time in accounting for a receivable than it is worth; the constant repricing of inventory becoming a major business expense. It is more than a nuisance from the earliest levels; it adds to every cost of doing business and to the price of everything. In doing so, it makes us poorer. But if not opposed from the beginning, inflation develops ardent supporters and often ends in hyperinflation and a collapse of the monetary system.

At what point does inflation give way to hyperinflation? When does it "run away"? Academic definitions vary, and are of little practical use in making predictions. Clearly when the inflation rate is so high that increases in prices are reported daily, or even hourly, inflation has run away; when the monetary authorities have to hurriedly print new banknotes with more zeros on the end—in 1946 Hungary issued banknotes denominated in 100 quintillion of its currency units—hyperinflation is under way. While fixed definitions of hyperinflation are arbitrary, it is useful for purposes of investing to examine runaway inflation from the point of view of the monetary authorities and their motivations as well as from the experiences and behavior of the populace at large.

When can one reasonably expect runaway inflation? Inflation can be thought of as a convenience or monetary tool when it is one of a number of means of financing the government. But it can be practically described as runaway when there is no other means of the government's financing its expenditures. At that point inflation becomes compulsory. The government must "inflate or die." At that point inflation spins out of control, climbing higher and higher. America's inflation of the last couple of generations has been mostly elective. It is perhaps at least fiscally conceivable, if not politically, that the $455 billion deficit of 2008 could have been eliminated in a combination of spending restraint and taxes. But we are at the point of no return now. The $1 and $2 trillion deficits on the immediate horizon cannot be financed by new taxes in a declining $14 trillion economy in which the people are already paying more than 30 percent of their income in taxes. And just as your credit card company wants to raise your rates and lower your limit—or cancel your credit entirely—just when you need it most, America's creditors, as we will see in the next chapter, are well aware of our circumstances. That means a growing reluctance to lend us more and higher rates for what we can borrow. Runaway inflation is not elective. The monetary authorities don't do it for fun. But allegiance to the institutions and authority of the governing classes prevails over conceding their impotence in the face of economic reality. They can be counted on to persist in their error, often for years at a time.

At some point there is a breakthrough in public consciousness, when it becomes widely understood that rising prices are not isolated to a few products, but that it is money itself that is becoming worthless. Prices go up far faster than the issuance of new money would suggest. Cash is trash. The great economist Ludwig von Mises called this, the awakening of the masses, "the crack-up boom."

> They become suddenly aware of the fact that inflation is a deliberate policy and will go on endlessly. A breakdown occurs. The crack-up boom appears. Everybody is anxious to swap his money against "real" goods, no matter whether he needs them or not, no matter how much money he has to pay for them. Within a very short time, within a few weeks or even days, the things which were used as money are no longer used as media of exchange. They become scrap paper. Nobody wants to give away anything against them.
>
> It was this that happened with the Continental currency in America in 1781, with the French mandats territoriaux in 1796, and with the German Mark in 1923. It will happen again whenever the same conditions appear. If a thing has to be used as a medium of exchange, public opinion must not believe that the quantity of this thing will increase beyond all bounds.

Von Mises is clear that in "the crack-up boom" a critical mass has been reached in which the monetary authorities, short of collapse, are incapable of containing runaway prices. In a period of rapid inflation, the money loses value faster than its supply has been increased, and gold rises higher than the quantity of money would suggest. So much for Chairman Bernanke's helicopter money.

In describing America's hidden debt in chapter 3 we introduced Richard Fisher, the president of the Federal Reserve Bank of Dallas, and relied on his description of the problem of unfunded liabilities. Fisher has the reputation of being something of a hawk on inflation, and in the May 2008 speech he was quite adamant that the Fed would not destroy the American economy by attempting to inflate that debt away:

> It is only natural to cast about for a solution—any solution— to avoid the fiscal pain we know is necessary because we succumbed to complacency and put off dealing with this looming fiscal disaster. Throughout history, many nations, when confronted by sizable debts they were unable or unwilling to repay, have seized upon an apparently painless solution to this dilemma: monetization. Just have the monetary authority run cash off the printing presses until the debt is repaid, the story goes, then promise to be responsible from that point on and hope your sins will be forgiven by God and Milton Friedman and everyone else.
>
> We know from centuries of evidence in countless economies, from ancient Rome to today's Zimbabwe, that running the printing press to pay off today's bills leads to much worse problems later on. The inflation that results from the flood of money into the economy turns out to be far worse than the fiscal pain those countries hoped to avoid. . . .
>
> Even the perception that the Fed is pursuing a cheap-money strategy to accommodate fiscal burdens, should it take root, is a paramount risk to the long-term welfare of the U.S. economy. The Federal Reserve will never let this happen. It is not an option. Ever. Period.

Fisher would have us believe that the Federal Reserve, the engine of inflation, stands as an iron barrier against the doomsday consequences of the fiscal authorities' irresponsibility. But there is no reason for the Fed to exist other than to provide cover for irresponsible fiscal authorities. One has to ask in any circumstance, as Professor von Mises has, why the traditional means of raising revenue, legislated taxes and lawful borrowing, have to be bypassed and supplemented by the surreptitious activities of the Fed to begin with. In any case, it was in May that Fisher provided us his adamant assurances, "The Federal Reserve will never let this happen. It is not an option. Ever. Period."

Months later there was another tone in a speech Fisher gave in New York. By this time IndyMac had been taken over by the FDIC, Fannie Mae and Freddie Mac had been nationalized, Lehman Brothers had filed for bankruptcy, the Fed had started serial giveaways of billions to AIG and had injected hundreds of billions of dollars of liquidity into the markets. Then on top of the federal debts, visible and unseen, that Fisher decried in May, Congress had been asked to cough up another $700 billion it didn't have for a bailout. In the aftermath of all that, on September 25, Fisher was less the adamant and more the supplicant:

> We are deeply submerged in a vast fiscal chasm. Which begs the question: Is it possible, now that so many distinguished senators and congressmen are proclaiming their concerns for the price tag of the Treasury proposal and are ardently defending the interests of the taxpayer, that one of the outcomes of this debate will be that Congress, which alone has the power to tax and spend, will finally face up to the task of squaring the nation's books?
>
> They can use this crisis as a call to arms for coming to grips with our fiscal predicament, or they can punt by asking our children and their children to do what they cannot bring themselves to do. Or, just as awful, they can turn to the Fed to print their way out of their dilemma and encumber future generations of Americans with the debilitating burden of debased money.

Two weeks ago, I was blessed with the birth of a grand-
child. Her name is Anna. For Anna's sake, I pray that those
with the power of the purse will take the high road and come
to grips with our nation's fiscal predicament either through
deft management or enlightened fiscal initiatives. And I pray
that Congress will resist the temptation to hinder the Federal Reserve's independence and instead allow us to implement policy unencumbered by political exigency. For if they
don't and the people who deliberate monetary policy in the
Fed's hallowed halls are no longer able to do their . . . best to
tell it like it is and act accordingly to provide the monetary
conditions for sustainable noninflationary growth, I will
fear for Anna's future.

There is poignancy in Fisher's remarks. But they may evoke a more
caustic reaction in those who realize that the Fed is both the architect
of the present crisis and the engineer of the dollar's long-term debasement. Far from a bulwark against a flood of congressional profligacy,
the Fed has been its enabler. Regardless of the condition of the Republic
when we finally emerge from the coming chaos, the first order of business must be to see that the Federal Reserve and its functions are abolished so that a sound monetary system can again emerge.

CHAPTER EIGHT

Toppling the Dollar

Your New World Order Is Waiting!

We have in many ways humiliated ourselves as a nation with some of the problems that have taken place here.

—Henry Paulson, U.S. Treasury Secretary

I think there is a question mark over the durability of any power that relies as heavily as the United States on importing capital and borrowing from abroad.

—Niall Ferguson

Made in China

If the monetary policy of Bulgaria is inflationary, the rest of the world doesn't even shrug. If the fiscal policy of Bolivia is reckless, the global economy is unaffected. Not so with the United States. Since the end of World War II, the U.S. dollar has been the reserve currency of the world. Just as central banks including our own once held gold and issued their currencies as a marker for gold, under the Bretton Woods agreement, foreign central banks have held U.S. dollars against which they issue their own currencies. Despite the abrogation of the U.S. promise of dollar/gold redeemability, the dollar standard has persisted. Almost two thirds of foreign currency reserves are held in dollars. As the world's leading reserve currency, the advantages for the United States are several. This dollar standard results in greater market demand for dollars and therefore a higher exchange rate than would otherwise exist. American consumers have been the beneficiaries of this additional demand for dollars. James Grant, editor of *Grant's Interest Rate Observer*, has described what the prerogatives and temptations of the reserve currency status are like by imagining if they were conferred on some little unsuspecting country that could go forth to consume more than it produces, only troubling itself to print currency to cover the difference. Wouldn't the inhabitants of such a favored land, he wonders, "spend a little more freely, eat a little bit better and speculate a little more readily than they had before their currency passed for good money the world over? Might they not take it upon themselves to wage a small war, if financial limitations had previously constrained them?"

In fact it has been a very sweet deal for Americans to have industrious people elsewhere in the world willing to sell the goods they make at real cost in materials and labor in exchange for paper money that can be printed willy-nilly. It has been an act of great unrecognized charity on their part to save rather than to spend, and to loan their savings to the United States government so that it can spend recklessly. The next generation of Americans who will have to pay tomorrow for today's consumption, wars, and waste may not have a voice in this affair. But our creditors do. They are under no obligation to continue funding the vote-buying programs of our Republicans and Democrats in Washington. And as they watch America's debts soar, some of the passengers aboard the Dollar/Debt Express have reached for the emergency cord in hopes they can stop the train and get off.

When Americans buy Chinese-made shoes and shirts at "everyday low prices," as well as electronics and furniture, and toys and games from the shelves of Wal-Mart or any other retailer, a portion of the dollars paid to the retailer in turn are sent to China to pay for the manufactured goods. The manufacturer of the Chinese products must pay its suppliers, utilities, plant, equipment, and workers in domestic currency. So those dollars are exchanged for local currency and end up in the hands of China's central bank and investment authorities. Those dollars don't do any good just sitting around in an electronic entry in the bank. They are spent or invested. Some are spent buying things from the United States. But China sells five times more to the United States than it buys, so most of those dollars will be invested. For example, in 2007 the United States bought $321 billion in goods from China, but sold only $65 billion to China. That means that China had a trade surplus with the United States (or the United States had a trade deficit with China) of more than a quarter trillion dollars ($256 billion). That surplus must be invested, most of it finding its way back to the United States.

China recently surpassed Japan as the world's largest foreign holder of U.S. Treasury securities, with $767 billion worth at the end of March 2009. Its total holding of U.S. Treasuries and agency debt altogether is thought to exceed $1 trillion, a figure that is estimated to be as much as 60 percent of its foreign exchange reserves. At the time Fannie Mae and Freddie Mac were seized, Chinese sources reported that the country had invested more than $400 billion in the debt instruments of the two institutions. The willingness of China to fund our debt and deficits to that extent has helped keep U.S. interest rates lower than they otherwise might have been. It has therefore been a subsidy for American debt and consumption. It is the equivalent of each individual American having borrowed $3,300 from the Chinese people. This is, to say the least, a peculiar state of affairs considering that per capita income in America is 8.5 times higher than that of China; that America has the sixth highest per capita income in the world, while China ranks at only number 100. It calls to mind the repeated admonition in the *I Ching*, the ancient Chinese "Book of Changes," that it is the way of fate to empty that which is full and to prosper the modest.

China's growth since substantial liberalization of the economy in 1979 has been remarkable, producing annual growth rates at or just under double digits for three decades now. It has not been lost on the Chinese people that they have created substantial pools of capital. China's young and increasingly urban consumers want to enjoy the fruits of their labor. Their spending is climbing. Still only 38 percent of GDP, Chinese consumption has a long way to go to reach U.S. levels, in which consumer spending accounts for almost 70 percent of GDP. But as U.S. consumers retrench with the mortgage meltdown, the Chinese government intends for domestic spending to make up some of the shortfall in economic activity and to that end may remove blocks to domestic consumption. In November 2008, China announced its own stimulus package of $586 billion. Like all such "stimulus" plans, it will be far less effective than letting people keep the money they have earned and spend it on their own real preferences. Even so, it must appear a strange foreign custom to the American governing classes that the Chinese government is spending money it actually has.

It should at least be noted that this stimulus expenditure is the dollar equivalent of China's holdings of U.S. Treasury securities. With the assertion of domestic claims for Chinese capital, U.S. interest rates will rise. But while expanding Chinese consumer demand may represent some competition for the Chinese capital that funds U.S. government debt, it is not the biggest threat by any means.

When Your Banker Has a Problem

A time-honored expression had it that if you owed your banker a thousand dollars, you had a problem, while if you owed your bank a million dollars, the bank had a problem. Adjusted for today's cheaper dollars, the adage could stand reformulation: If you owe your bank ten thousand dollars, you have a problem. If you owe your bank ten million dollars, the bank has a problem. As a key banker for an indebted United States, China has a very big problem. But as institutional holders of bundled mortgages are learning, eventually there comes a time to face up to reality and square the books.

Like codependents in a standoff, the United States and China constantly bicker about exchange rates. It may seem peculiar that the United States should be too unhappy about a relationship that allows it to produce paper dollars at almost no cost for which valuable goods are exchanged, but unhappy it is. Washington's insistence is to get less for its money, as though a country can become wealthier by debasing its currency. While most shoppers want the most they can get for their dollar, the United States wants less. Instead of 8 Chinese yuan for each dollar, Washington wants only 5.5. The objective is to make American goods, steel, heavy equipment, and agricultural products cheaper in China. The cost of the adjusted exchange rates would be borne by

American shoppers who would find the value of consumer goods they buy in places like Target and Wal-Mart jump as much as 30 percent virtually overnight. Of course, as prices for Chinese goods rise, other Asian competitors like Vietnam would likely fill the void. And its negative impact on China's dollar earnings means U.S. interest rates would have to tend higher to attract other buyers of U.S. debt. This perpetual bickering over exchanges rates is one of the problems of both the nationalization of trade and of a fiat, irredeemable currency. Robert Mundell, winner of the Nobel Prize in economics, has commented about this surrealistic squabbling between countries that are one another's best customers:

> When the international monetary system was linked to gold, the latter managed the interdependence of the currency system, established an anchor for fixed exchange rates and stabilized inflation. When the gold standard broke down, these valuable functions were no longer performed and the world moved into a regime of permanent inflation. The present international monetary system neither manages the interdependence of currencies nor stabilizes prices. Instead of relying on the equilibrium produced by automaticity, the superpower has to resort to "bashing" its trading partners which it treats as enemies.

It was in this bickering environment in the second half of 2007, with whispers of trade wars in the air, that Secretary Paulson went to China to lecture its officials about their currency. This is another case of a Treasury head who should have been minding affairs closer to home. After all, at the time the dollar was in the middle of a two-year slide, setting new daily lows against the euro. But Paulson thought to demand that China adjust its dollar exchange rate "without delay." China's response came from two quarters; the Chinese state media called it "the nuclear option."

China should use its huge foreign reserve holdings as a "bargaining chip," said Xia Bin, a finance official in the cabinet in July. Then in August, in the Chinese government's English-language paper where it was certain to be noted in the Western world, He Fan, an official at China's leading official think tank, offered a reminder that China could pull the trigger if it wished:

> China has accumulated a large sum of U.S. dollar holdings. Such a big sum, of which a considerable portion is in U.S. treasury bonds, contributes a great deal to maintaining the position of the dollar as an international currency. Russia, Switzerland, and several other countries have reduced their dollar holdings.
>
> China is unlikely to follow suit as long as the yuan's exchange rate is stable against the dollar. The Chinese central bank will be forced to sell dollars once the yuan appreciated dramatically, which might lead to a mass depreciation of the dollar.

It was the first time a threat to dump dollars had been made explicitly and it caused a stir. Paulson dismissed the prospect of China's selling its holdings, telling CNBC, "I think it's absurd, frankly." On Fox News, President Bush said, "It would be foolhardy of them to do that." A *New York Times* editorial entitled "Irresponsible Threats" called talk of Chinese dollar selling "stupefying." The editorial also assured its readers that China's central bank had announced it had no plans to sell its dollars. As though such plans would be announced.

Paulson was whistling past the graveyard by calling the threat absurd. Thoughtful observers like Paul Craig Roberts, assistant secretary of the treasury in the Reagan administration, had been warning for years of China's growing influence over the dollar and U.S. interest rates. That leverage extended to American foreign policy as well. Roberts put it succinctly: "A country whose financial affairs are in the hands of foreigners is not a superpower."

As Paulson continued to downplay the possible impact of China's triggering the "nuclear option," Roberts wrote that if Paulson didn't understand the dependence of U.S. interest rates on China's purchase of Treasuries, "Bush had better quickly find himself a new Treasury Secretary." Since the United States doesn't have any reserves or other means to fund China's share of Treasury and agency debt, he said, such a sale would result in monetary ruin:

> . . . the main support for the U.S. dollar has been China's willingness to accumulate them. If the largest holder dumped the dollar, other countries would dump dollars, too.
>
> The value and purchasing power of the U.S. dollar would fall. When hard-pressed Americans went to Wal-Mart to make their purchases, the new prices would make them think they had wandered into Neiman Marcus. Americans would not be able to maintain their current living standard.
>
> Simultaneously, Americans would be hit either with tax increases in order to close a budget deficit that foreigners will no longer finance or with large cuts in income security programs. The only other source of budgetary finance would be for the government to print money to pay its bills. In this event, Americans would experience inflation in addition to higher prices from dollar devaluation.
>
> This is a grim outlook. We got in this position because our leaders are ignorant fools.

Those are sharp words, but the idea that mention of the economy's vulnerability was "absurd" merited them. The possibility always existed that the escalation of an unexpected event—the "Wang Wei" spy plane incident of 2001; the March 2009 incident involving the USNS *Impeccable*, a surveillance ship off China's coast; or another American war (Iran? Pakistan?)—could trigger the Chinese "nuclear option." But the greater likelihood is of gradual disinvestment by China through attrition. Serious officials, rather than being dismissive, would have to contemplate several very real possibilities for disinvestment. The U.S. economic slowdown resulting in reduced Chinese foreign exchange earnings, competing Chinese domestic demand for the capital, and concerns of inevitable dollar depreciation are all very real reasons to expect that Chinese investment patterns can change. There is no evidence that U.S. officials have any plan other than inflation to deal with real-world economic circumstances that are already under way.

Rewind a year to the takeover of Fannie Mae and Freddie Mac. It was widely met in populist circles ("You don't see anybody in Kansas getting bailed out!") with suspicion that it was more about keeping China in the U.S. debt game than it was about keeping Americans in their homes. The case was persuasive on its face. As investor Jim Rogers said in a Bloomberg interview, "The people who bought debt in Fannie Mae and Freddie Mac can read a prospectus. They can read it. It says it is not guaranteed by the government. Anybody who can read a balance sheet knew that both of those companies were a sham and they had problems." But China, the largest foreign holder of Treasury debt, was also the largest foreign holder of Fannie and Freddie debt, followed by Japan. Fannie and Freddie's precarious fiscal conditions were well known long before the takeover. The commitment of $200 billion for preferred stock and other guarantees may have been reassuring for the agencies' bondholders, but it didn't do much for American homeowners. The takeover represents money the government doesn't have for investments it hadn't guaranteed in the cause of arresting the falling housing market, which it cannot do. Making the federal guarantee of the agencies' bonds explicit in the face of the stock collapse shows concern for the bondholders, Chinese and Japanese among them. Ironically, however, except for inflation, those guarantees can only ever be effected by borrowing more money from . . . places like China and Japan! America's bankers have a problem.

Brand Name America

Just as the costs of the Vietnam War were instrumental in the collapse of the Bretton Woods gold exchange monetary system, Bush's elective war in Iraq will be noted as the straw that broke the dollar standard that has prevailed since 1971. There was always something inherently unstable about the neoconservative fantasy of a "unipolar world." Empires do extend themselves into collapse. But it was more than just the dollar cost of war and empire. There were other consequences, harder to calculate but nonetheless real.

It was, to be sure, a war that would pay for itself, according to then–deputy secretary of defense Paul Wolfowitz. Pay for itself? Not so fast! Economist Joseph Stiglitz, a Nobel laureate, and his coauthor Linda Bilmes made a serious attempt to calculate the cost of the war, including its hidden costs. The conclusion became the title of their book, *The Three Trillion Dollar War*. That is a staggering cost, especially since the U.S. debt was less than $6.5 trillion when the war began. Even so, on my Phoenix radio program Stiglitz said they believe the actual cost is more likely to be $4 or $5 trillion.

Among the difficult costs to ascertain is the war premium on the price of oil that the prolonged Iraq escapade and years of saber-rattling toward Iran have entailed. During some periods in which fears ran high that the disruptions were about to spread, that extra cost may have run as high as $20 to $40 per barrel, depending on developments. It was an enormous transfer of wealth from Americans to Mideast oil sheikhs, Putin's Russia, and Chávez's Venezuela. With more than 20 billion barrels of crude oil imported during the period and a war costing trillions, the Iraq adventure has proven to be a very efficient means of decapitalizing the country. The fear premium on oil only began to subside in the waning days of the Bush administration as the prospect of an attack on Iran diminished.

Even more difficult to determine were the costs "brand name America" paid with growing resentment of the country and its policies. Studies on the commercial impact of the war repeatedly found foreign consumers rejecting American products on the basis of the war. A 2007 BBC poll reported on average half of respondents in twenty-five countries believed the United States plays a negative role in the world. Americans clearly sense the shifting attitudes. A recent Pew Research study shows seven out of ten Americans believe their country is less respected than in the past. And in response to the credit collapse, people across the world are reported to fault America for economic problems that are developing in their countries as well.

Militarism has proven an inadequate compensation for the loss of America's industrial base and manufacturing jobs. Chalmers Johnson, the author of a best-selling trilogy on American foreign policy, including *Blowback*, published shortly before 9/11, in which he tried to warn America about unexpected consequences from its clandestine foreign activities, calls our massive military expenditures "military Keynesianism."

> By that, I mean the mistaken belief that public policies focused on frequent wars, huge expenditures on weapons and munitions, and large standing armies can indefinitely sustain a wealthy capitalist economy. The opposite is actually true.

The ultimately impoverishing reliance on armaments as a substitute for a vanishing industrial base; harm done American commercial interests around the world; indirect costs including the transfer of billions of dollars of American wealth overseas because of the fear premium on the price of oil; and budgeted and other inescapable dollar costs of the war—all of the foregoing are among the clear economic concomitants of the war. They tell part of the story. But the war also created new alliances in nervous response to the "world's lone superpower," as the formulation went. Eyeing the Bush doctrine and the contrived rationale for the invasion of Iraq, these new bedfellows raced into one another's arms in hopes of offsetting the wobble of the "unipolar world."

As the United States has been a party to it itself, the syndrome should be quite familiar: Nikita Khrushchev's Soviet Union sought to warm relations with the United States as its conflicts with China grew. Similarly Mao Zedong welcomed Nixon's diplomatic advances to China in part because of China's fear of the Soviets and their military presence on the Chinese border. That Sino-Soviet rift, long and intense, makes China and Russia's recent mutual cooperation all the more notable. That cooperation has now become substantial and it is evident that it is driven by apprehension about the United States. Border disputes between the countries have been settled, treaties have been entered upon, and astonishingly, in 2005 China and Russia conducted their first ever joint military exercises. Currency agreements are next, agreements that do not have a role for the dollar. Wise people know that wars are best avoided when it is possible to do so. Shallow people embark on wars of choice when the correlation of forces seems to make their victory certain. But when Benjamin Franklin wrote, "There never was a good war, or a bad peace," he was suggesting that not only are wars costly in many ways, they can also have unintended consequences. One of the consequences of the current war is hastening the end of the dollar standard.

Dumping Dollars

It was one of those stories that was fun to tell whether it was confirmed or not, so it was widely reported. In 2007, as the U.S. dollar was tanking in foreign exchange markets, the world's highest-paid supermodel (according to *Forbes*), Gisele Bündchen, had demanded that Procter and Gamble pay her in euros instead of dollars to represent one of its hair products. The story got a lot of play because it fit the times, and after all she is a supermodel. But it was covered to a degree inversely proportional to its economic impact.

Contrast that with a story of real impact that was hardly reported at all. Despite the fact that the dollar had rallied 8 percent from the time of the supermodel story, *Asia Times* reported in November 2008 that Japanese economists were calling for the U.S. Treasury to issue bonds payable in yen. "If concerns over U.S. Treasuries continue to grow, no one will want to buy them. Yen-denominated U.S. Treasuries would make it easy for foreign investors to buy them," said one economist. "The U.S. will be forced to issue foreign currency–denominated U.S. Treasuries in its hour of need," said another, dubbing them "Obama Bonds." "The U.S. cannot finance its deficit by itself. The U.S. financial system cannot survive without foreign investors."

Calls for an alternative to the dollar standard have been accelerating. At a Russian/Chinese conference in Moscow in October 2008, Chinese premier Wen Jiabao added his voice: "We need to diversify the global currency system, to support its stability through the use of different currencies." His remarks had the moderation of diplomacy-speak. But a different tone came through loud and clear in the *People's Daily*, China's official party newspaper: ". . . the United States has used the U.S. dollar's hegemony to plunder the world's wealth," said Shi Jianxun, a professor at Shanghai's Tongji University. His front-page commentary called for trade between Europe and Asia to be conducted in euros, pounds, yen, and yuan. On another front, discussions have been under way for some time between China, Japan, and South Korea for a euro-like "Asian Currency Unit." As 2008 came to a close, plans to wean itself from the dollar standard became overt, as China announced a pilot program to settle certain foreign trade in its own currency instead. The first steps include initiating the use of the yuan in the settlement of trades between Chinese industrial regions and both Hong Kong and Macao; the program begins to displace the dollar as the unit of settlement as Chinese exporting areas are allowed to begin using yuan for trade with the major southeast Asian nations.

At the Moscow conference Russian prime minister Vladimir Putin made the inevitable call for Russia and China to gradually adopt the use of their own currencies in bilateral trade. "The world has gotten itself into trouble with its heavy reliance on the dollar," Putin said. Russia may move the idea along; it has already begun a trial program of trading its primary export-blend oil in rubles. Venezuela is among a number of OPEC nations that have diversified some of their reserves out of dollars and into euros, while a majority of Iran's oil exports are now priced in euros, and it now sells oil to Japan in yen. It would be a mistake to consider Venezuela and Iran outliers on the dollar issue. While both countries' motivation for a change in OPEC oil pricing may be as much political as economic, the economic reasons remain compelling. Other OPEC members, noting dollar problems, have pushed for a change as well. "Maybe we can price the oil in the euro," said OPEC secretary-general Abdalla El-Badri in an interview that suggested member nations had been having lively discussions about a pricing change.

One has to suspect that a pricing change might not be gradual in the face of escalating dollar inflation. Just as supermodel Gisele Bündchen may have preferred to be paid in euros, during the inflation of the 1970s singer Bette Midler demanded payment in gold South African Krugerrands to perform overseas. When it was inevitable that the Bretton Woods dollar gold exchange standard couldn't last, France could send warships to pick up its gold in New York. Under the existing dollar standard, there is nothing to pick up. Those that get out early can pre-serve their capital; others will be left holding the "IOU Nothing."

There is reason to believe that Persian Gulf region money is moving out of dollars and into gold. In November 2008, Gulfnews.com reported a two-week Saudi gold buying spree of about $3.5 billion. That summer Iran officially denied that it had moved $75 billion from European banks (probably for fear of its being frozen by U.S. sanctions), but by November an adviser to President Mahmoud Ahmadinejad confirmed without detail that the country was moving reserves into gold.

At the same time China was reported in a number of accounts to be considering increasing its gold reserves from six hundred tons to four thousand, to diversify its dollar risk. Stories of that kind can be hard to source and can sometimes be planted by someone hoping to make a quick profit in the commodities market. But the question should be whether such a move would be prudent for China, which otherwise has all its eggs in the dollar basket.

In our discussion of likely dollar dumping, U.S. banknotes outside the country deserve consideration. On entering Baghdad in 2003, U.S. troops found hundreds of millions of dollars in cash in the hideaways of Saddam Hussein's cronies. One stash of $112 million in Federal Reserve notes was discovered, another of $650 million in shrink-wrapping bundled by the Federal Reserve Bank in New York. A subse-quent investigation revealed that the banknotes, originally shipped to Switzerland, had made their way to Iraq by way of Iran.

Nobody really knows how much U.S. currency is being held over-seas. There is almost $900 billion in circulation altogether. Alan Green-span has testified that more than half of U.S. currency is held outside the country. These are dollars held by gun runners and drug traffickers; by Ethiopian pirates and Russian oligarchs. These are dollars sent back home to Mexico by illegal aliens working in the United States; dollars paid to bribe officials in foreign lands, and even dollars held by people in places like Venezuela and Ukraine and Zimbabwe who don't trust their own currencies. The holders of all these dollars, U.S. legal tender, believe them to represent a claim on the goods and services of America. As dollar depreciation accelerates, this currency can race back into the country, bidding up prices seemingly overnight, as it adds fuel to the fires of inflation.

Just as those dollars exist in the form of actual currency, there is the much larger problem of the dollars serving as currency reserves in foreign central banks. In mid-2008 data from the International Monetary Fund, covering two thirds of the world's central banks, foreign currency reserves topped $7 trillion. Sixty-two percent of the reserves identified as allocated to a specific currency, a total of $2.73 trillion, are held in U.S. dollars, virtually all in U.S. Treasuries. It is not a serious problem only if they all agree to hold those dollars forever.

In many ways it is like the story of the old man who called his doctor, his priest, and his lawyer to his bedside as he lay dying. "As you know," he managed to whisper, "I have no heirs, so I've decided to see if you really can take it with you. I'm giving each of you an envelope containing $100,000. You are to put the envelopes into my casket just as they lower me into the ground."

They all solemnly agreed and at his burial soon thereafter each slipped an envelope into the casket. Later over cocktails and reminiscences, the priest had an attack of conscience. "I have to confess," he said, "that our homeless program has been a little short of funds, so I only put $80,000 in the envelope and gave the other $20,000 to the homeless." The doctor said, "I have to confess as well, that I put $50,000 in the casket and gave the rest to the children's ward at the hospital."

The lawyer glared at them. "I am deeply disappointed in you both. And I want you to know that I placed in his casket my personal check for the entire $100,000!"

Since 1971 the United States has tossed check after check into the vaults of central banks around the world. But the people to whom those checks are written have not been dead, only sleeping. They are beginning to stir.

CHAPTER NINE

The Authorities Are in Charge

Or So They Think!

. . . if we face a monopolist we are at his mercy. And an authority directing the whole economic system would be the most powerful monopolist conceivable.

—F. A. Hayek

The more prohibitions there are, the poorer the people become. . . . The greater the number of statutes, the greater the number of thieves and brigands.

—Lao-tzu

The Command Economy

America is transforming itself, without forethought, debate, or pause, into a command economy. A command economy is a top-down, state-controlled economy directed by planners and bureaucrats, boards and bodies, administrators and authorities. A command economy is not characterized by mutuality of interest and agreement between parties. It relies on edict. A command economy, as the name implies, orders the affairs of a nation by coercion. In a free economy goods and services are bought and sold by consent; business transactions are based on agreement; contracts depend upon a meeting of the minds of the parties involved. In a command economy government sets prices, controls and directs resources, and oversees production and consumption. Free economies produce prosperity; command economies produce poverty. The transformation of America is already taking place at breakneck speed, even before the current economic crisis is full blown. Historical precedents insist that as conditions worsen, the transformation into a command economy will accelerate.

It is astonishing that this should be taking place, especially at a time in which three billion people around the globe have rejected the poverty, want, and shortages of their command economies to begin to experience the blessings of abundance. It is not as though object lessons are wanting. China's stunning economic growth, its modernization and rising living standards are the result of nothing more complicated than freeing the command economy. Although lessons abound, Americans are choosing—or perhaps failing to choose and therefore letting the choice be made for them—to go in much the same direction as the command economy of postwar Great Britain. That period saw the nationalization of entire sectors of the British economy, a currency crisis and prolonged economic decline including crippling unemployment and choking inflation. The reasons that the United States would choose to follow a pattern that hollows out economies the way it did the British are many. But as a symptom, although not a cause of this self-inflicted harm, look to the modern American politician. For today's breed of politician, power is their very passion. Their every concern and the entire public debate about politicians centers around the use of power. How may power best be exploited and aggrandized? Who is to be bailed out, who is to be plundered to pay for it? Who is to be subsidized, who penalized? Who shall be taxed and who shall be paid? In contrast, the founders looked upon power very differently: How can the use of power be limited? How can it be divided against itself? How can it be kept in check? In yielding to the former and to their command economy, the current generation of Americans, blessed with so much, will be the shame of the ages.

Anyone believing the evidence for the looming command economy is being overstated need look no further than the speed at which American finance has been nationalized in the current crisis. Legislators voted an initial $700 billion bailout package, but in no time the taxpayers ended up with more than eighteen times that, $12.8 trillion in loans, spending, and guarantees. And to make clear who is really in charge, the giveaways are accompanied by a refusal of the authorities to disclose who is getting what and what kind of collateral, if any, is being given. The trend was dramatically illustrated in October 2008. In a development that played out like a scene from *The Godfather*, the CEOs of the nine largest banks in America, dealmakers and negotiators in their right, were ushered into a room at the Treasury Department in Washington and handed a one-page document agreeing to sell preferred shares to the government. They were told by Henry Paulson, according to the *New York Times* account, that they must sign it before leaving. The chairman of Wells Fargo protested that his institution didn't have problems with toxic mortgages and didn't need a bailout. Too bad. "It was a take it or take it offer," said one insider. An online writer for *The Wall Street Journal* favorably likened Paulson's commandeering of the banks to Reagan at the Berlin Wall. "History often carries an air of inevitability," he gushed.

If there is inevitability to America's becoming a command economy, it is a sorrowful day for human freedom. The Central Plan of the command economy is incompatible with dissent, disagreement, individual preferences, and your own plan, whatever it may be. If the Central Plan is to prevent foreclosures on homeowners who can't pay, then the plans of individuals whose resources will be used to prevent those foreclosures must give way. If your individual plans and the Central Plan are in conflict, you will have to give up your plan. As we have noted, a free economy rests on agreement, but a command economy is constructed of coercion. One of the reasons (among many to which we have referred in this book) that a command economy produces poverty has to do with the diversion of productive human effort. In a free economy people provide services that are sought by others and they are rewarded for doing so. Each individual's own wants and needs are met to the extent he finds ways to serve others. But in a command economy enormous amounts of human effort are expended in attempts to influence or control the Central Plan. This activity produces no new wealth. It only seeks to divide what wealth already exists.

The command economy is not the exclusive province of either the left or the right, Republican or Democrat, Communist or Fascist,

Stalinist or Nazi, Pol Pot, Mao, Chávez, or Ahmadinejad. It is what they all have in common. Just as war is the health of the state, economic turbulence is the state's opportunity for self-advancement. As the unseen and destructive consequences of each new command initiative unfold, new plans are created and commands issued to undo the latest harm. In the current sequence, the Fed used its monetary monopoly to create artificial credit conditions; the cheap money fueled a housing boom, which, like all bubbles, popped; the monetary and fiscal authorities rushed in to bail out the banks; the only means they have of bailing out the banks is to borrow or print more money. As individuals seek to protect themselves from the destructive effects of the command economy, new measures are taken to prevent them from doing so.

It is these new measures that are the focus of this chapter.

Wage and Price Controls

It was a moment of that self-deprecating humor that people found endearing in Ronald Reagan. During a televised debate in the 1980 presidential campaign as inflation raced along at double-digit rates, a reporter asked about invoking wage and price controls. Reagan answered that wage and price controls don't work, and they didn't work in ancient Rome when the emperor Diocletian tried them. "I'm the only one here old enough to remember!"

Reagan shouldn't have had to go back as far as the Roman Empire to discredit wage and price controls, since they had yielded their destructive results just a few years earlier when implemented by President Richard Nixon. There was a reason Nixon was called "Tricky Dick." It is clear from the subsequent release of the Nixon White House tapes that he knew wage and price controls would be counterproductive, but he was willing to unleash their injurious effects on the country as a whole in hopes of winning some advantage in his reelection bid.

Wage and price controls are the first refuge of the governing classes in inflationary times. Price increases are first noted by the public at the grocery store and for everyday necessities. When it becomes apparent the household budget is being stretched to its breaking point, a cry goes out: "The government must do something." The call for the government to put a lid on prices by fiat or by edict reflects a confusion of cause and effect, because the government already did do something. It inflated the supply of money and credit. As long as the public perception of inflation is that it is a natural and spontaneous phenomenon, politicians, both the crafty who know better, and the clueless who don't, will escape accountability for it and will propagate schemes to cap prices. Late in his first term, with consumer prices rising at about 5 percent, Nixon announced his distinctly Leninist-sounding "New Economic Policy." He ordered a freeze on all wages and prices in the United States. It is not exactly clear how Nixon derived the authority to do this, but rather than an outcry of indignation, many of the nation's business leaders and the public at large supported the plan. The stock market responded the next day with a record price rise. (A note of irony inescapable in a discussion of inflation: the day's record move of the industrial average was only 33 points!)

Nixon's wage and price controls included a freeze on wages, prices, and rents, and extended to calling for a freeze on corporate dividends. He also announced the creation of a "Cost of Living Council," which would be run by Donald Rumsfeld and his deputy Dick Cheney. Although Nixon's August 1971 announcement was for a ninety-day price freeze, the program went through four separate phases that lasted ten times that long, until April 1974. An iatrogenic disease is one introduced by the treatment of a physician. If rising prices were the ailment from which the economy suffered, Nixon's prescription of wage and price controls proved to be bad medicine with its own iatrogenic disease. Its most debilitating symptom? Shortages.

Costs of some raw materials such as cotton were allowed to rise, but the costs of finished products made of those materials were not. So the finished goods were not made. Store shelves emptied. Farmers discovered it cost more to raise poultry than they could recoup selling it at the controlled prices. Chickens were drowned before they consumed more costly feed. The same thing happened with ranchers and feedlots that would lose money bringing cattle to market at the controlled prices. There were low prices for beef posted in the supermarkets, but the meat counters were empty. Because Nixon was afraid of political reaction to the creation of price inspectors crawling under the tables and peering from behind curtains at every American business transaction, he styled the mandatory price controls as "voluntary." But they were only voluntary in the sense that paying income taxes is "voluntary." And he held the threat of IRS audits over businesses that failed to comply.

The story is told of the woman who found a butcher out of compliance with the price controls. When she complained that a particular cut of meat was $1.19 a pound instead of 89 cents a pound as it was across the street, the butcher suggested she just go buy it there. "But they're all out," she replied. "Ma'am," the butcher shot back, "when I don't have any, mine is eighty-nine cents a pound, too!" Perhaps apocryphal, but revealing, is the claim that price administrators didn't account for the extra transportation costs involved, so toilet paper became scarce in Hawaii.

The wage and price controls required some manufacturers to cut quality and retailers to cut warranties to meet the artificial prices. If balancing your new tires had been free, now it was extra. If delivery had been free, now it cost. As an unintended consequence some prices ended up higher as middlemen proliferated to evade the price controls. Some products were sold to straw men in Canada only to be sold back into the United States at the uncontrolled prices of imports. Oil passed through additional and unnecessary hands as price markups were allowed in the subsequent sales of petroleum. Lumber was drilled through and patched up so that it could be sold as a manufactured product. In the end Nixon's burlesque created distortions, inconvenience, and shortages, but prices continued to rise. During the period of the controls prices rose at an average annual rate of 6 percent; when most controls expired, prices quickly played catch-up and hit an annualized rate of more than 12 percent in late 1974.

During episodes of wage and price controls it is tempting to think that perhaps something has been forgotten in the American character, because price controls really aren't about controlling prices, which after all have no volition of their own. They are about controlling free people who are now forbidden from engaging in noncoercive commercial activities. Perhaps as price controls wreak their economic toll, the people will remember that liberty is manifested through economic freedom. Imagine freedom of worship if the government owned all the places people could gather. Imagine freedom of the press if the government controlled the supply of newsprint.

But maybe there is no DNA code for freedom in the American psyche. Maybe the nation has coasted for more than two hundred years on the vision of a few of the founders and the experiment with freedom has run its course. Perhaps it is a replication failure of the liberty gene. If so, the failure began several generations ago. Germany's stunning economic recovery miracle after World War II took place over American and British objections. In 1948 the German economy remained as broken and as nonproductive as it had been three years earlier when the war ended. The Allied occupation government had a command economy in place complete with wage and price controls and rationing, some of which were remnants of the defeated Nazi government. Goods were scarce. Much of commerce consisted of primitive barter in cigarettes, chocolate, and nylon stockings. It was in this environment that economic official Ludwig Erhard, knowing that the occupying military governors would be away and not quickly able to object, went on nationwide radio on a holiday weekend and abolished the controls.

General Lucius Clay was the American military governor in Germany at the time. He told Erhard that his advisers insisted lifting the controls was a terrible mistake. "Pay no attention to them, General," said Erhard, "My advisers say the same thing."

The results of lifting price controls were immediate and dramatic. Stores that had been all but bare were stocked full of goods in no time at all. Instead of spending their hours in miserable lines waiting for the scarce staples of life under a command economy, people returned to productive activity. Employment expanded as the economy added 6 million new jobs between 1950 and 1960, while the unemployment rate fell from 10.3 percent to 1.2 percent. Over the decade annual economic growth averaged 8 percent. Industrial production soared by 25 percent in 1950 alone, and by 18 percent the next year. Germany was rebuilt; prosperity was restored. Truly it was an economic miracle.

During the postwar occupation of Germany, the American and British authorities banned F. A. Hayek's seminal 1944 book *The Road to Serfdom*, for fear it would offend the Soviets. Hayek's work described the way in which a central economic authority's planning put a government at war with its own citizens, how it must become increasingly coercive in order to prevail, and how the coercive machinery of the central plan, once erected, can be employed to any coercive end. Violation of price controls was a capital offense in Diocletian's Rome and in the French Reign of Terror. But those are not the exception; price controls have been accompanied by brutality throughout history. Dr. Murray Rothbard cites more recent episodes, cases that have been widely overlooked:

> Why did Chiang Kai-shek "lose" China? The main reason is never mentioned. Because he engaged in runaway inflation, and then tried to suppress the results through price controls. To enforce them, he wound up shooting merchants in the public squares of Shanghai to make an example of them. He thereby lost his last shreds of support to the insurgent Communist forces. A similar fate awaited the South Vietnamese regime, which began shooting merchants in the public squares of Saigon to enforce its price decrees.

Despite these dangers and their demonstrable ineffectiveness throughout the ages, wage and price controls remain a political favorite. It is inevitable that a thunderous demand for them will arise in the high-inflation periods ahead. Often in their initial appearance wage and price controls will masquerade as "voluntary." The more aggressively they are implemented, the more certain it is that the economy will grind to a halt. As a commercial collapse proceeds it is soon joined by a collapse of the social order.

Prices and Rationing

With the notable exception of war and slavery, there are few things governments do that are as damaging to the natural abundance of a free economy as continual interference with prices. No activities are undertaken as universally as price interference. Indeed, meddling with prices is virtually the all-consuming passion of modern governments.

What demands repeating of this obsession is that it is really not prices, which have no volition of their own, but parties to commercial transactions that are being controlled in this chronic busybody-ism. The government, deciding to favor one party against another, intrudes in mutually voluntary relationships to mandate prices. Sometimes governments set minimum prices or price floors. These encourage overproduction and result in gluts and waste. From *Saturday Night Live* many will remember comedian Chris Farley's hilarious portrayal of the character Matt Foley, a motivational speaker who lived in a van down by the river, and subsisted by "eating a steady diet of government cheese." That government cheese was the result of the glut produced by government price interference. Well-connected parties commonly use their political clout to have politicians force the public to pay artificially high prices for their goods. Sugar is a good example, as sugar-growing families are subsidized by the public, which is forced to pay prices almost twice the world market rate for sugar. The political calculation is that it amounts to a small price per consumer that can go unnoticed, but that it means big profits for the politicians' grateful contributors. Ethanol production is also heavily subsidized. *The Economist* reported in December 2007 that there were two hundred different government subsidies in the ethanol program, requiring taxpayers to fork over a whopping $1.90 per gallon to producers. Minimum wage laws are another example of price floors. They produce labor surpluses or unemployment. Such laws forbid people whose skills are worth less than the minimum from working.

But price ceilings, maximum prices, are the predictable nuisances of inflationary periods. And it is those maximum prices, as described in the last section, which produce shortages. In such cases, the government sides with consumers and against producers. To understand the harm this does, it is worth spending a moment on the function of prices in a free economy. Prices mediate or reconcile supply and demand. Generally when supplies are abundant, prices come down. When supplies are scarce, prices rise.

In a free economy it might be useful for consumers concerned with high prices to think of them as the antidote to high prices. That's right: high prices are the answer to high prices. When prices of items or products are high, some consumers will adjust their preferences, reducing demand. They may entirely forgo satisfying their desire for a particular product or find a substitute for their need. Meanwhile producers note the high prices and profit opportunities and step up their production of the products. Before long, demand falls off while supplies increase and prices begin to subside. Similarly, low prices are the antidote to low prices. When prices are low, consumption often increases, while some producers decide to turn their efforts to more profitable activities. Demand has increased while supplies have diminished, which leads prices to rise. This is a typical dynamic of the price system found in a free economy.

Politicians interfere in this dynamic in an inflationary economy with price ceilings. The artificially low prices enforced by law keep consumption at higher levels than would otherwise pertain, while disappearing profit margins on fixed prices result in reduced production. Demand is high, supplies are low, and shortages result.

When shortages occur, there are two ways for the scarcities to be allocated: by price or by rationing. Several years ago a pipeline delivering gasoline to Phoenix broke. Deliveries were interrupted. Shortages appeared. Lines formed at gas stations and fights even broke out. Some people began following gasoline delivery trucks, hoping to find ample supplies. And at some gas stations prices started going up. Of course, it was a big topic for days on my Phoenix talk show. One caller waiting in a long line, down to nothing but fumes in his tank, hoped the gas wouldn't run out before his turn at the pump. "My wife is about to give birth any time now. She could wake me up in the middle of the night ready to go! I've got to have gas!" So I asked if he wouldn't prefer to pay a higher price and not risk waiting in line and perhaps still not getting any gas. His answer was obvious. He would rather pay more, even if it meant he had to cut spending somewhere else, or eliminate unnecessary automobile trips.

But talk turned at once to rationing and charges of price gouging, which is music to the ears of politicians. They were ready with their one-two punches to make the situation worse: price interference and rationing. A headline in one of the Arizona newspapers read, "PHOENIX GASOLINE SHORTAGE—GOVERNOR LOOKS AT RATIONING." Arizona's attorney general had made no secret that he wanted state and federal antigouging laws, that is, caps on prices. But there were many reasons for prices to go up in the face of the shortages. Some stations were concerned about replacement costs; what if they sold their gasoline inventories at the prices that prevailed before the shortages and yet their next delivery was at substantially higher prices? Would they have to borrow money, or recapitalize their businesses to afford to fill their underground storage tanks? So they raised prices. Tanker drivers went to Tucson to load fuel for delivery in Phoenix. They didn't have to go, but they spied a profit opportunity. Some had to wait around up to ten hours to get fuel. Does the governor think they shouldn't have made the trip? Was their time free? Would Phoenix motorists have been better off had the tanker drivers stayed home and watched baseball? To assure quick supplies, Phoenix vendors offered California refiners higher prices than they were getting there to make deliveries to Phoenix. Were they colluding in a way that would be actionable by a headline-seeking attorney general? Would it have been effective had they offered refiners the same price they were getting in California?

Government price interference can really hurt consumers in emergency situations. In areas with severe weather, hardware stores may stock plywood that goes unsold for extended periods, and make up the extra inventory expense with higher prices when homeowners need to quickly patch up storm damage. The higher prices at the time help keep supplies available when the first buyer gets only what he needs for the emergency instead of taking up more of the inventory for later projects while he's at it. Are the victims of a natural disaster really better off if workmen in nearby states don't have any incentive to load their pickup trucks with supplies and chainsaws and tools to remove toppled trees and patch roofs where they are needed?

These questions shouldn't need to be asked. But rationing is the first-born child of wage and price controls. It is inevitable that politicians will respond to scarcities—a problem of their own making to begin with—by instituting rationing. Rationing deprives an economy of its resilience. It's "a dollar waiting on a dime," as people stand in line for hours, otherwise unproductive, to get rationed goods. In the command economy of postwar Germany worker absenteeism was an enormous burden. Work was secondary; people had to forage and queue up for hours to get the staples of life. In the free economy after the "Economic

Miracle," rampant absenteeism came to an end. No one ever seems to ask if the people would really rather stand in lines for hours to get a stale loaf of Soviet bread from the state commissary, or if they prefer to choose their favorite bread from a selection of dozens of fresh choices at a grocery store in a free economy.

Scarcities can be allocated by price or by rationing. Each method of allocation has its attributes.

Allocation by Price	Allocation by Rationing
Relies on agreement between willing buyer and seller	Relies on coercion of both the seller and the buyer
Provides for increased supplies	Impairs supply
Reduces marginal demand	Increases demand
Minimizes demand on consumer time	Endless queuing
Disempowers politicians; minimizes politics, connections, social standing, and favoritism	Empowers politicians; maximizes influence peddling, bribery, and political corruption

For all the attributes of price allocation, none will trump the politician's attraction to power, which is always at a high premium in a command economy. Given that rationing empowers the governing classes, one can be sure that shortages produced by wage and price controls will soon be followed by rationing. Yes, even in America.

Currency Controls and Reporting

Like wage and price controls and rationing, currency controls proliferate during a monetary crisis. In this age of identity theft, computer hacking, employees stealing customer records, credit card data, and even medical records, not to mention home invasion robberies, there are plenty of legitimate reasons for people to want their financial transactions private and anonymous. But the government has made itself the implacable foe of those seeking confidentiality in the conduct of their affairs. Imagine nothing more devious than buying your spouse an expensive piece of jewelry for Christmas and having the invoice or a copy of the check with your home address lying around in the store offices for any employee to see. But a desire to do business anonymously and in cash invites the suspicion of government agents.

It starts with a requirement that businesses file reports with the IRS for cash transactions of $10,000 or more. But if a husband and wife each withdraw $5,000 from their account, they may have committed the crime of "structuring," intentionally conducting their affairs so that they don't meet reporting requirements. It gets worse. If you decide to withdraw an indeterminate amount of cash less than $10,000, it may seem that you are avoiding reporting requirements, and if so, the bank is required to file a "Suspicious Persons Report." And they are not allowed to let you know that they are doing so.

An increasing number of people are running afoul of these measures. An April 2008 *Forbes* story relayed a few accounts of people who found themselves under criminal investigation:

- A young couple who received gifts of cash at their Greek wedding. They didn't want to wait in line to fill out paperwork so they made a series of smaller deposits.
- A New York couple, restaurateurs, made a series of cash deposits that triggered a "structuring" investigation. The feds grabbed $400,000 from their bank account even though they demonstrated that it was all legitimately earned and taxes were paid on all of it.
- The government took $240,000 from the brokerage account of an Illinois couple, claiming they used multiple bank accounts and kept cash deposits to $8,000. But they had a different account for each motel they own, and room rates of $47 to $55 a night.

Then there is the case of New York governor Eliot Spitzer. Spitzer resigned his governorship in March 2008 after the *New York Times* reported his involvement in a sex scandal. Spitzer was revealed to be "Client 9" of a high-priced prostitution service called Emperors Club VIP. According to investigators, Spitzer had paid $4,300 to a $1,000-an-hour call girl who went by the name Ashley Dupré. Perhaps Spitzer should have resigned or been charged for conduct for which he locked up other people as attorney general. That is a separate issue. But Spitzer was done in when he withdrew his own money from his account at his bank. The bank reported a cash withdrawal to the IRS. The IRS called in the Justice Department and the FBI. Federal wiretaps ensued.

It is important to understand that these reporting requirements and the criminalization of private financial behavior are only the beginning. The established practices are the baseline upon which the command economy will erect new regulations, criminal statutes, and surveillance practices in the monetary crisis. It is a baseline congested with precedents that the authorities of the Washington Party will evoke again and again as they try to stamp out the symptoms of monetary mismanagement, while the underlying causes go treated.

Perhaps it is worth a moment speculating about the measures that might be invoked in a monetary breakdown and compare the speculation to reality:

SPECULATION: **In a monetary breakdown your access to and the liquidity of your investments in the markets and exchanges can be imperiled or even frozen.**

REALITY: In January 1980 the Board of the Commodities Exchange adopted a rule limiting trading in the surging silver market to "liquidation only." That meant that silver investors could only sell their positions. The board that made the sudden decision included four members representing major short positions in the market.

REALITY: In September 2008, the SEC, under pressure from the Treasury and the Fed, issued a ban on short-selling stock in 799 financial companies. Before long it added another couple hundred companies to the list. The ban was an attempt to prop up the market and interfered with the market's function of price discovery in assessing very real toxic mortgage risks held by financial companies, risks that every investor would want known.

SPECULATION: **In a monetary breakdown the government may try to stop you from moving your money out of the country or investing it abroad.**

REALITY: In 1968 President Johnson implemented mandatory controls on foreign investments and on loans made abroad. The headline in the *New York Times* on January 2, 1968, read, "JOHNSON ACTS ON DOLLAR: CURBS INVESTING ABROAD AND ASKS CUTS IN TOURISM."

SPECULATION: **In a monetary breakdown the government may confiscate pension plans and retirement accounts. It may institute forced savings schemes or other appropriations. It may insist that safety deposit boxes be opened in the presence of an examiner.**

REALITY: In October 2008 the U.S. House Education and Labor Committee heard testimony from an economist proposing replacing 401(k)s and IRAs with government retirement accounts.

SPECULATION: **In a monetary breakdown the government may confiscate your personal wealth.**

REALITY: In 1933, under threat of ten years' imprisonment and fines of $10,000, Americans were ordered to turn their gold coins over to the government. Thereafter it was a felony for Americans to own monetary gold in the United States or elsewhere.

Currency controls are generally implemented to restrict flight capital as people seek to move their wealth to safer havens. Often they are used to try to maintain some artificial and untenable exchange rate, or to prevent the usage of an alternative currency. While no one has to pass a law to compel the usage of sound money of self-evident value, the creation of currency controls impedes the circulation of money and the robust commerce necessary to a prosperous people.

SECTION IV

WHAT
TO
DO

CHAPTER TEN

What to Do

Overview

We long ago reached the point at which government's grand solutions took precedence over personal freedom. In the midst of another Great Depression, would any politician let your freedom or the sanctity of what you've earned get in the way of his so terribly urgent program?

—Harry Browne

Because there is opportunity in every crisis, *The Dollar Meltdown* has carefully described our crisis: a frenzy of bailouts and stimulus spending that have lit the fuse on America's powder keg of debt. And a frenzy it has been. By the end of March 2009 the government had spent, loaned, or issued guarantees in the bailout equal to $42,000 for every man, woman, and child in America. Because this is on top of the existing debts, both explicit and concealed, that have been piling up for years, you were shown how massive and unsupportable that debt has become. A short history of money followed, with a description of successful monetary systems and their contributions to civilization, followed by instructive case histories of monetary systems gone awry and the destruction that occurs in their wake. Grounded in the differences between the two, we turned next to inflation, from the way it has been created through history to the sophisticated means the monetary authorities employ to inflate the currency today.

How a crisis presents itself is critical to seizing the opportunities that accompany it. That discussion in the previous section about the way a monetary crisis unfolds is among the most timely and critical in the book. The economic conditions that prevail during a crisis are magnified by the international status of the dollar. When those holding dollars around the globe decide they don't want any more or don't want them any longer, the impact on prices here can become evident overnight. That problem is compounded by the near inevitability that a currency crisis will be met with a variety of destructive reactions: wage and price controls, rationing, and currency restrictions. It is impossible to predict the severity of such measures in advance. For example, in imposing wage and price controls, President Nixon, ever crafty, was reluctant to unleash a swarm of enforcement officers on the public. He was about to begin his reelection campaign, and having served in the Office of Price Administration in World War II, knew something about the public resentment such steps could engender. But such measures as he did implement were destructive enough. It is almost universal that the authorities' response to a currency breakdown—of their own making to begin with—exacerbates the crisis. This forewarning will forearm you in your investment and financial decisions and help you take advantage of opportunities in the days ahead.

All of this is vital prologue to this part of *The Dollar Meltdown*: "What to Do." This is the payoff for all you have learned. It is here that you will discover how to invest for the dollar meltdown, with specific advice you can use today to avoid pitfalls and to protect your assets and profit from the opportunities that are always implicit in a crisis.

The monetary lessons of the past are plain to see. It is self-evident that the Dollar/Debt Express cannot go on. The recommended investments follow quite readily from the principles (*"wealth cannot be created out of thin air"*) and precedents (*"irredeemable paper currencies do not last"*) we have explored. Still, you should know how I became acquainted with these lessons, principles, and precedents, and why I am eager to share them with you.

When I was a young teenager in the mid-1960s, and the government stopped using real silver in most of its coins, my father began keeping the actual silver coins—dimes, quarters, half-dollars—that passed through his hands in change and depositing them in a large decorative vase in the living room, while the new base metal coins that appeared in 1965 were spent and passed along. Although he was a philosophy professor, there was nothing specialized or academic in his actions. It was simply rational economic behavior that does not have to be taught and was being practiced at the same time by perhaps millions of people across the land, just as it had been for thousands of years. You may remember Gresham's law from chapter 4: bad money drives out good. People hold on to the money that has superior value and pass along inferior money. I quickly learned that the value of the coins comes not from the name of the issuing government, the images represented, the face values inscribed, or even the stirring mottoes themselves. Trusting in God is one thing; trusting in government is another.

Only a year or so before that I had come upon an image from the period of the great German inflation that made a deep and lasting impression on me. It was of an older woman weeping in utter desperation at her impoverished circumstances and the complete worthlessness of her life savings. As children we all learned the story of the grasshopper and the ants. But this didn't fit the story. Here was someone who had practiced the industry and thrift the story commended, but who was left helpless despite it. I knew that her story and the silver coins in the vase in the living room were somehow related: in both cases there was something wrong with the money. A seed had been planted.

I was serving in the army, outside the country as a news anchor on an armed forces television network, when President Nixon announced his wage and price controls and repudiated America's promise to redeem its dollars in gold. It was a Sunday evening, August 15, 1971. Ever the politician, chief among Nixon's concerns was that his Sunday night prime-time announcement of the change would preempt the popular television show *Bonanza*. As I watched the broadcast from the newsroom, I knew that Nixon's actions would have a long-term impact on the dollar and the country. I began to wonder exactly how events would unfold and vowed to follow them carefully. I had a lot to learn, but every day for the next few years was like a class in the conditions described in this book: shortages, unemployment, dollar destruction, strains on the middle class and business, inflation, deficits and debt, the costs of war, taxes, currency manipulation, recessions, and stagflation.

Why did prices suddenly rise dramatically? And why were we subjected to a continuous series of booms and busts? Was Karl Marx right? Was it somehow endemic to capitalism, that we were consigned to these destructive episodes of systemic distortions and painful corrections? And I wondered why the conventional wisdom never seemed to see what was coming.

It was then I found that my questions had already been answered. I discovered the Austrian school of economics. It is called Austrian economics not because it is practiced in Austria—it isn't—but because many of its founders and proponents such as Ludwig von Mises and Nobel laureate F. A. Hayek were Austrian. From the perspective of a humane appreciation of free people and free markets, the Austrian school economists provided clear explanations of the business cycle of booms and busts that bedevil our economy and showed how they are needlessly caused by central bank policies. They advanced a theory of money and credit that accounted for inflation and deflation and much more. But even more important for investors, Austrian economics has great predictive power. Austrian economics allow the investor to tell the difference between a sustainable bull market, one driven by net new savings, and a bubble, driven by the artificial creation of credit. The Austrian economists and those employing such analysis were at the forefront, warning of the current market debacle while it was in the making. Time after time, the intellectual coherence and predictive power of this school of economics has been demonstrated, in contrast to other schools, usually Keynesian, which, in their attachment to deficit spending, have dug us into our current hole of debt. So great is this Keynesian influence among the governing classes that we just keep digging in deeper.

The practical applications of what I had discovered showed up during the Carter presidency, when I became convinced that the dollar was in trouble and that gold and silver were about to take off. In 1978 I became a broker for one of the nation's largest precious metals and currency dealers. The period developed into the highest peacetime inflation in the country's history, and I was there throughout the dollar crisis and the runaway bull market in gold and silver. There is little in these markets that I haven't seen. (One unforgettable memory of the time: leaving my office at the end of the day, going home to change out of suit and tie and into work clothes so I could help the overwhelmed security crews in our bank vaults move the virtual flood of silver we were buying from around the world on behalf of Bunker Hunt as he famously accumulated a good deal of the world's silver.) I wrote for a number of the popular investment newsletters of the time, spoke across the country on behalf of an international gold trade association, and have given perhaps hundreds of public talks, seminars, and broadcast interviews about geopolitics, economics, and the other subjects of this book. While in the years since I have been a stockbroker and president of a precious metals and commodity futures brokerage house, most memorable for me have been the people from whom I have learned. I have been especially fortunate to have known and discussed over dinner and into the night the issues in this book with many men of great economic wisdom such as the late Dr. Murray Rothbard and Nobel Prize winner Dr. Milton Friedman. Twenty-five years ago, hosting monetary conferences in California and Arizona, I arranged for a little-known Texas congressman who understood sound money and Austrian economics to be the keynote speaker. Even then, Ron Paul was able to speak with foresight and wisdom about what the prevailing economic policies would mean for the future.

Upon returning to my roots in broadcasting in the 1990s, I specialized in geopolitical and economic issues. Regular visitors on my Phoenix talk shows over the years have included investor Jim Rogers, Addison Wiggin of *The Daily Reckoning*, and influential analyst Mish (Michael Shedlock), each of whom has had regular weekly segments on the *Charles Goyette Show*. They, along with Peter Schiff, Robert Prechter, Robert Kiyosaki of "Rich Dad" fame, and many other respected market observers, have been among welcome and frequent guests who sounded a warning about the crisis as it built.

For many years I hoped that the United States could avoid a financial calamity. I have been visible in a small way in the national debate both in public speaking and as an outspoken talk show host in trying to influence public policy. But with the citizenry's willingness to go along with a costly and unnecessary war, and the growing fiscal recklessness of the Republicans and Democrats, it has become apparent that the opportunity for collective action to avert the most serious economic episode in the United States since the Great Depression has passed. It is a shame that that should be the case, but consequences of a generation or two of reckless policies can hardly be wished away. I began to turn my own efforts away from messages to the public at large about saving our peace and prosperity, and toward individuals, people like you, the readers of this book, in hopes that you can be assisted in weathering the now inevitable storm and in profiting along the way.

The Recommendations

The investment recommendations that follow come in four categories, the portfolio equivalent of a balanced diet with four basic food groups. Unlike some books that make investment recommendations, no attempt is made here to apportion your investments among these groups as a percentage. The circumstances of each reader are highly personal and it is my experience that rather than strictly adhering to such recommendations, people will adjust their portfolios to their own suitability and comfort level. That is an approach I endorse. Get started on paper by dividing the money you have for this program equally four ways for each of the categories that follow. Then start making adjustments, taking careful thought for your personal circumstances. If you own a hardware store in a farming community and expect to do well as agricultural commodities rise, you might wish to deemphasize that component of the recommended investments, diversifying by adding more weight to another. If you spend a lot of time behind the wheel and your cost of living will rise sharply as energy prices climb, you may want to hedge that risk by allocating more to the energy component of your portfolio. Someone with a small amount of money may invest the entire amount in gold coins, while an experienced investor with an already diversified portfolio will act on one or two specific recommendations that represent special profit opportunities. Even so, I do recommend that you allot your investments among the four categories to the extent you are able.

The four categories represent investments in enduring monetary vehicles (although gold and silver each merit a separate chapter, think of them both as part of this category), in the world's preeminent form of energy, in the basics of life, and in financial conditions that unfold over time. You will note there are no trendy retailers in the mix. Not so many years ago one of the nation's most visible mutual fund managers wrote a best-seller in which he suggested "hanging out at the mall" as an investment strategy. Of course, that was another easy credit period during which the Fed engineered the Fed funds rate down from 10 percent to 3 percent in less than five years, running the Dow and the S&P 500 up some 60 percent. The same fund manager displayed a photo of Fannie Mae's headquarters alongside family pictures in his office and wrote glowingly about Freddie Mac and Fannie Mae's new practice of bundling up packages of mortgages into what we all know now as "mortgage-backed securities."

Undoubtedly someone will come up with a new fast food idea that will sweep the land or a trendy retail concept that will have high school kids saving their lunch money. But these days the idea of checking out the malls for the next big stock opportunity sounds uncomfortably similar to hanging around at the racetrack trying to get some tips. The hottest trend at shopping centers now is "for lease" signs and the big box retail locations are emptying out. Fed interest rate manipulation that had people stalking the malls for the next big thing when they should have been saving for their futures is the kind of policy that has left the credit markets dilapidated today. Today there's no room for the Fed to manipulate interest rates down another seven percentage points.

In the pages that follow then, we go back to the basics. You won't find the next digital entertainment products or hot technology, and nothing about condos in Cancún. In the midst of snowballing socialization, medicine and health care can't be suggested as investment sanctuaries. Nor can finance in its nationalized forms like Fannie Mae and Freddie Mac. Instead you will learn about havens of safety and opportunity, just plain sensible things like: 1) *real money* (gold and silver); 2) *real energy* (oil); 3) *real things* that real people need (agricultural and raw materials); and 4) *a realistic assessment* of the economic environment (depreciating dollars and higher interest rates).

In each of these four categories of investments you will find one or more *core recommendations*. These have been chosen as the most appropriate recommendations for the achievement of our investment objectives. You may simply invest just in the core recommendation in each category, or if there are two core recommendations, divide your investment between them. Most categories have *also recommended* investments. Although not our preferred investments for the category, these vehicles are suitable, and may serve as handy diversifications for larger portfolios, or for personal needs and preferences. Several additional investment opportunities are included as *deserving mention*. These are specialized opportunities within each category that may be of interest as you explore the general themes of the book and plan the allocation of your investments. A reluctance to invest in equities is evident throughout this book for reasons made plain, including the socialist breezes wafting through Washington. But when, in the slightest of bows to conventional wisdom, stock fund investments are covered, they will be found in the second or third categories.

It should go without saying that all investments have some risk and may not be suitable for everybody. You are urged at each turn to read disclosure documents and regulatory filings as well so that you can make well-informed decisions. No tax advice is intended in this book. You should check with your own tax adviser for the taxation impact of any investment you make.

In the 1970s, as the postwar Bretton Woods standard was breaking down after a generation, no one made as much money for investors as did the late Harry Browne, who wrote with great wisdom about the coming dollar devaluation. Now, more than a generation later, as the dollar standard collapses, I have taken a couple of cues from Browne. The first is in seeking to arm you for more than just the investment conditions of this year, the next, and the year after. I have wandered through history, monetary theory, and economic principles to help you recognize syndromes, remember precedents, and be equipped to make sound judgments so you can profit from both the expected and the unexpected, now and in the future.

Second, I have approached making these recommendations in a spirit of modesty. They are designed to protect what you have, to insulate you as much as possible from a monetary breakdown, and to guide you to substantial profits along the way. But they are also made bearing in mind the unexpected and highly unlikely event of a sudden transformation in the hearts and minds of the governing classes, consisting of a newborn sense of financial responsibility, and a newfound commitment to sound money and to the economic liberty that is the author of prosperity. Even in that unlikely case, you will still do very well indeed with these recommendations. A period of new political enlightenment will demand a redeemable currency, oil will still make the world go around, a growing population will still need food and water, and interest rates cannot stay near zero in an environment in which money is not created out of thin air. In other words these are investments that you can buy and hold through the dollar meltdown. They will do well if we are dragged kicking and screaming to our senses by a breakdown, just as they will perform well if a light should dawn before it gets any darker.

CHAPTER ELEVEN

Investing in Gold

Glittering Opportunity

To be long gold is, in a grand thematic way, to be short the social-ization of risk.

—James Grant

O gold! I still prefer thee unto paper, which makes bank credit like a bank of vapor.

—Lord Byron, *Don Juan*

What to Buy and How to Buy It

I have on my desk at least a dozen forecasts for the price of gold, all made by people of some experience and knowledge. Someone in Hong Kong is calling for gold to hit $1,500 to $2,000 per ounce before long. Here's one for $1,650. Several are for $2,000. Another, this from Citigroup's chief technical strategist, says it could blow right past $2,000 by the end of 2009. Another has a range from $5,300 to $53,000 per ounce based on remonetization of gold. Here's one from somebody in Dubai who says "the price per ounce of the yellow metal will tip the $4–5,000 an ounce level." Another forecasts $10,000 per ounce.

All of these forecasts are possible. And yet no one knows. How fast will the dollar crisis unfold? The answer seems to be faster than anyone can foresee. With each passing day U.S. budget forecasts become more laughable. Just months before fiscal year 2008 ended the Bush administration forecast a budget deficit for 2009 of $482 billion. That was $74 billion higher than it had predicted six months earlier. A guess of $2 trillion would have been closer. It may be fascinating to try to predict the gold price, but it is impossible. Americans have not even begun to buy gold. Imagine the market reacting to the buying power of each American family buying a few coins. One ounce per family member would be 305 million ounces of gold. That's 9,486 metric tons, almost four years of new mining production. Some will buy far more than one ounce of gold. Add in the dollar holders around the world attempting to beat one another out the dollar door and into gold. And then remember Ludwig von Mises' description of "the crack-up boom," the breakdown that takes place within weeks or days as the realization spreads that the currency is just a scrap of paper. When those things begin to happen, gold can run through targets of $2,000, $3,000, or $5,000 an ounce like a hot knife through butter. As we said in the first chapter, your primary concern will be "How many ounces of gold do I have?" rather than "What is the dollar value of my gold?"

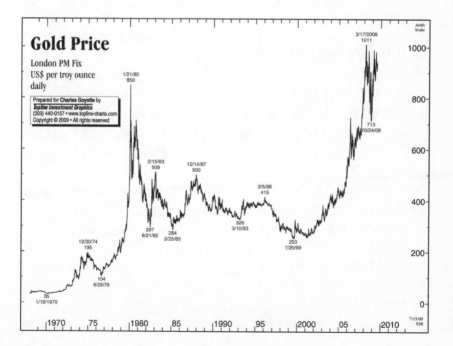

Much of the following description of the markets and mechanics for investing in gold applies to silver as well. But let's concentrate first on gold.

What to Buy

Someone once called gold "capital on strike." If the currency of the day is rapidly being debauched, you are being victimized and it makes sense for you to stop participating in this victimization. Put your money in real money. Begin now to buy gold, in the form of one-ounce bullion-type gold coins. Bullion coins are those that sell for prices based on their gold content and not for their rarity, date, or condition as judged by a collector. The most widely traded one-ounce bullion coins are the U.S. Gold Eagle, South African Krugerrand, and Canadian Maple Leaf. Others include the Austrian Philharmonic, Australian Kangaroo, Chinese Panda, and U.S. Buffalo. Each of these coins contains one troy ounce of actual gold content, but because pure gold is slightly soft, a couple of them (Gold Eagles and Krugerrands) have a total weight of just over an ounce; the small amount of added alloy makes the coin harder. These coins are recommended because of their convenience and portability and because each of these coins is instantly recognizable and liquid around the world for its uniform gold content. They are traded at prices generally within a few dollars of one another.

We have disclaimed any intention of offering model portfolios consisting of a certain percentage of each class of asset in this book's recommendations. But so you will have a place to begin, you should consider starting with 25 percent of your portfolio in physical gold and silver that you take in your possession. Remember you are putting your money into an enduring form of money.

While you will need to be concerned with what you pay (we'll get to that), do not spend a lot of time worrying about the price of gold. Because the monetary situation is precarious, it is important to act. Somehow it always seems that if you buy today, the price will go down tomorrow. But if you don't buy today, the price will go up tomorrow.

There are other gold bullion products including smaller coins of fractional ounces and a variety of bars weighing 1, 10, 1 kilo (32.15 troy ounces), 100, and 400 troy ounces. Bullion bars can be acquired at lower prices than one-ounce bullion coins, and those bearing the hallmarks and serial numbers of Credit Suisse and Johnson Matthey are acceptable trading items in the industry. In their one- and ten-ounce sizes, they are also acceptable for monetary investors. Kilo bars are becoming more widely traded as well. Even so, my recommendation for most people stands—to invest in one-ounce bullion coins. But if you do choose to buy bullion bars, by all means stick to the recognized hallmarks mentioned above and the one-ounce, ten-ounce, and kilo sizes. Otherwise, since you are going to take delivery of your gold yourself, the depositories' chain of custody is broken and you may encounter delays and even have to wait for some of the larger bars to be assayed when you sell.

The Market

There are several components in the price at which gold, silver, and other precious metals are bought and sold. They are the prevailing price of gold or silver, often called the market or "spot" price, the premium of the specific item, the "spread," and the dealer's commission or markup.

The "spot" price refers to the price of a commodity of a standard quality and quantity for immediate delivery on an exchange. Increasingly the industry refers to just the "gold price" or the market price. This is an important benchmark price; if spot gold goes up $100, the value of the gold you own has typically gone up $100 as well. It is important for you to ask for the spot or gold price when you get a quote for specific precious metal coins or products. Because the gold market trades globally around the clock and is a sensitive barometer of economic events, prices fluctuate constantly. When you make inquiries about buying and selling, in the time it takes you to hang up and call a competing dealer, the underlying gold price, or spot price, may have moved substantially. If so, your price comparisons for a specific coin will be on an unequal basis.

Premiums

You can check crude oil prices in the morning paper or online, but you would not expect to get a quart of Pennzoil motor oil at a price that is the fractional equivalent of the spot or world market oil price. Similarly, gold coins and bars require minting, marketing, and distribution. This cost is called the premium and is usually a few percent over the gold price. While the premiums can fluctuate, rising in a period of product shortage or higher demand, and falling in quiet markets, for the most part the premium stays with the coin, so that you pay more than the gold price when you buy coins, but the price at which you sell also contains a premium over the gold price. Therefore some of the bullion bars with slightly lower premiums may seem to represent a price advantage over bullion coins, but that advantage may amount to very little when you sell.

Spreads

Precious metals are traded among market-makers and brokers around the world on the basis of a bid-ask spread, just as you find in currency and stock markets. In making a market, a dealer will offer to buy a product such as Gold Eagles at one price, the "bid," and sell them at a price a few dollars higher, the "ask" or "offer" price. It is the difference between the bid and ask prices that keeps market-makers trading, making products available when you wish to buy and providing market liquidity when you wish to sell. Think of a retailer with inventory that sits on the shelves for long periods of time with few buyers. To cover his costs, his markup for those items will have to be higher than for inventory that turns over faster. Similarly in precious metals, the more actively a product is traded the narrower the spread, the difference between buying and selling prices, will be. In a fast-moving or volatile market, spreads will widen as the dealer seeks to protect himself from sudden price changes.

Commissions

The broker or dealer selling you precious metals will charge a commission for his services. Usually commissions on bullion coins and bullion bars are no more than a few percent. Sometimes the commissions are explicit and show up on your invoice or statement, and sometimes they are built into the asking price of the coins or bars. If you are going to comparison shop, be sure you are being quoted complete "out the door prices." If you are having your gold shipped to you, make sure the quotes you get include shipping and insurance.

To review, the bullion coins you buy will be sold to you at the dealer's "ask" price, which represents a premium of a few percentage points above the gold or spot price. In addition to that, or built into their asking price, will be a commission, also of only a few percent. When you sell, the dealer will pay you the "bid" price for the coins, and will charge a small commission as well. Take physical possession of your coins. Do not leave them with the dealer or let the dealer store them for you.

Where to Do Business

There are two kinds of places to buy gold and silver: precious metals brokerages and coin shops. You shouldn't have to slink down a dark alley in a tough part of town to do business in a dusty old coin shop filled with antique helmets from World War I. Such places do exist, plenty of them. On the other hand there are gold brokerage firms that would sell you the Brooklyn Bridge if you were willing. My preference is a precious metals broker because of their capabilities. If you had an account or a history of doing business with a brokerage house, in January 1980 when silver went into a steep parabolic climb, you likely could have called your broker and sold your silver over $50 an ounce over the phone—before you could make delivery of the metals. In a few days it was down to $35. But it's better to do business with a good, reputable coin shop that provides good service at fair prices than a brokerage house that pressures you to make the wrong investments.

A stockbroker does not keep an inventory of the shares of every company that trades on hand in case you happen to call and want to buy a few shares. A broker enters the market on your behalf and buys and sells on your instructions and with your money. While many times a well-capitalized gold brokerage house can fill your order on the spot, accepting your payment and handing you your gold, that is not the industry standard. Most often you are expected to pay first at the time you place your order, and then take delivery of your order a few days later. But since dealers capitalize the trades they do with one another, there is no reason you shouldn't ask them to do the same for you. The gold price moves from minute to minute, but your broker can execute your trade and lock in a fixed price right on the telephone. At that point the broker has actually executed the trade on your orders or adjusted the firm's house position for your order. You will be given a confirmation number with your order and a printed or e-mailed copy of the transaction. Generally firms will require you to remit funds the same day, often by a bank wire. For large orders a deposit may be required before it can be executed. Some dealers may want a credit card number, not to charge your account for the order, but to cover their exposure if the price should move down and your payment is not received. These procedures are a great convenience provided to you by the broker. (Imagine asking a stockbroker to buy shares for you when you have no money in your account!) Check fraud is fairly common and cashier's checks are sometimes counterfeited as well. So if you pay by check or cashier's check, the dealer will have to wait until the check has cleared before delivering your gold. Upon receipt of good funds, your gold will be shipped to you by registered insured mail, or available for pickup if you are dealing with a local company.

The process works the same when you sell. You can agree to sell at the prevailing price and your order will be executed on the phone. You are responsible for delivering or shipping and insuring your shipment to the dealer the same day and will be paid the agreed-upon price upon receipt. While most dealers have procedures that are close to this description, there can be some variation between dealers and depending on market conditions.

A personal referral can be helpful in finding a reputable broker. You can look for longevity as a guide to a firm's stability, and check with the Better Business Bureau to see if complaints are frequent and if they are resolved. Such steps can be helpful, but most important of all is to be clear about what you want and what you do not want.

First of all, you want the bullion coins recommended above, U.S. Gold Eagles, South African Krugerrands, and Canadian Maple Leaf gold coins. Many dealers will immediately try to switch you from bullion coins, which sell based on their gold content, to rare coins. These collector coins, called numismatic and seminumismatic, are pushed aggressively by some dealers, because the premium, the spreads, and the commissions are high. Markups of 20 to 50 percent are quite common, and they are often substantially higher than that. There is not usually anything deceitful in such markups if they are disclosed. While bullion brokers, as noted above, enter the market on your behalf, rare coin shops, like automobile dealers or other retailers, generally have to maintain a costly inventory. Costly inventory means high markups. Markups of these proportions may be acceptable to hobbyists and collectors; dealers and their salespeople make out well, investors not so well. Imagine the underlying price of gold having to double before you are in a profit position on rare coins investments. In writing this section I spot-checked a number of dealers for their latest sales practices and can tell you that virtually all of them immediately began trying to switch me into collector coins, mostly pre-1933 U.S. gold coins, $20 Liberty and $20 St. Gaudens gold pieces. The pressure sales tactics were relentless, the stories ranged from the laughable to the outlandish. It is true that these coins can have a day in the sun in certain market conditions, but owning them for investment has been a disappointment for many people. In any event, since you understand the economic picture and the future of the U.S. dollar, your objective is to own gold for its monetary properties.

Let me spend another moment on this. The dealer and his agent want to sell you high-profit-margin coins. They have overhead to pay, mortgages, car payments, and kids to put through school. That is not your problem. Often the sales pitch has to do with selling you high-profit-margin coins to protect you from the government's confiscation on the grounds that coin collections will be exempt. That may or may not prove to be true if and when gold confiscation takes place. But the reason there are so many of those coins still around to be purchased is that Americans only turned them over in small numbers during the last confiscation. If there is a monetary breakdown, you are almost certain to be better off if you purchased two or three gold coins with your money instead of only one. If need be, keep this book by the phone when you call to place an order, or take it with you to the dealer, shrug your shoulders helplessly, and read the following sentence aloud or point it out to the broker: BUY ONLY BULLION COINS; DO NOT BUY NUMISMATIC COINS.

Other Ways to Own Gold

This book is written to help you protect yourself from the unconsciona-ble mismanagement of the fiscal and monetary authorities. But there are more needless risks than just the governmental ones. Among them are institutional risks. These include risks associated with banks, insur-ance companies, brokerage houses, stock and commodity exchanges, and money managers. And there are credit and counterparty risks. Among those are the risk of nonpayment, default, and bankruptcy by individuals and entities who are party to a loan, contract, or investment in which you have an interest. In addition to governmental insolvency and currency depreciation, it has been a season rich with banking and other institutional, credit, and counterparty failures and frauds. It is as though we are trying to survive artillery fire while traversing a mine-field and being strafed from the air.

Still, one cannot be entirely isolated from the calamities of the soci-ety of which we are part. There will be times in which it is appropriate and profitable to participate in the public square of financial life. A couple of examples will describe such opportunities.

Although precious metals can be held in a tax-deferred Individual Retirement Account (IRA), they must be held by an institutional custo-dian. You will pay for the shipment of your gold and silver, and a storage fee as well. If you are not going to have hands-on possession of your pre-cious metals in the retirement account yourself, is there a way to invest in them that saves you money, and allows you to buy and sell or trade from gold to silver and back if you wish, in a way that is affordable? There is.

It is a reality that some people will wish to actively trade in precious metals markets for reasons of their own. Some may be reluctant to hold U.S. dollars even for a short time and may wish to add gold and silver investments to their portfolio beyond their core physical holdings. From time to time people may wish to park their money in precious metals assets, to add to and withdraw money as need arises or for expected expenditures. Some will want to speculate. Can this be done with minimal transaction costs? It can.

Exchange-Traded Funds

Exchange-traded funds or ETFs are one of the most popular developments of the investment markets in recent times. ETFs are like mutual funds, but they trade throughout the day on a stock exchange. Among the reasons for the growing popularity of ETFs are their low expense ratios and certain tax efficiencies. (You should seek specific and additional information about taxation from your tax adviser.) Like stocks, ETFs can be traded with market, limit, and stop-loss orders and can be sold short. ETFs are traded in bid-ask markets like those described above in the bullion markets, the spread representing the difference in price between what a market-maker will pay a seller and what it will charge a buyer. When markets are very thinly traded, they will have wider bid-ask spreads. When that is the case, the expense of a round trip of buying and selling can become more costly than is appropriate for rapid and frequent buying or selling. Since day-trading and "scalping" the market in hopes of achieving small profits in small price movements is not a recommended approach here, none of the spreads of the vehicles recommended should be a prohibitive consideration. Even so all of the core recommendations have sufficient volume and liquidity that the spreads are completely reasonable.

One other caution about ETFs before providing recommendations, and it is a caution that is important enough that it will be made again later in another context. With the success of ETFs there has been a proliferation of leveraged funds, funds that are managed to produce results that are a multiple, sometimes twice or more, of the performance of the underlying index or commodity. They often have names that make them easy to identify, like 2X, Double Long, Double Short, or Ultra. There is nothing inherently wrong with these leveraged instruments, and they can be valuable tools in the hands of financial professionals who need to insure some commercial activity or hedge against a market risk. Otherwise they are like gambling. A simple example that is used often in the industry will illustrate the way in which leverage can work against you. It compares an investment in an index with a market price of $100, and supposes that the market goes up 10 percent one day, and down 10 percent the next.

A 10 percent increase on the first day means a nonleveraged $100 investment would be worth $110. Falling by 10 percent the next day would mean a loss of $11 (10% of $110 = $11), so the investment, despite moving both up 10 percent and down 10 percent, would now be worth $99, less than where it started.

Now let's apply the same two-day market action to a leveraged fund that is designed to double the price movements of the index. Starting again at a market price of $100, a 10 percent rise on the first day means a 20 percent movement in the leveraged fund, up to $120. The next day the market moves down 10 percent, so the leverage fund drops by 20 percent, or $24 (20% of $120 = $24), and is now down to $96. After two days of seemingly offsetting price movements, the original investment has lost 4 percent of its value.

As that process repeats for some time, even if the price remains in a narrow trading range, the losses in a leveraged investment can add up fast. None of the ETFs or other funds among the recommendations here employ that kind of leverage, and you should be wary of using leveraged ETFs for anything but specifically designed commercial purposes of short duration.

Because it filled a need to make gold-based investments accessible in a new way, one of the real ETF success stories is SPDR Gold Trust, an exchange-traded fund (New York Stock Exchange symbol: GLD) that you can buy and sell in a stock brokerage account. The shares you buy represent a fractional, undivided interest in the trust, the assets of which are invested in gold bullion. When the fund was initiated each share of the trust represented one tenth of an ounce of gold, but the trust sells small amounts of gold to pay its expenses so now shares trade at a price slightly less than one tenth of an ounce of gold.

Since its establishment in 2004, GLD has been hugely successful and is the most active of any ETF recommended in these pages. It has made investing in gold accessible to institutional investors like pension funds that had not previously been able to have a position in bullion. Now GLD is one of the largest gold owners in the world, with more than the central banks of Great Britain, Russia, or China and about the same holdings as Japan's central bank. In May 2009, GLD held over 35 million ounces of gold, valued at more than $33 billion.

The fund's expenses are low, charging 0.40 percent a year. Couple that low expense with discounted brokerage fees, and the costs of buying and selling GLD can be quite advantageous compared to bullion. The trust also makes available on its Web page a complete list of the individual gold bars it owns. Before investing, read the prospectus at spdrgoldshares.com.

iShares COMEX Gold Trust (New York Stock Exchange symbol: IAU) is another ETF that invests in gold bullion which is held in custody as the property of the trust. Like GLD, IAU's price is modeled after one tenth of an ounce of gold and its expenses are a modest 0.40 percent per year. Created in 2005, IAU is not as large as GLD. In May 2009, IAU held more than 2.2 million ounces of gold valued at more than $2 billion. You can learn more about IAU at the iShares Web page. Read the prospectus before investing: ishares.com.

Bullion dealers mostly react negatively to the bullion ETFs, in part for competitive reasons. They are correct that an unallocated individual interest in bullion held in trust is not a replacement for ownership and physical possession of gold, our first recommendation. But GLD and the other bullion trusts around the world are providing a valuable service creating stockpiles of precious metals in nongovernmental hands. As such these market developments can become keys to the eventual development of a sound monetary system.

Undeniably the bullion ETFs have been a component of the gold bull market since their creation. In a period of monetary breakdown, the bullion ETFs can act like a booster rocket strapped to the price of gold and silver!

Gold Stocks

You will need to step into the financial system for virtually every other type of investment you make. But not gold. It is the one monetary instrument not dependent on trust, institutions, or governments. In general you should save your exposure to the financial world's institutions for other recommended investments that cannot be held in person. Because one need not invest in gold and silver stocks and mining shares to invest in gold and silver, stocks do not appear among our core recommendations. It is unfortunate that this is so, as they have been very attractive investments in the past and remain so today in some ways. But these are not ordinary times. Today's challenges are extraordinary. Property rights are likely to be tested as never before in our history. When governments need money, they find it. Dividend income is an easy target for revenue-hungry legislators. As Venezuela faced collapsing oil revenue in 2008, President Chávez began seizing gold mines. It does no good to protest that the United States is not Venezuela. Remember the delight Chávez took in "Comrade Bush" nationalizing American finance.

Even so, old habits die hard. There will be a class of investors who will only invest in stocks. And the leverage that mining shares provide—as metals prices rise, current production and reserves become more profitable—is undeniable. Among the risks of gold shares are geopolitical ones, management risk, labor and environmental risks. Those risks are all old hat to experienced gold stock investors. But these times also bring a new quality to which we must adjust. The deleveraged economy means lower levels of investing. Market valuations, price/earning ratios, and risk assessment are all changing. Expect long-term wariness from stock-shocked American investors. It is as though time and tide have receded for the stock markets. Their old ports and harbors don't welcome as they once did. Hazards, once submerged and unknown, have run so many ships aground that they are now apparent.

Those who have established a comfortable position in our core recommendations, and wish to own gold shares as well, should remember that in a portfolio of two or three gold stocks, a problem with just one can do substantial damage. A very convenient way to invest in gold shares is with Van Eck's Market Vectors Gold Miners ETF (New York Stock Exchange symbol: GDX). This provides excellent diversification away from the risk of any specific company. It holds stocks in all the world's leading gold and silver mining companies, including Barrick, Goldcorp, and Newmont, in its mix of thirty-three small-, mid-, and large-capitalization public companies. GDX seeks to correspond before expenses to the price and yield of the Amex Gold Miners Index. GDX has an expense ratio of 0.55 percent. The fund recently held mining investments in the following countries, listed in descending order of exposure: Canada (59.9 percent), South Africa (13.9 percent), United States (13.0 percent), Australia (4.9 percent), United Kingdom (4.3 percent), and Peru (4.0 percent). You can learn more about GDX and access the prospectus, which you should read before investing, at www.vaneck.com.

Taxes and Bureaucracy

In chapter 9 we discussed some of the reporting requirements for dealing in cash. In general, your broker or dealer will report to the IRS any payment of cash, or series of payments that are related transactions, for amounts of $10,000 or more. This reporting requirement extends to the use of cash equivalents, cashier's checks, money orders, and other monetary instruments, even if they are less than $10,000, as part of cash transactions. Increasingly precious metals dealers are refusing to take any cash in transactions.

Bear in mind, these reporting requirements are directed at the use of cash, and are not specific to the coin or bullion markets. In other words, the simple act of purchasing gold or silver is not a reportable event. Neither you nor your dealer is required to report purchases made with personal checks, bank wires, and cashier's checks unless they are part of cash transactions described above.

When you sell precious metals to your broker, he is required to report some items to the IRS. The industry Council for Tangible Assets is a trade association of precious metals dealers. It advises its members to file an IRS Form 1099b when clients sell them certain gold, silver, and other bullion products, including one-ounce Krugerrand, Maple Leaf, and Mexican Onza gold coins, U.S. silver bags, and some bars. In general remember that you must report capital gains in precious metals as you would any other investment. Be sure to keep records of your purchases and sales for reporting purposes.

The IRS classifies precious metals investments as "collectibles," whether bullion, coins, or even in ETFs. That's right, the IRS lumps them right in there with "any work of art, any rug or antique. . . ." The tax rate for collectibles is 28 percent versus 15 percent for most long-term capital gains. (The government really doesn't want you to own this stuff!) Contact your tax adviser for specific information.

Frequently Asked Questions

QUESTION: **Can I leave my gold and silver in storage with the dealer?**

ANSWER: No. Don't let your dealer hold on to your gold and silver. It's not that your dealer may not be trustworthy, but too many people have lost too much doing that, either through mismanaged brokerages or through fraud. It's an unnecessary risk, easily avoided.

QUESTION: **Then what do I do with it? Where do I put it?**

ANSWER: Many people have a place to keep their gold in their homes. Others prefer to keep it locked up in a safety deposit box.

QUESTION: **But in the last chapter you raised the issue of confiscation and the possibility that safety deposit boxes may have to be opened in the presence of an inspector.**

ANSWER: Anything can happen and it is useless to consider the possibilities when it is too late. For the time being safety deposit boxes may be safe. You are likely to be better off buying gold and keeping it in a safety deposit box if you must, than not having any at all. But do keep in mind that we have already experienced bank runs in the current crisis. Banks can close in the event of a monetary breakdown or a bank holiday.

QUESTION: **What about the risk of the exchange-traded funds like GLD being nationalized? That's a lot of gold up for grabs.**

ANSWER: The growing mountains of gold in exchange-traded funds may indeed be an attractive target for government plunder, even though the $35 billion in market capitalization early in 2009 of the two gold ETFs is not enough to make a dent in the government's financial predicament.

But the real motivation for controlling people's economic behavior is often actually for purposes of social engineering, and not financial at all. Issuers of fiat currencies are always hostile to gold and must suppress it at the first hint of a challenge. If a wholesale abandonment of paper dollars begins to build, it is to be expected that private gold stockpiles would become a target.

There is usually plenty of warning before command economies begin wholesale confiscation. In the 1930s gold coins began disappearing from circulation months before they were confiscated.

QUESTION: **How can you tell when something like that will happen? What are the warning signs?**

ANSWER: The governing authorities will do anything at all to keep themselves in power and to keep their game going. Watch the usual sources of revenue. Is it becoming harder for the government to borrow? Are new taxes failing to produce? If you are not under any illusions about what they will do, you'll recognize the signs when they are about to grab your gold.

Such actions are usually implemented under cover of a calamity: war, a devastating terror attack, economic collapse, civil disruption. Depending on the severity of the crisis, rather than confiscation, the authorities may find it more expedient to use onerous taxation to profit from private gold stockpiles. The tax system is already in place and gold is already the target of punishing tax treatment. But this discussion provides a good opportunity to reiterate that your core position in both gold and silver should consist of real metals in your possession.

QUESTION: **Are you saying I should break the law if the government calls in all the gold?**

ANSWER: No. You are required to obey all laws that are legal. There are penalties for not doing so.

QUESTION: **My broker says you are wrong about numismatics.**

ANSWER: Of course he does.

QUESTION: **But he says there are big profits in rare coins.**

ANSWER: Maybe you'd like to invest in rare postage stamps and Star Wars memorabilia, too.

Look, by definition the supply of these rare coins is fixed, more or less, right? They aren't making any more of the pre-1933 U.S. gold coins. So let's look at demand. It is not unusual for collectibles to appreciate in periods of inflation. But if the inflation goes on long enough, the economic damage spreads and people begin thinking more about making ends meet, and not so much about Chinese ceramics or rare coins. The universe of buyers shrinks.

If you want to be a coin collector, collect coins. Many people find it to be a delightful hobby. But don't confuse that with positioning yourself for a monetary crisis.

QUESTION: **How do I know my gold coins are real? What about counterfeits?**

ANSWER: It's not really a problem with the bullion coins recommended here. Anybody who handles gold coins would recognize a counterfeit gold coin by its weight, feel, and even its sound instantly. Few things weigh or feel like gold. Lead and silver are so much lighter that counterfeits of either would be instantly noticeable. Platinum is actually a little heavier than gold, but since it costs more, there is no advantage to counterfeiting "gold" coins with platinum. Tungsten is closer in weight but difficult to mint. To satisfy yourself, deal with reputable and experienced people and ask to see and hold several types of gold bullion coins.

Interestingly, almost all the counterfeiting of gold coins is confined to numismatic coins. Counterfeiters will use real gold or sometimes a lesser-carat gold to counterfeit coins that sell for premiums well above the gold price. Since you are not buying numismatic coins, this will not be a problem for you.

Recommendations

Core Recommendation
A core position in physical gold bullion coins. Buy and take possession of either U.S. Gold Eagle, Canadian Maple Leaf, or South African Krugerrand one-ounce gold coins. For larger portfolios bullion bars of established hallmarks can supplement an initial position in coins.

Also Recommended

Precious metals exchange-traded funds, after the core physical positions have been taken, based on personal needs and circumstances:

SPDR Gold Trust ETF, NYSE symbol: GLD
iShares COMEX Gold Trust ETF, NYSE symbol: IAU

Deserving Mention

Market Vectors Gold Miners ETF, NYSE symbol: GDX, a well-diversified fund holding an index-based portfolio of gold and silver mining companies.

CHAPTER TWELVE

Silver

Who Says It's Second Place?

Take a silver dollar and put it in your pocket, never let it slip away.

—Bob Dylan, "Endless Highway"

. . . of silver no one ever yet possessed so much that he was forced to cry "enough."

—Xenophon, "On Athens"

The Silver Baron

In March 1979, with silver trading between $6 and $7 per ounce, I listened carefully as famed oilman and silver investor Bunker Hunt, normally reticent, spoke candidly at a private investment conference with which I was associated. Hunt alluded to the deterioration of the dollar and an ultimately futile attempt some months before by the International Monetary Fund to bail out the sinking U.S. dollar. Despite efforts of the sort, Hunt expressed the view that such bailouts have only very short-term impact and that it would take an enormous amount of courage under the circumstances to put money in paper currency. As the silver baron warmed up to his subject he suggested it would be a good idea to establish a hedge against the dollar's troubles and he spoke about silver with great enthusiasm. Relative to gold, said Hunt, silver is enormously undervalued.

Ten months later silver traded above $50 an ounce. That is the equivalent of more than $130 an ounce in today's dollars. It was a move so powerful that it would be the equivalent of the Dow Jones Industrials exploding from 10,000 points to around 80,000 in less than a year. What was driving the interest of the Hunt brothers and some of the other global superrich that were aggressively buying silver that year? That's part of the silver story.

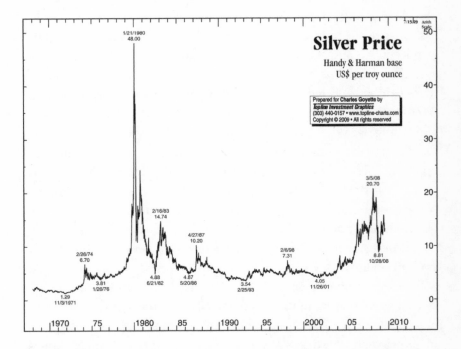

Silver shares the monetary virtues of gold. It is desirable, durable, fungible, divisible, and scarce. At least a dozen languages use the same world for both silver and money. Indeed, silver has served as money longer and in more widespread usage than gold. Conventional investment wisdom sees silver in light of its industrial demand. Indeed, ever-growing industrial applications for silver have long eclipsed its monetary role. Silver is the most electrical and heat conductive of any metal. It has the highest light reflectivity and sensitivity. It is highly chemically reactive and is among the most malleable and ductile of the metals. It is highly resistant to corrosion.

Because of these qualities more than half of the demand for silver is now industrial, followed by jewelry and silverware. The use of silver in photography has fallen sharply with the development of digital technology, but growing industrial demand elsewhere has more than made up the difference. Much of that industrial usage is for electronic applications. Silver is in high demand for use in printed circuits, electrical contacts, batteries, and highly critical circuitry in aerospace and weaponry. Consumer electronics silver demand includes its use in flat-panel display screens, cell phones, iPods, CDs, and DVDs.

To assess the industrial demand for silver, it is helpful to understand a concept economists call *price elasticity* or *elastic demand*. Generally speaking, when the price of goods or services rises, the demand for them can be expected to fall as some consumers forgo or find substitutes for them. Demand that is highly sensitive to price changes, rising and falling, is said to be *elastic*. Elastic demand tends to moderate price increases: as prices move higher, demand falls off, just as demand picks up when prices move lower. But the demand for silver is said to be relatively *inelastic*. In many of its uses there are no acceptable substitutes. And silver usually accounts for only a small part of the total cost involved. Silver contacts make cell phone keypads and computer keyboards dependable at the cost of only a few cents per unit. Manufacturers won't cease to use silver in these applications if the price rises. Nor will the Pentagon stop acquiring cruise missiles and torpedoes because of a substantial jump in the cost of the silver components.

The same kind of analysis can be applied to the supply of silver. Most silver production is dependent on the mining of other metals. Almost two thirds of the world's mined silver is a by-product of the mining of base metals copper, lead, and zinc. Because of the economics involved, producers are not spurred to increase their output of silver by an increase in silver prices alone. Silver represents too small a share of their revenue.

World silver demand in both 2006 and 2007 was about 900 million ounces. New mine production has been meeting 70 to 75 percent of that demand, with 20 percent filled by the recovery of silver scrap. (Some silver recovery from photographic applications and X-rays may be lost with the decline in photographic silver usage.) The remaining gap of 5 to 10 percent has been filled by government sales. The Silver Institute reports that after several years of heavy selling, Chinese stockpiles have been so reduced that more such dishoarding is unlikely. Similarly, U.S. government stockpiles that totaled billions of ounces after World War II have been depleted. Other government silver stockpiles have been similarly depleted as well.

In an industrial slowdown, in recessions and depressions, silver demand may appear sluggish, while the long-term supply/demand fundamentals for silver are almost wildly bullish. But in our era, with the valuelessness of irredeemable paper currencies exposed, it is surging investor demand that will help drive the price of silver. Just as it was thirty years ago.

When Bunker Hunt, his brother Herbert, along with other family members, powerful Saudi interests, and a small handful of other global silver bulls were buying aggressively, it was not because they were interested in using silver in industry. Certainly Bunker Hunt knew the facts about silver, about its distribution in different hands around the world, and about supply/demand fundamentals. Industrial demand was a necessary but insufficient part of the story. After all, there were other industrial commodities with compelling supply/demand fundamentals. But there is something else about silver. Silver is a monetary commodity. It was silver as a store of value in the face of dollar destruction that drove Hunt and the other silver investors who ended up controlling as much as 280 million ounces of silver.

The double-digit rate of consumer price increases of the mid-1970s had eased off a few points, but in the month that Hunt spoke about silver, consumer prices were rising again, back to over 10 percent annualized. And they kept climbing to a rate that registered 14 percent just twelve months later. The silver buyers were entirely correct in not trusting the government's management of the dollar. They were wholly justified in their concern about inflation and hyperinflation. It is understandable that they wanted to preserve their wealth. As for Saudi silver buyers, their concern about the depreciating value of the dollars they were taking in exchange for their appreciating oil was justified by experience. But in a characteristically revealing incident, at that time the Federal Reserve expressed to commodity exchange officials its concern that the dollar was being weakened by the bull market in gold and silver. The truth, as ever, was that the Federal Reserve was destroying the dollar's purchasing power, and driving the Hunts and altogether ordinary people in every city and town in America to buy gold and silver.

The silver bull market was stopped by a number of events. Several rules were enacted by the exchanges to force the silver buyers to sell, but the most egregious of them came on January 21, 1980, when Comex, the Commodity Exchange, adopted a rule to squeeze the silver buyers who might reasonably be expected to want to take physical delivery of what they had bought, and to benefit the short sellers who had sold silver they didn't have and now wanted out of the deal. The exchange board declared an emergency that limited silver trading to "liquidation only." No net new buying was allowed. Commodity trading authority Paul Sarnoff, who watched the market action close-up, wrote about the incident in a 1980 book called *Silver Bulls:*

> The longs now had no place to go, no normal market to absorb their holdings. They found themselves now locked in perilously by Comex rules—rules formulated by the board including at least four members representing firms that held the majority portion of the shorts in all the outstanding open interests.

It took more than that to break the silver market. The Federal Reserve under new chairman Paul Volcker instituted a policy of strict credit controls aimed at redlining gold and silver buyers; and while evincing a determination to rescue the crashing dollar by raising interest rates dramatically, the action had a collateral effect the Fed would have also wished: leveraged silver (and gold) buyers would be washed out by interest rates several points above the new stratospheric prime rate of 15.75 percent. (Eventually the Fed funds rate peaked at 20 percent and the prime rate at 21.5 percent under Volcker.)

But the tale of silver baron Bunker Hunt and the market is told here for two reasons. The incident strips away the veneer that the exchanges are market-neutral institutions devoted to fair exchange. Sarnoff wrote that the governing of the exchanges "was designed to break the silver price and benefit the trade member shorts." Such institutional self-serving underscores the importance of the recommendation that you take physical delivery of a core holding of precious metals.

Second, the event illustrates that silver's monetary role has not been forgotten. Although no central bank holds silver in monetary reserves, in the late 1970s, before today's digital technology for cameras and imaging, when silver was indispensable for photography and medical X-rays, silver's monetary desirability still quickly eclipsed industrial demand as the dominant factor in the market price of silver in the face of rapid dollar depreciation.

Today, America's financial condition is much more grave than it was when silver last exploded. The federal debt then was not even a trillion dollars; today it is $12 trillion. The country's manufacturing base was intact then; today it is being clobbered by foreign competition. In 1979 the country ran a $31.6 billion deficit; that would be a rounding error today. The deficit back then was a mere 1.4 percent of GDP; now it's almost 13 percent. The total federal budget in 1979 was $478 billion; *just the deficit in 2009 will be four times as much or more!* In 2009, the Obama government will have to borrow almost half of every dollar it spends.

Gold's movement in 2002 over $300 and its march to $1,000 in 2008 and again in early 2009 is market confirmation of its monetary role as a dollar alternative. While silver is secondary to gold as a monetary metal, below $20 an ounce the market isn't yet even accounting for silver's monetary virtue. A currency crisis will instantly thrust silver back into its role of a superior store of value where it will serve in a (perhaps non-circulating) monetary capacity. Judging the future by the past, the price increases may be spectacular!

The Gold/Silver Ratio

One tool that can be useful in allocating precious metals investments between gold and silver is the gold/silver ratio. You can think of it as how many ounces of silver it takes to buy one ounce of gold. The ratio is determined by dividing the price of gold by the price of silver. For example, if gold was $1,000 an ounce and silver was $20 an ounce, the ratio would be 50 to 1; the gold price at 50 times the price of silver. If gold was $1,000 and silver was at $100, it would make a gold/silver ratio of 10 to 1.

Through the nineteenth century the United States and other countries attempted a bimetallic standard consisting of both gold and silver coins circulating with a fixed rate of exchange of 15 or 16 to 1 between them. Like all the cases of government price fixing we have highlighted in this book, the bimetallic standard was unworkable. Bimetallism's rate of exchange must overvalue one metal while undervaluing the other. Unresponsive to real-world changes in supply and demand, an artificial ratio could not reflect the impact of new gold supplies from discoveries such as in California's Gold Rush. As gold became more plentiful (and cheaper), it took fewer silver coins to buy it; silver was relatively more valuable. Coins with the higher precious metals value, higher than the arbitrary government rate, in this case silver, would be hoarded or melted and sold; debts would be paid with the cheaper coinage. By 1853, five years after the California Gold Rush, Congress had to reduce the silver in the coinage to keep coins from disappearing. No artificial price or ratio can ever accommodate always changing supply/demand realities like the silver bonanza of the great Comstock Lode ten years later, much less the mushrooming demand for silver in our electronic and digital age.

Left to move freely and thus reflect real economic conditions, the gold/silver ratio has moved from ancient times, when two ounces of silver could buy an ounce of gold, up to 100 to 1 in 1991. It should be noted that the gold/silver ratio cannot tell you whether the price of gold or silver is going to go up or down. If, for example, gold is $1,000 and silver is $20, that ratio of 50 to 1 will remain unchanged if both fall in half to $500 and $10 respectively, just as it remains 50 to 1 if both double with gold at $2,000 and silver at $40. While it cannot tell you if the price will rise or fall, the ratio can be a useful indicator of whether one metal is undervalued relative to the other. When the Hunt brothers' buying drove silver to $50, gold topped out at $850. On their way the ratio briefly moved below 15 to 1 and at the top of the market produced a gold/silver ratio of 17 to 1. Silver was clearly ahead of itself relative to gold. Reflecting the current industrial orientation of the silver market, silver prices fell sharply as the recession and credit crisis developed in

2008. When the ratio hit 85 to 1, silver looked very convincingly inexpensive relative to the gold price, and as such you could emphasize silver in your portfolio with some confidence.

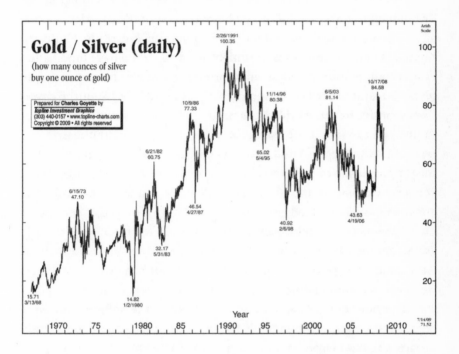

The experience of 2008 also reveals a characteristic of the silver market: While the prices of gold and silver are closely correlated, silver's price is more volatile than gold's. Silver fell more sharply than gold did during its late-2008 correction as investors, stunned by the extent of the financial collapse, demonstrated a greater willingness to part with silver than with gold. Gold corrected 30 percent from its earlier high of $1,000 all the way down to $700; silver diverged as it fell by more than half from its March high of $21 to $9 in October. But this greater volatility can be the investor's friend. Look for silver to fall more than gold in a bear market and to outperform gold in a bull market. When gold rises in a currency crisis, silver may seem to play catch-up at first. But when monetary demand for "the poor man's gold" hits the smaller silver market, it's off to the races.

Buying Silver

The procedures and prices of the physical silver market work the same as in the gold market, with spot prices, premiums, spreads, and commissions. One of the most convenient ways to own silver—and in the event of a monetary breakdown a form that you will be exceptionally grateful to have—is U.S. silver coins. The pre-1965 U.S. silver coins, dimes, quarters, and half-dollars, trade in "bags" with a face value of $1,000. That means a bag of 10,000 silver dimes, or 4,000 silver quarters, or 2,000 silver half-dollars, each "bag" of which would have a nominal or face value of $1,000. Whether dimes, quarters, or halves, these coins were minted with 90 percent real silver. These are not collector coins, but the circulated coins that were used in everyday commerce until 1965. Because they are used coins, they are referred to in the trade as "junk silver" or "junk bags." Accounting for some wear from circulation, each bag, weighing about 54 pounds and the size of a gallon paint can, contains about 715 ounces of actual silver content. Be aware that in periods of tight supplies such as late 2008, the premium on silver bags can be high, while at times the premium can actually be slightly negative, that is below the spot silver price. These are not investments to be traded, but an important part of your monetary self-protection, and they should be purchased and held.

It is strongly recommended that each family have a portion of its core precious metals holdings in this form. Each coin is a small unit of silver of widely known value in a familiar form. They provide a ready bread-and-butter purchasing power for emergencies and in the event paper money is finally rendered useless. Silver bags are not just a head-for-the hills investment. It is a convenient and liquid form to hold silver. The coins never require assaying and unlike silver bars that cannot be divided, silver bags need not be sold in their entirety. Silver coins may be purchased and sold in full bags and in fractional bags.

Silver is also available in bars in 1-, 10-, 100-, and 1,000-ounce bars of unalloyed silver, .999 purity. While the 1,000-ounce bullion bars are an industry standard for commodity markets and depositories, they are generally not suitable for an investor taking physical possession. Although each bar is hallmarked and stamped with its weight and purity, the weight of the bars can vary by as much as 10 percent. At times buyers will require them to be assayed and they can be a real challenge to ship. Because they generally carry a low premium over spot, the 100-ounce bars are most suitable for investors. They are convenient and easy to move and weigh exactly 100 troy ounces. As with gold bullion, buy only the widely traded hallmarks. In 100-ounce silver bars that means Engelhard and Johnson Matthey. Do not buy bars produced by nonrecognized refineries, even if there is no question about the purity of the silver or the integrity of the refiner. Demand for nonstandard bars can be quite weak in a rising silver market, causing delays and difficulties when selling. The 1- and 10-ounce silver bars (again of the major hallmarks only) and 1-ounce silver coins such as the U.S. Silver Eagles and the Canadian Silver Maple Leaf coins have higher transaction costs but are suitable for smaller investments.

Other Ways to Own Silver

What the exchange-traded funds GLD and IAU do with gold, iShares Silver Trust (New York Stock Exchange symbol: SLV) does with silver. Created in 2006, SLV is off to a fast start with 268 million ounces of silver in trust, valued at $3.8 billion, in May 2009. Because an equivalent value of silver is heavier, more costly to ship, and takes more room to store, it should not be a surprise that the estimated annual expenses of SLV are slightly higher than gold at 0.50 percent per year. SLV also makes available for download a complete list running more than five thousand pages detailing the individual silver bars owned by the trust.

You can learn more about SLV at the iShares Web page. Read the prospectus before investing: ishares.com.

Recommendations

Core Recommendation
A core position in U.S. silver coinage. Buy and take possession of pre-1965 U.S. silver coin "bags." Available in full or fractional bags.

Also Recommended
100-, 10-, and 1-ounce silver bars of major recognized refineries Engelhard, Johnson Matthey.

Also Recommended
1-ounce U.S. Silver Eagles and the Canadian Silver Maple Leaf silver coins.

Also Recommended
Precious metals exchange-traded fund, after the core physical positions have been taken, based on personal needs and circumstances:

iShares Silver Trust ETF, NYSE symbol: SLV

CHAPTER THIRTEEN

Oil

Still Making the World Go Around

It is clear our nation is reliant upon big foreign oil. More and more of our imports come from overseas.

—George W. Bush

Wow, it seems shocking that a product of finite supply gets more expensive the more we use it.

—Jon Stewart

The Myth of Energy Independence

"I will set a clear goal as president: In ten years, we will finally end our dependence on oil from the Middle East." President Barack Obama accepted his party's nomination with those words in August 2008. "Now is the time to end this addiction," he said, aligning himself with the promises and platforms of every president since Richard Nixon. For Nixon it was Project Independence. It would end America's reliance on foreign oil producers by 1980. It failed before we got there, so in 1977 Jimmy Carter declared his energy initiative to be the "moral equivalent of war." In his concern that "our nation's independence of economic and political action is becoming increasingly constrained," Carter bequeathed us a new bureaucracy, the Department of Energy. How's the department doing on the independence front? It does not explore the remote corners of the earth for oil; the heads of the enterprise do not raise capital for the enormous risks of locating petroleum, nor do they risk their own lives and livelihoods; they do not recover, refine, transport, or market a single barrel of oil or put a dollar's worth of gas in your tank. But they have managed to spend a half trillion dollars over the years anyway.

Oh, and the country imports 1.25 billion barrels a year more now than it did when the department was created. And domestic production of crude oil today is only about half what it was when it peaked in the 1970s. Today we are not more independent, we are more dependent than when the department was created.

Promises of energy independence have more to do with politics than with economic reality. In modern and complex energy markets, where the petroleum is pumped out of the earth is a matter that borders almost on irrelevance, for just as water flows downhill, oil flows to the highest bidder. To illustrate the point Charles Peña, senior fellow at the Independent Institute, cites Great Britain's experience during the oil price spike in 1979. Although effectively energy independent because of its North Sea production, the country was still hit as hard by higher prices as Japan, which was dependent on imported oil.

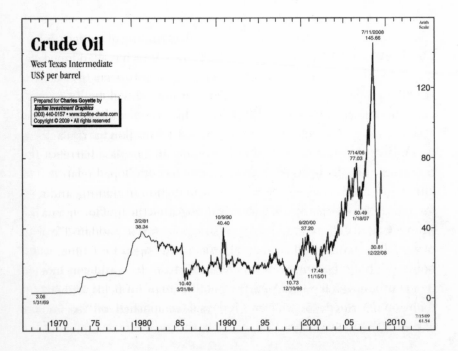

All the rhetorical smoke about energy independence has been swept aside in a thorough and important book on the issue, *Gusher of Lies: The Dangerous Delusions of "Energy Independence,"* by Texas energy journalist Robert Bryce. Energy independence is neither doable nor desirable, says Bryce. Instead of longing for some bygone era, the United States needs to face today's reality of energy interdependence. Bryce points out that Saudi Arabia, although it sits on 260 billion barrels of oil reserves, imports 83,000 barrels of gas and other refined products every day, while Iran with 130 billion barrels of oil imports 40 percent of its gasoline. The sophistication and integration of the global market, Bryce says, are crucial:

> Indeed, America is getting much of the energy it needs because it can rely on the strength of an ever-more-resilient global energy market. In 2005, the U.S. bought crude oil from 41 different countries, jet fuel from 26 countries, and gasoline from 46. In 2006, it imported coal from 11 different countries and natural gas from 6 others. American consumers in some border states rely on electricity imported from Mexico and Canada. . . .

The Chinese seem to have a healthy understanding of modern energy interdependence. An oil exporter until 1993, China has abandoned ideology for reality. China is now busy securing its future energy needs by deploying not troops, but deal makers, around the globe. In a grand capitalist manner, China seems to have discovered it's cheaper to buy energy than it is to steal it. China imported 1.5 million barrels a day in 2000; by 2030 it is expected to be importing 10.9 million barrels a day, half from the Gulf region. Already China has developed relationships with Saudi Arabia that involve joint participation in refining and marketing Saudi oil in China. In Iraq, China became the first foreign nation to sign a multibillion-dollar oil deal since the fall of Saddam Hussein. U.S. sanctions on Iran have left that field wide open for China, which now gets about 5 percent of its oil imports from Iran and continues to invest in the development of additional Iranian oil fields. Other Gulf region countries with which China has established oil ties include Kuwait, Oman, Syria, and Yemen.

If the entire globe is China's target of opportunity, Africa is the bull's-eye. Angola is China's largest oil supplier, while it is active in the pursuit of oil and other commodities such as coal, copper, and cobalt there and in Sudan, Nigeria, Zambia, and the Congo. When Bush went to Africa in 2008, it was like Rockefeller passing out dimes to children. Bush gave away hundreds of millions of dollars of the taxpayers' money in foreign aid and boondoggles. The Chinese look for and get projects that provide resources and earn a return. Elsewhere China's reach for oil extends to nearby Kazakhstan and Russia and farther away to this hemisphere, in Venezuela and Canada. China has even leased land in Cuba for oil exploration.

Bryce points out that China is getting all the oil it needs from the Persian Gulf without a single soldier on the ground there and saving hundred of billions in military expenditures at the same time. Chalmers Johnson tells of asking an official of import-dependent Japan thirty years ago what it would do if a hostile power sank one of its supertankers in the straits around Singapore. "Call Lloyds Insurance Company," he replied, making the point that it is cheaper to build a new tanker than to build and maintain a navy to patrol the shipping lanes from the Persian Gulf to Japan. The Arab oil embargo of 1973 is the rallying flag raised as a justification of an imperial energy policy. But Bryce makes the wholly inconvenient point that there was no shortage of crude oil in America during the embargo. To the contrary, imports actually went up in both 1973 and 1974. Oil is a fungible commodity in a global marketplace. The Arab oil producers could stop direct sales to the United States, but had no control over the secondary market. Once oil hit the open market the producing state had no control over where it ended up. Prices did rise at the time of the embargo, driven by the breakdown of the gold-exchange Bretton Woods agreement. At the same time gas lines were forming. The gas lines were very real, but what created them? It is our old nemesis: government price-fixing. As refining oil into gasoline at prices mandated by bureaucrats became a money-losing proposition, shortages developed.

A global empire of foreign entanglements and foreign aid drains the wealth of the people, under the rubric of energy independence. Less costly but no less outrageous are energy subsidies. And nothing in the energy pork barrel smells as bad as ethanol.

Ethanol gobbles up almost a quarter of America's corn production to produce just a few percent of its automotive fuel. Corn alone raked in $51 billion in subsidies between 1995 and 2005; ethanol has been directly subsidized to the tune of about $80 billion. But that may not even tell the full story, since ethanol is the beneficiary of almost two hundred individual tax breaks. Ethanol subsidies have been estimated to run as high as $1.90 per gallon. Charlie Munger, the vice chairman of Warren Buffett's Berkshire Hathaway Corporation, was asked about ethanol at the company's 2008 shareholders' meeting. Munger was dismissive of ethanol as an economically unjustifiable fuel that runs up the price of food as well. "Running cars on corn is about the stupidest thing I ever heard of," he said. "More energy is used producing ethanol than it creates and that's without considering the damage to the topsoil producing fuel when we could be producing food."

Munger is on to something when he says the production of ethanol consumes more energy than it creates. By one estimate that factors in the farm production costs of planting, fertilizing, pesticides, plus distillation and transportation, ethanol consumes 30 percent more energy than it produces. Ethanol proponents say it's not that bad, some insisting that ethanol has a positive energy output of 25 to 30 percent. Even at that level, Bryce, cited earlier, concludes that gasoline has an energy profit of at least twenty-two times that of corn ethanol. So uneconomical is ethanol that all the billions in subsidies have not been enough for the industry to stand on its own feet. An ethanol industry trade group, the Renewable Fuels Association, ended 2008 looking for a billion-dollar bailout and $50 billion in loan guarantees, on top of the massive subsidies it already receives.

One really doesn't have to compare input/output ratios to conclude that it is farm state senators driving the ethanol component of energy policy. One only has to look at the subsidies and ask what the viability of ethanol would be without them. It appears to be about the same viability as Carter's $20 billion SynFuels boondoggle that was supposed to produce millions of barrels of synthetic gasoline a day by 1990. If the economic case for ethanol were real, the Senate would not have had to legislate the production of 36 billion gallons of ethanol by 2022; the market would have demanded it and the incentive of profit would have produced it. President Obama, long an ethanol booster (he was after all a senator from corn-growing Illinois and worked hard for his 2008 victory in the Iowa caucuses), even went a step further. He authored a bill that would mandate the production of 50 billion gallons by 2030.

America's energy policy is a chimera, a monstrous patchwork of contradictory extremes: a counterproductive militarism coupled with a pretend devotion to energy independence. Both are driven by the barely disguised opportunity for political plunder. By squandering trillions of dollars today on fanciful undertakings that do not pass the test of hard accounting, America is robbed of resources it will need to buy energy in the future. The lion's share of America's foreseeable energy needs will only be met by buying petroleum from a far-flung and complex global energy market. It would be helpful to have a strong and valuable currency when shopping for energy. But in its absence, many, many units of a cheap currency will have to do.

The Myth of Proved Reserves

Why did oil reach an all-time high of $147 a barrel in July 2008? According to Ali Al-Naimi, Saudi Arabia's oil minister, it was because the market feared Saudi oil reserves had topped out. There was certainly more to it than that. The dollar's weakness played a major role in spiking oil prices in 2008, as it bottomed out against the euro. Gold's powerful moves to all-time highs only months before corroborated the diminishing dollar's roll in the price of oil.

But just as much of our current credit crisis is born of overvaluation of assets, there is a growing concern that nation-states have substantially overstated their petroleum reserves. For some it is a way of buttressing their currency valuations. For others ample incentive for widespread exaggeration is created by the OPEC policy of establishing members' market quotas as a proportion of their stated reserves. In 2007 the former head of Saudi Aramco oil production suggested that

300 billion barrels, a quarter of stated global petroleum reserves, may be merely speculative. At a London oil conference Sadad al-Husseini claimed, "Reserves are confused and in fact inflated. Many of the so-called reserves are in fact resources. They're not delineated, they're not accessible, they're not available for production." It is the kind of thing that oil producers like having said as the market is talked higher. Still there seems to be ample corroboration of his point. When OPEC began basing production quotas on reserves, most of the member nations began making substantial increases in their reported reserves, increases of 300 billion barrels, matching al-Husseini's figure for reserves that are only speculative. In a display of candor, an Iranian oil official has claimed that Iran's official reserves are vastly overstated. In 2006 *Petroleum Intelligence Weekly* reported that Kuwait had only half its officially stated reserves, a report the country's former oil minister said he was unable to deny. Several years ago Mexico found itself having to cut its official stated reserves in half.

Because proved reserves are those reasonably certain of recovery given prevailing political conditions and technological means, they are bound to change. But one thing is clear. Oil recovery made possible by improvements in technology can be enormously expensive, at least in places where much of the low-hanging petroleum fruit has already been picked. Al-Naimi, Saudi Arabia's oil minister, made reassurances about Saudi oil reserves on CBS's *60 Minutes* in December 2008. But the story said less about proved reserves than it did about the enormous expense of tapping new reserves. Lesley Stahl's report displayed one oil project that demanded removal of 100 million cubic feet of sand dunes just to build an airstrip, while a 400-mile pipeline had to be constructed in an unforgiving terrain in which temperatures can reach 135 degrees. Another, at the Khurais oil field, is described as the biggest oil project in history. Because of inadequate pressure, a 150-mile pipeline was built from the sea to pump in 84 million gallons of seawater each day. Peak Oil, the theory that world oil production has reached its maximum level, has to contend with a moving target. New drill bits and recovery methods make oil accessible at places it couldn't be tapped years ago. But it all comes at a cost. Equipment wears out; infrastructure has to be maintained. Russia has been able to boost its proved reserves in western

Siberia with new technology, but when Russian oil production dipped in 2008, it was because of insufficient reinvestment. Deeper water, and more remote and harsh environments, inevitably leads to delays and interruptions and adds to the cost of production.

Global Demand

By the end of 2007 as a combination of war and a tanking dollar sent oil racing toward $100 a barrel, a new recession was already getting under way. When oil peaked seven months later, on July 11, 2008, at $147 a barrel, it topped off an impressive run. Oil had risen 600 percent from the end of the last short recession in November 2001. But some analysts were calling for still higher prices. A month after the high, Goldman Sachs suggested oil would end the year at $149. Others had been talking about prices reaching $200, $300, and even $500. A familiarity with the history of prior oil price spikes might have sobered their overexuberance. Big moves up in energy almost as a rule trigger recessions.

The 1973–75 recession set in as the oil embargo quadrupled prices; the 1980–82 recession came on the heels of oil prices more than doubling as a result of the 1979 Iranian revolution and the outbreak of the Iran-Iraq war; and with the advent of the first Gulf War oil ran up from below $20 to over $50, and a recession ensued. The role of oil price spikes as the straw that breaks the back of an economy already loaded with unsustainable excesses is not widely discussed, but the load of higher energy prices stresses household budgets, strains marginally functioning businesses, and begins to expose malinvestments throughout the economy.

The global recession spelled contracting demand. The Energy Department calculated that U.S. petroleum consumption for 2008 would show a drop-off of 5.8 percent from 2007 levels, and furthermore that reduced global consumption in 2008 and the expectation of even lower demand in 2009 would represent the first consecutive years of decline in three decades. As oil skidded—its fastest fall in history— from $147 to $34 just five months later, gasoline prices fell as well. The average U.S. price of gas peaked in July 2008 at $4.11 per gallon. By

December it had fallen to $1.66. Even with gas lower than it had been since 2004, the sting of $4.00 gasoline is not likely to be forgotten by drivers for some time. The destruction of demand caused by high prices can persist even after prices have fallen back. As American consumers began moving massively to smaller cars after the oil shocks of the 1970s, average fuel consumption declined and continued to do so for years even after the price of gasoline had retreated sharply. By the end of 2008, in response to the recent price shocks, plants making SUVs were closing left and right. On December 23, General Motors closed an Ohio plant that had turned out 3.7 million large SUVs.

In response to lower gas and oil prices, OPEC nations, having already agreed to production cuts of 2 million barrels a day in the fall, announced an additional cut of 2.2 million barrels a day in December 2008. Altogether OPEC agreed to reduce oil production by 14 percent in hopes of halting the sliding prices. OPEC agreements are notorious for being honored for only about five minutes after the meeting breaks up. As former U.S. House Speaker Tip O'Neill once said, "All politics is local." For governments like Ahmadinejad's in Iran and Chávez's in Venezuela, that means international agreements be damned. They have to pump even more furiously at lower prices to meet the promises of the demagoguery that brought them to office back home.

But Saudi Arabia and most of the other Arab OPEC states appeared both determined and financially capable of holding the line on production. Although Russia is not an OPEC member, its production is falling as well, although for other reasons.

The demand news was bearish: demand destruction and a global recession of unknown duration. But the bearish news was quickly assimilated by the market and was reflected in the 2008 lows.

In discussing rationing in chapter 9, we described high prices as the antidote to high prices. Sensitive to new developments, oil prices provide a clear illustration of this principle. Spiking prices lead to economizing by consumers, whether they simply cut back on driving or shift to more fuel-efficient cars. Soaring energy prices contribute to a slowdown of industrial and other business activity. And rising energy profits can capitalize the discovery and development of new supplies. All these things occurred as oil closed in on $147 a barrel. But just as market dynamics that make high prices the answer to high prices, low prices become the antidote to low prices.

It takes years for new petroleum projects to come online and hit their production targets. But it took just a few short months after oil's all-time highs for lower prices to have their impact. New investments fell off. Production plans and expansion projects were shelved. Smaller wells in the United States were taken out of production. Expensive oil sands projects would have to wait. Ethanol producers, always subsidy dependent even at high energy prices, began going bankrupt. In response, prices began a new march up and hit $60 by May 2009.

The International Energy Agency's annual survey of energy issues, *World Energy Outlook 2008*, issued in November, projects global oil demand, even accounting for the economic slowdown, to grow from 82 million barrels per day in 2007 to 106 million barrels per day in 2030. But current world demand is met by oil fields many of which are in decline, so the new production that has to be brought online is not just the 24 million barrels a day difference between current and future demand. An unprecedented survey of the production trends of eight hundred existing oil fields reveals something alarming. Rates of decline in fields that have passed their production peak are expected to rise from 6.7 percent now to 8.6 percent by 2030. Nobuo Tanaka, the IEA's executive director, highlights the challenge and scope of investments that will be needed to keep up with declining production. "Even if oil demand was to remain flat to 2030, 45 million barrels a day of gross capacity—roughly four times the current capacity of Saudi Arabia—would need to be built by 2030 just to offset the effect of oilfield decline," Tanaka says. That is, to repeat, if demand were to remain flat. But with projected demand growth, more than 60 million barrels per day of new production will have to be made available between now and 2030. The total amount needed is more than three-fourths current oil capacity, demanding an estimated investment of $8.4 trillion for exploration and development. What about nearer term? The report anticipates that 30 million barrels per day of new capacity will be needed by 2015. Including the electricity sector, altogether $26.3 trillion will need to be invested in energy between now and 2030. It is investments that constrain production, the report concludes. Investment capital is more difficult to achieve generally in a global slowdown and substantially less available in the oil business as profit margins are squeezed by low prices. "The era of cheap oil is over," says Tanaka. The longer prices stay low, the less spent on development and production infrastructure and the bigger the breakout when prices climb.

The changing demand picture can be seen in the emerging economies. Most of the demand growth through 2030 identified in the IAE 2008 report will come from places like China, 43 percent, and India, responsible for 20 percent. The growth in demand in oil-producing nations themselves is an important consideration for the availability of future supplies. China, a net oil exporter through the 1970s and 1980s, has been a net importer for more than fifteen years. Indonesia, an OPEC member since 1961, gave up its membership in 2008 because it is no longer a net exporter. Thanks to its North Sea production, Great Britain became a net exporter in 1980. In the last few years it has again become an importing country. Mexico is consuming a greater share of its declining production. But most interesting is the IEA 2008 report's identification of the Middle East as a major new source of energy demand, expected to account for 20 percent of growth through 2030. Predictable in a rising market, resource nationalism was growing as oil prices climbed. Venezuela and Russia both demonstrated the syndrome in 2007, as oil companies operating there were forced to turn over ownership stakes to state-owned companies. Exxon and ConocoPhillips both chose to leave Venezuela. The risk of nationalization reduces the availability of badly needed development capital; the certainty of socialized ownership and management will hamper efficiency and production. But resource nationalism is not just to be expected in the environment of rising prices. As domestic demand for more of its own energy production rises in the Persian Gulf states, as suggested in the IEA study, it is bound to be accompanied by a rise in resource nationalism as well. After all, if the U.S. government can waste billions of its taxpayers' dollars on an ill-starred quest for energy independence, should oil-rich nations be any less susceptible to appeals to autarky and nationalism? It is unreasonable to expect that, in the face of Gulf oil producers' own developing economies and growing energy needs, cheap and easily printed scrip-money will be welcomed in exchange for commodities that are in great global demand.

Priced in Dollars

The purchasing power of the dollar is a central concern of this book, just as it is central to energy economics. Since most global oil sales are denominated in dollars, a reckoning is demanded: How susceptible is oil pricing to dollar deterioration? The answer is very susceptible. As the United States piles trillions of dollars of new debt faster and faster on its balance sheet, as the hidden debt silently grows mostly unnoticed, as major wars continue, as bailouts are given and guarantees extended with a recklessness that defies accounting, the rest of the world must question the creditworthiness of U.S. debt and look at the dollar with the suspicion that someone will get fleeced. OPEC has seen this sort of thing before. The memory may have grown fuzzy on the part of the monetary authorities, but the cartel once relied on the British pound as a pricing unit, before abandoning the pound for the dollar. As we pointed out in chapter 7, the organization repeatedly announced in the 1970s that a change in the value of the dollar would mean a change in oil prices. Within a few years of Nixon's delinking the dollar from gold, oil prices quadrupled. Ten years after Nixon's act, prices had risen 1,000 percent. As crude broke through $100 a barrel at the beginning of 2008 and the dollar continued sinking against the euro, the repricing of oil was a frequent topic of discussion among OPEC member nations. OPEC secretary-general Abdalla El-Badri said such discussions were "lively," and in several interviews conceded that such a change from the dollar could be made, and that if it were, it would not take as long to implement as the change from the pound sterling to the dollar had taken.

Let us be clear: OPEC will not precipitously abandon the dollar. The announcement of such a sudden move would end the dollar's reserve currency status overnight. Hundreds of billions of dollars of international trade (OPEC had sales of $676 billion in 2007) would be repriced overnight. Oil importers would no longer need to hold large dollar accounts for future purchases; currency traders would sell dollars around the world, and central banks would race one another to the dollar exit; the dollar would plummet, gold would skyrocket along with silver, the euro, and other currencies; a period of economic chaos would ensue.

The consequences of a sudden move of that nature are understood. OPEC has the same problem as China with its dollar reserves. Some OPEC member nations have enormous dollar reserves themselves, which would collapse in value. Short of war, neither entity is likely to want to invoke the "nuclear option" of dropping the dollar. But to say that OPEC will not precipitously announce dollar regime change is not to say that it is willing to long be victimized by dollar destruction. It is more likely to beat a cautious retreat, moving at a moderate pace at first, becoming hasty later.

Even as the next powerful waves of inflation get under way, OPEC can hope to stay ahead of the dollar's deterioration when market prices begin to outpace the rate of inflation. Rather than holding dollars as in the past, OPEC is likely to designate a basket of currencies as a pricing unit, consisting mostly of dollars and euros, with some British pounds, Swiss francs, Japanese yen, and even a few other currencies. OPEC contingency plans for basket-of-currency pricing appear to have been in the works for some time. Already many Gulf nations exchange their dollars for euros and make deposits in Europe anyway, for fear of the increasingly frequent U.S. practice of freezing foreign assets as a tool of foreign policy. The adoption of a basket of currencies would be announced as an inclusive move, accommodating other nations, and not as a defense against the plight of the dollar. At some point along the way, producers will begin to exchange dollar revenue for gold and money substitutes, at first surreptitiously as appears to be taking place now, and then at an accelerating pace and openly. It is entirely possible that an OPEC currency basket would contain gold, if not in its first appearance, certainly before long. The pricing structure would foreseeably include a gold component of perhaps 5 or 10 percent at first, more later.

None of this should be viewed as idle speculation. Movement in this direction is further along than is widely recognized. Members of the Gulf Cooperation Council (six Persian Gulf states: Bahrain, Kuwait, Oman, Qatar, Saudi Arabia, and the United Arab Emirates) are ironing out details for a common currency and a central bank. Gold is certain to have a prominent place in the plan. At a 2008 year-end summit meeting, the Council's assistant secretary-general, Mohammed Al Mazroui, told *Gulf News*, "We first have to decide on the location of the Central Bank, then the Central Bank and Monetary Council will have to decide on the gold reserves for the Central Bank."

But a change in global oil pricing, even introduced gradually, will herald the end of dollar supremacy just the same as if it were done precipitously. The dislocations will be as great as if the dollar regime ended suddenly, but they will be drawn out and perhaps more painful for their duration. The only thing certain is that the investments recommended in this book will be the beneficiaries.

Investing in Petroleum

If there was a silver lining in the credit collapse, for consumers it was the fall in gas prices. For investors it was the opportunity provided by the collapse in oil prices. It is a fact of life that people will line up like lemmings in a market's blow-off top: dot-com stocks and real estate come to mind. But it's more difficult to interest anyone when prices are low: the Dow at 800 in 1982, or $34 oil at the end of 2008. This instinctive skepticism ("Why should I buy that? Look how cheap it is! Nobody's buying that!") is actually a useful trait when it protects people from throwing their money away on things that have no real value or expectation of market demand. But it may keep them from exploiting opportunities.

It is because oil must be among the first beneficiaries of the monetary and fiscal authorities' destruction of the dollar that it is recommended as a significant part of your portfolio. As the dollar bubble bursts, oil prices can move explosively. "Black gold" actually outperformed gold as the dollar began breaking down and hit new lows during the first leg of the bull market. The fact that the global recession drove the price to lows that could not last should make the case for the addition of oil to your portfolio even more compelling.

While this recommendation of oil is predicated on the dollar's woes, if war breaks out, you will be grateful indeed to have oil as a part of your portfolio. Any war in the Middle East can drive oil prices. An India-Pakistan conflict threatens to involve nuclear weapons and will draw in other regional players. The Israeli-Palestinian conflict can become a full-scale regional conflagration at any time as well. The Iraq War is not over, and Sunni-Shiite hostilities there may erupt anew. President Obama is committed to an escalation and prolonged presence in Afghanistan. Indeed, Obama's military posture in the region may be more similar to Bush's than many of his early supporters would find reassuring. The hawkishness of his appointees, his willingness to make military commitments, and the propensity of new presidents to show they are "tough" suggests that we are not through quite yet with immoral and budget-busting wars of empire.

A subtheme of our recommendations is the advisability of insulating oneself as much as possible from avoidable governmental and institutional risks in the derailing economy. In an economic crisis, energy producers are among the first industries nationalized. The complacent may react to the prospect of nationalized oil with the thought that "it can't happen here." But in a crisis, it can happen here. Much of American finance was nationalized in the current crisis without a peep of protest. Given a monetary calamity, energy can be nationalized in the wink of an eye. In the past, America has nationalized the telegraph lines and railroads, coal mines and even trucking. President Truman used the pretext of the Korean War to intervene in a labor dispute and try to nationalize the steel industry. Senator Edward Kennedy and others called for the nationalization of American oil companies as far back as the 1970s. Given a war with Iran and the Strait of Hormuz shut down, oil companies could be nationalized overnight. It can happen here.

As oil prices first moved up past $100 a barrel, there was talk in Congress about nationalizing refining and other oil companies. But if nationalization seems drastic and remote, at some point a substantial windfall profits tax is a virtual certainty. On the campaign trail promises of windfall profits taxes on oil companies were a big applause line for candidate Obama. Since then he backed off, at least while prices were low.

Institutions such as oil companies are subject to the caprices of governmental authorities as they bobble about from one "solution" to another in a crisis. Accordingly, investing in petroleum stocks cannot be recommended at this time when property rights are insecure. The erratic policies to which companies are subject can be minimized by investing as closely as possible in petroleum itself, rather than stocks.

Oil is the world's most important actively traded commodity and is absolutely indispensable to the functioning of modern civilization. It is not an exaggeration to say that at this point in human history everything economic is conditioned by oil. If we are concerned about both the nationalization and taxation of oil companies, can you hedge your future energy consumption now, before prices return to former highs? Short of constructing enormous storage tanks in your backyard, what are the best opportunities to participate in oil's future right now?

The United States Oil Fund (New York Stock Exchange symbol: USO) is an exchange-traded fund (a class of investments introduced in the recommendations for gold and silver) that suits our purposes.

Unlike the gold ETF GLD, USO does not buy and store oil in depositories. It seeks to approximate the percentage movements of West Texas Intermediate (WTI) light, sweet crude oil delivered on the spot market. The WTI price is the benchmark commonly used when oil prices are cited in news media, and is the most actively traded oil futures contract. The fund uses futures contracts and other financial instruments to achieve its objectives, but specifically advises on its Web site that it does not seek to use leverage and targets a one-to-one relationship between its assets and oil exposure. USO has an acceptable expense ratio of 0.45 percent and posts its daily holdings on its Web site. Launched in 2006, USO is a fund of almost $3 billion at the end of April 2009 that withstood the sharp and sudden market sell-off and performed as well as could be expected. And it allows individuals an alternative means of participating in commodities markets without undertaking the personal leverage risk of investing directly in commodities and options. Before investing, read the prospectus at unitedstatesoilfund.com.

A related, although smaller, ETF in the same family is the United States 12 Month Oil Fund (New York Stock Exchange symbol: USL), launched in 2007. It also seeks to track the approximate percentage movements of light, sweet crude oil (WTI) based on the average of twelve different months of futures contracts on the New York Mercantile Exchange. This averaging can dampen some of the technical disparities that occur in the market. USL's expense ratio is a little higher than USO's, 0.60 percent. Read the prospectus, available at the same site, unitedstatesoilfund.com, before investing.

Because of the political risk it is hard to recommend direct oil investments in much of the world now. Direct investments in kleptocracies like Mexico and Russia are out of the question except as small parts of well-diversified portfolios. Canada is another story. Canada is a rule-of-law nation that operates a fiscal surplus and a balance of trade surplus. It has the world's second-largest proved reserves and is the United States' largest supplier of oil. Canadian Royalty Trusts oil and natural gas producers deserve a mention in this section because of their advantageous structure. Royalty trust units trade like stocks and have been prized for their dividends. The royalty trusts own producing oil and gas assets that generate income and cash flow. Because these trusts are not corporations, if they distribute their earnings to trust investors they have not been subject to corporate income tax. Trust investors have thus earned substantial dividends that have ranged to as much as 12 and 15 percent and even higher as oil prices climbed. With declining prices for their production, those yields have not been sustainable and dividend reductions have been the order of the day.

Despite the prolonged prosperity in Canada, politicians there began hungrily eyeing hundreds of millions of dollars in tax revenue that might be had if the trusts were taxed like corporations. As you have probably guessed, laws were changed and beginning in 2011 the trusts will have to begin paying corporate income taxes. What happens after that is unclear. Some trusts have accumulated tax advantages that may shelter income and keep them paying dividends for a year or more after the change. Some may convert to corporations and use earnings to explore and develop additional resources.

Until then, dividends continue albeit at lower rates. But a bull market in energy will mean higher distributions and higher unit prices. U.S. investors need to be aware that Canada will apply withholding taxes of 15 percent on distributions; consult your tax adviser before investing. Here are three established Canadian Royalty Trusts that represent a profit opportunity you may wish to investigate. All three trade on both the Toronto and New York stock exchanges.

Baytex Energy Trust (Toronto Stock Exchange symbol: BTE.UN; New York Stock Exchange symbol: BTE), an oil and gas investment trust with producing properties in Alberta, British Columbia, and Saskatchewan, produces over 40,000 barrels of oil equivalent per day, weighted about 60 percent to heavy oil. Consult the company's Web site before investing, baytex.ab.ca, for regulatory filings and more information.

Enerplus Resources Fund Trust (Toronto Stock Exchange symbol: ERF.UN; New York Stock Exchange symbol: ERF) is an oil and gas income trust with a diversified portfolio of crude oil and natural gas assets located in western Canada and the United States. Production expectations for 2009 are 91,000 barrels of oil equivalent a day: 58 percent natural gas, 42 percent crude oil and natural gas liquids. Read investor information and regulatory filings before investing at enerplus.com.

Penn West Energy Trust (Toronto Stock Exchange symbol: PWT .UN; New York Stock Exchange symbol: PWE) is the largest conventional oil and natural gas producing income trust in North America, producing more than 190,000 barrels of oil equivalent a day from a portfolio of assets across the Western Canadian Sedimentary Basin. Penn West's production of crude oil and natural gas liquids as of March 31, 2008, was approximately 57 percent, natural gas 43 percent. Before investing, read the regulatory filings and other important information at pennwest.com.

Recommendations

Core Recommendation

Invest in a core energy position with USO, the United States Oil Fund, an exchange-traded fund that tracks crude oil, as a hedge against high inflation, energy depletion, and war.

Also Recommended

USL, the United States 12 Month Oil Fund, also tracks crude oil and is a suitable energy investment.

Deserving Mention

Canadian Royalty Trusts, oil and gas income trusts, can experience a major rally as energy prices recover. In the meantime the yields remain attractive for the time being. Baytex Energy Trust, BTE; Enerplus Resources Fund Trust, ERF; Penn West Energy Trust, PWE.

CHAPTER FOURTEEN

Real Things

Can't Live Without 'Em

One generation passeth away, and another generation cometh;
but the earth abideth forever.

—Ecclesiastes 1:4

Wealth is the progressive mastery of matter by mind.

—Buckminster Fuller

Agriculture

When investment legend and commodities bull Jim Rogers says that
ten years from now instead of twenty-nine-year-old stockbrokers
driving Maseratis, it will be twenty-nine-year-old farmers, he's making
an important point about the shifting economy. People's spending hierarchies experience dynamic changes in lean economic times. People
can live without the excesses of Wall Street. They can live without Hum-
mers, McMansions, and flat-screen TVs in every room. But they can't
live without food. The world can get along just fine with less so-called
investment banking. It can't get along with less farming. This goes for
the rest of the world: a growing population needs additional food.

Since 2000 Asia's growth has been equal to almost one and a half
times the total population of the United States. In 2008 the United
Nations estimated the world population to be 6.7 billion. By the time
children who entered the first grade that year graduate, the world

population will have grown by another billion people, or roughly the population of the entire Western Hemisphere today.

THE PROJECTIONS AT A GLANCE					
Population (millions)	1979–81	1997–99	2015	2030	2050
World	4,430	5,900	7,207	8,270	9,322
Developing countries	3,259	4,595	5,858	6,910	7,987
Industrial countries	789	892	951	979	986
Transition countries	382	413	398	381	349

United Nations Food and Agricultural Organization

Agriculture demand growth is a certainty. Government contributed to the food anxiety of 2008 as subsidies displaced the planting of wheat to corn, which was diverted to ethanol. Meanwhile, corn, heavily subsidized by the U.S. taxpayer for years, has been dumped in Mexico, swamping growers there. Those who might have been competitive with U.S. corn at market rates (not having to pay the additional transportation) have been put out of business by subsidized corn at the expense of the American taxpayer.

A middle class has been developing in both China and India. This growing prosperity means richer diets in places that have long been used to subsistence standards. Think about it in these terms: America's rich may drink more expensive wine and dine on food prepared by celebrated chefs, but for the most part the American middle class eat as well as Britney Spears, Tom Cruise, and Warren Buffett. (After all, Buffett and Bill Gates dine together at McDonald's.) As the Chinese people have prospered their caloric intake has risen. Malnutrition has been disappearing from the cities. In urban areas, young Chinese boys are on average 2.5 inches taller than thirty years ago. Obesity is beginning to become a problem. If the trend continues, before long China's middle class will eat as well as its upper class. With growing affluence they can be expected to eat more secondary foods, such as milk and meat. Since it can take eight pounds or more of grain to raise one pound of meat, agricultural demand grows in a way that is not limited to just the increase in population.

THE PROJECTIONS AT A GLANCE					
Calorie consumption (kcal/capita/day)	1961–63	1979–81	1997–99	2015	2030
World	2,283	2,552	2,803	2,940	3,050
Developing countries	1,960	2,312	2,681	2,850	2,980
Industrial countries	2,891	3,135	3,380	3,440	3,500
Transition countries	3,154	3,389	2,906	3,060	3,180

United Nations Food and Agricultural Organization

What is the impact of this additional demand on food production, and for our purposes, on food prices? It means that people in the developing world will be bidding their productive efforts (for that is what currency ultimately represents) against the productive efforts of people in the developed world. Their productivity has grown in value; ours has not kept up. In the global auction for food, these new billions of people will be stronger bidders. No matter what happens to food production, whether it goes up, down, or stays the same, there are more bidders of greater means at the auction. Prices in terms of U.S. dollars will climb.

The Department of Agriculture reports that food accounts for 35 percent of household expenditures in China. Only 5.7 percent of Americans' household expenditures go to food. That percentage will go up, particularly when a currency of declining value is used to bid in global auctions.

Natural Resources

Deng Xiaoping, the Chinese reformer, has to be given enormous credit for cracking open a door to the middle class for such a great number of the world's people. The fall of the Soviet Union opened it a little wider. India, too, has been slowly shedding its socialist somnolence. With an added entrée to the developed world thanks to the English language left behind by British occupiers, India has experienced annual growth of 7 percent for a decade and falling poverty rates. With the heel of the boot off the people's necks, and with property rights being asserted, prosperity becomes a prospect. It isn't always a straight line of progress. There was a time in Beijing when property owners on certain streets were mandated to be merchants. Old habits of command economies die hard. But the world has been revolutionized as billions are welcomed to share in the hard-won advances in human living conditions. That means an inexorable demand for the things that things are made of: copper for power lines, steel for automobiles, aluminum for refrigerators and other appliances, zinc for paint, and lead for batteries. The growth of the global middle class is a long-term affair with a long way to go.

Meanwhile, back in the United States, a few years ago the Federal Reserve began using a new price index for reports to Congress. Instead of the Consumer Price Index, the new number to watch was called "core inflation," which was computed by stripping out the prices of food and energy. It has been widely suspected of being an attempt to soft-pedal the truth about how fast prices are rising, and perhaps it is. It is not a number of much value anyway, since everything that lives depends on food and energy. In any event, neither of these government numbers, the core inflation rate or the Consumer Price Index, are likely to long fool anybody who actually has to try to make a household budget work. Nor does the contrivance of core inflation have any traction in these pages. On the contrary, our core recommendations include both food and energy. Much about the pursuit of oil and global consumption patterns we described in the last chapter applies to raw materials. Having dealt with oil there, this chapter provides a digest of investments in agriculture and other natural resources, commodities that have a greater impact on the conditions of daily living than do stock averages and that can be expected to do well in a declining currency.

Investing in Real Things

When I was a young boy, my father used to say, "I'm not interested in words. I want deeds!" Paper money is to hard assets what words are to deeds. Empty representations and hot air have had their day on the stage. As the present economic crisis draws the curtains aside, more people will discover that the Washington wizards are like the Great and Powerful Oz, unable to create wealth by printing a piece of paper. The real things that people need to live, food and water, and the hard assets from which real life-improving things are made, will become profit opportunities, because in times of monetary turbulence nobody needs much convincing that food and hard assets are primary havens. Here are selected investment vehicles that are constituted to do well, beginning with agricultural commodities.

PowerShares DB Agriculture Fund is an exchange-traded fund (New York Stock Exchange symbol: DBA) that invests in futures contracts of widely traded agricultural commodities, equally divided among four: corn, sugar, soybeans, and wheat. Since the prices don't move in tandem, the fund is rebalanced each year to the 25 percent weighting of each of the four commodities. Although incidental to our objective, three of the four commodities, corn, sugar, and soybeans, have biodiesel fuel applications. DBA was created in January 2007. Its managing owner, DB Commodity Services LLC, is a wholly owned subsidiary of Deutsche Bank AG, a major German bank, operating globally in seventy-three countries. The fund is liquid, has a recent market capitalization of more than $2 billion, and an expense ratio of 0.75 percent. As always, read the prospectus before investing. It is available at dbfunds.db.com.

Making a nice natural resource supplement to the agriculture fund is a base metals fund that consists of commodities contracts in three industrial metals, aluminum, zinc, and copper. PowerShares DB Base Metals Fund (New York Stock Exchange symbol: DBB) rebalances its portfolio once a year to equal weights of one third for each of the three key metals. This is a somewhat smaller, but nevertheless fast-growing fund, with a recent market capitalization of about $230 million. It is tightly focused on industrial metals without components of gold or silver, which have already been addressed in our recommendations. It has an expense ratio of 0.75 percent. Be sure to read the prospectus before investing. You can find it at dbfunds.db.com.

The Hard Assets Producer fund represents broader diversification. An ETF based on Jim Rogers's global commodity equities index, Hard Assets Producer (New York Stock Exchange symbol: HAP) is the world's first global hard assets equities fund, launched September 2008. We have referred to Rogers several times in this book. He is a cofounder of the Quantum Fund and a well-known international investor, was a creator of The Rogers–Van Eck Hard Assets Producers Index, and serves as chairman of the RVE Index Committee. HAP is designed to replicate that index, which recently consisted of 271 companies in the United States and forty other countries that produce and distribute hard assets and hard asset products and services. These include energy, agriculture, base metals, precious metals, and forest products. Water and renewable energy (solar and wind) are also included. The index and fund are designed to be a pure equity play in these commodities, including only companies that derive at least 50 percent of their revenue from the targeted commodity, except for the water component, which demands 25 percent of revenue from water.

The fund may provide some leverage during a bull market. According to Van Eck, during five years of the commodity bull market ending July 31, 2008, commodity producer equities outperformed the underlying physical commodities themselves, 262 percent to 73 percent. This is so because, as a hypothetical example, in a commodity like copper, prices can rise a mere 10 percent and yet provide a greater increase of, say, 25 percent in the producer's profitability as his production costs will not have jumped commensurately.

One of the fund's interesting innovations is that it allocates its investments based on global consumption of a commodity. Accordingly, recently 39.7 percent was in energy, 29.2 percent in agriculture, 21.6 percent in industrial and precious metals, reflecting that ratio of global demand for those sectors. With close to $50 million under management, the Hard Assets Producer fund, HAP, is a truly global fund, with less than half of its exposure in the United States. The funds expense ratio has been initially capped during its launching phase at 0.65 percent, but that may increase. This fund should appreciate substantially in an environment of a depreciating dollar. Before investing, be fully informed. Read the fund's prospectus, which you can find at vaneck.com.

Another fund, well diversified among the wealth that comes from the earth, is the SPDR S&P Metals and Mining ETF (New York Stock Exchange symbol: XME). The fund invests in a portfolio of stocks, seeking to replicate, before expenses, the performance of the S&P Metals and Mining Select Industry Index. A recent snapshot of its top five holdings included Freeport-McMoRan Copper (copper, gold, and molybdenum), Alcoa (aluminum), Newmont Mining (gold), Peabody Energy (coal), and Nucor (steel). Recently a $600 million fund, XME has an expense ratio of 0.35 percent. Before investing read the prospectus found at spdrs.com.

For one-stop shopping in a commodity ETF, take a look at Power-Shares DB Commodity Index Tracking Fund (New York Stock Exchange symbol: DBC). The fund invests in a spectrum of six commodities, both hard and soft, with an energy bias. It is rebalanced annually in the following base weight percentages for the commodities: light sweet crude oil, 35 percent; heating oil, 20 percent; aluminum, 12.5 percent; corn, 11.25 percent; wheat, 11.25 percent; and gold, 10 percent. DBC, with an expense ratio of 0.75 percent, pioneered making commodities investing available in ETFs and has grown to a recent market capitalization of more than $2.3 billion. The prospectus, which you should read before investing, is available at dbfunds.db.com.

When Jim Rogers saw that we were entering a long-term secular bull market for commodities, he decided to start a commodities index fund. Just as the stock market has index funds that follow the S&P 500, the Dow Jones Industrial Average, or some other index, Rogers looked for a commodities index as the basis of his fund, one that was well thought out and representative of the dynamics of global economic change. What he found was disappointing. One index weighted oil and orange juice equally. "I don't know about you," said Rogers, "but in my life oil plays a much larger role than orange juice." Although half the world eats rice every day, he found none of the existing indices included rice. As Rogers wrote in his 2004 book *Hot Commodities*, what he was looking for didn't exist. So he created it. The Rogers International Commodity Index takes a global view of the economy and raw materials prices.

Today the Rogers International Commodity Index (RICI) is the broadest such index, consisting of a basket of energy commodities (44 percent of the fund), metals (21.10 percent), and agricultural components (34.9 percent). It is a sensitive and valuable indicator of global commodity prices. Based in part on global consumption patterns incorporating both developed and developing countries, it reflects the value of futures contracts on thirty-six physical commodities, from eleven different exchanges in five countries. The commodities range from oil, the most heavily weighted commodity in the index, to those familiar to U.S. consumers such as wheat, cotton, copper, coffee, and sugar, and right on through to commodities more prominent outside the United States like azuki beans and greasy wool.

The following chart shows the commodities in the index with their relative weightings:

Product	Weight
Crude Oil	21.00%
ICE Brent Oil	14.00%
Wheat	7.00%
Corn	4.75%
Cotton	4.20%
Aluminum	4.00%
Copper	4.00%
Soybeans	3.35%
Gold	3.00%
Natural Gas	3.00%
RBOB Gasoline	3.00%
Soybean Oil	2.17%
Coffee	2.00%
Lead	2.00%

Product	Weight
Live Cattle	2.00%
Silver	2.00%
Sugar	2.00%
Zinc	2.00%
Heating Oil	1.80%
Platinum	1.80%
ICE Gas Oil	1.20%
Cocoa	1.00%
Lean Hogs	1.00%
Lumber	1.00%
Nickel	1.00%
Rubber	1.00%
Tin	1.00%
Soybean Meal	0.75%
Canola	0.67%
Orange Juice	0.66%
Oats	0.50%
Rice	0.50%
Palladium	0.30%
Azuki Beans	0.15%
Barley	0.10%
Greasy Wool	0.10%
Total	100%

Source: *RICI Handbook*

Although Rogers launched a private fund that tracks the index, there is a way to invest in the performance of the RICI in publicly traded products.

Exchange-traded notes (ETNs) are useful ways of tracking an index. Structured products similar to ETFs, they can be bought and sold on the stock exchange through your brokerage account during the trading day and can be shorted. Unlike ETFs, exchange-traded notes are just that, notes. They are not funds; they are unsecured, unsubordinated debt securities. They have a maturity date, although they can be actively traded until maturation. The tax treatment of ETNs differs from that of ETFs. (Be sure to check with your tax adviser.) They do not represent any kind of ownership interest in a commodity or stock. ETNs are notes backed by the credit and solvency of the issuing bank, and thus have a layer of risk not found in ETFs. The credit rating of the issuer is a part of the valuation of the ETN. Although the issuer is typically a large and formidable financial institution, so too were Bears Stearns and AIG at one time. Indeed Lehman Brothers was the issuer of three ETNs, including both a raw materials and an agricultural one. The ETNs ended up being delisted and worthless in the unfolding demise of Lehman.

The advantage of the ETN is the access it provides to participating in the performance of a market benchmark, less investor fees. In the case of an ETN linked to the RICI, it provides a cost-effective means to replicate the performance of thirty-six global commodities priced in four different currencies in eleven different markets around the world, with an exchange listing and liquidity.

Elements are ETNs managed by Merrill Lynch, with a suite of four products linked to the Rogers Index, one linked to the performance of the broad index itself, and three linked to specific subindices: agriculture, energy, and metals:

> Elements ETN Linked to Rogers International Commodity Index Total Return (NYSE symbol: RJI). The ETN is linked to the performance of the entire basket of thirty-six weighted commodities of the global economy in the RICI.
> Elements ETN Linked to Rogers International Commodity Index Agriculture Total Return (NYSE symbol: RJA). Providing exposure to the agriculture subsector of the RICI, this ETN is linked to the value of a basket of twenty agricultural commodity futures contracts.

Elements ETN Linked to Rogers International Commodity
Index Energy Total Return (NYSE symbol: RJN). This
ETN is linked to the performance of the subindex of
the RICI representing the value of a basket of six energy
commodity futures contracts.

Elements ETN Linked to Rogers International Commodity
Index Metals Total Return (NYSE symbol: RJZ). Representing the value of a basket of ten metals commodity futures contracts, this ETN is linked to the metals
subindex of the RICI.

The note issuer of each of these ETNs is the Swedish Export Credit
Corporation, a financial institution owned by the government of
Sweden. Access the prospects for each at elementsetn.com.

These four ETNs are worthy of your attention and may be appropriate for some readers. In other circumstances they might even be among
the core recommendations here. The Rogers International Commodity
Index is certainly the foremost guide to global commodity values. But
because of the precarious nature of the times and widespread loss and
risk throughout the financial world, exchange-traded notes as a class
cannot at this time be among the recommendations of this book.

Rogers has identified three long-term commodity bull markets in
the last century, most recently from 1968 to 1982. Their average duration has been just over seventeen years. And while a new one appears to
have gotten under way, Rogers himself counsels to expect setbacks in
the life of a long-term commodities bull market. But such setbacks provide an opportunity to enter the market at lower prices.

Frequently Asked Questions

QUESTION: **What about investing in water? There's a lot of talk about
a growing population and not enough water.**

ANSWER: It's a popular topic. More mouths to drink . . . more mouths to
feed: farming is responsible for about 70 percent of water consumption.
It all means more water. One of the biggest problems with water is

distribution. The earth has apparent excesses of water in some places sometimes (think New Orleans and Katrina), and droughts elsewhere (the Dust Bowl in the 1930s). In many of the places where the agricultural land is seriously degraded, the stresses on arable land are due to erosion from flooding or poor irrigation. All these are conditions that can be normalized to some degree, but it takes capital.

It should be a familiar dynamic to readers at this point: Would people rather have ample water at higher prices or no water at nice low prices? The more strain there is on water supply, the higher prices should go, spurring innovation and efficiencies in water usage, alleviating the crisis. But almost everywhere you turn, water and government go hand in hand. The water industry is highly bureaucratic and highly regulated, altogether not conducive to producing abundance or profits.

The Hard Assets Producer fund, HAP, has a small water component which is enough for now.

QUESTION: **What about steel? America was built on steel. America moves on steel.**

ANSWER: You've answered your own question. If America were to start cranking out cars as it did in the old days, steel would become attractive. But even an auto bailout will not be able to turn that clock back. It may be that a massive public works program from the Obama administration could result in some increased steel demand. But it also means more dollar destruction and a poorer nation.

There is a steel ETF, but I recommend that if you want steel in your portfolio, you do it with the SPDR S&P Metals and Mining fund, XME, which is diversified, but has some steel.

QUESTION: **I get the food investments. And I get the precious metals. But what is it you like about the base metals, at least in a slow economy?**

ANSWER: All the base metals are cyclical and can use some growth. As we suggested in answering the prior question, it is prudent to be diversified in them. But the best thing about investments in base metals is the barriers to competition. Between first-world environmentalism and third-world socialism, it's amazing anything gets mined and refined at all. Farmers can change crops in a season in response to high prices of some food. But it takes years and an enormous amount of capital to enter the metals and mining industry.

And remember, we're investing for a period of monetary turbulence. People will want to exchange wasting assets for just about anything durable.

QUESTION: **What about timber? That's agricultural.**

ANSWER: There's an ETF for everything. There's an agribusiness ETF with the symbol MOO. There's one for timber with the symbol CUT. The Hard Assets Producer fund, HAP, has a timber component. Before taking a more significant position in timber, however, bear in mind that there are almost 19 million unoccupied homes in America and the number of bank-owned properties continues to rise.

QUESTION: **You recommend a lot of commodity ETFs, in oil, agriculture, and hard assets.**

ANSWER: We are using ETFs to "position trade" commodities. That means we have identified long-term economic trends—the dollar/debt crisis—that will be reflected in commodity prices.

The long-term economic trend was set in motion with the creation of the Federal Reserve in 1913; it was accelerated with the nationalization of gold in 1933; it shifted into high gear with the severing of the dollar-gold linkage in 1971. Today's credit crisis and the compounding debt were implicit in those events. Now challenges to American global economic hegemony, bailouts, stimulus packages, and the recession and its accompanying deficits are driving the trend to a climax.

The development of ETFs has made these commodity investments accessible in a way that they have not been before. We are using ETFs so that we can invest in these markets without the leverage, margin calls, or emotional toll of second-to-second price changes. You do not have to be mesmerized by price fluctuations on a screen. You do not have to give up your real job to become a day trader the way so many did in the dot-com bubble. You do not have to have perfect timing to enter and exit the market. You are not generating commissions by trading in and out of commodities. You are simply investing in real things and getting them in exchange for "magic" money that was created by Washington wizards. And everybody eventually learns that there's no such thing as "magic."

Recommendations

Core Recommendation
Invest in a core food position as a hedge against rising food prices and a depreciating dollar. Use DBA, the PowerShares DB Agriculture Fund, an ETF investing in agricultural commodities.

Core Recommendation
Add base metals to your portfolio with PowerShares DB Base Metals Fund, DBB, consisting of commodities contracts of three prized industrial metals, aluminum, zinc, and copper.

Also Recommended
To add broad diversification to your portfolio with hundreds of companies engaged in the production and distribution of hard assets around the world, make a core "real things" investment in the Rogers–Van Eck Hard Assets Producers Index, HAP, an equity ETF.

Also Recommended
For a broader investment in the mined riches of the earth there is the SPDR S&P Metals and Mining ETF. XME invests in a portfolio of stocks of major companies producing copper, aluminum, coal, steel, and more.

Deserving Mention
Six commodities in one fund, PowerShares DB Commodity Index Tracking Fund is mostly energy with agriculture and metals too. The fund, DBC, invests in light, sweet crude oil, heating oil, aluminum, corn, wheat, and gold.

Deserving Mention

The four Elements ETNs Linked to Rogers International Commodity Index Total Return: RJI, linked to the performance of the entire basket of thirty-six weighted commodities; RJA, linked to the twenty commodities of the RICI agriculture subsector ETN; RJN, an ETN linked to the performance of the RICI subindex of six energy commodity futures contracts; RJZ, an ETN linked to the ten-metal commodity subindex of the RICI.

CHAPTER FIFTEEN

Bonds

A Crash Course

If something cannot go on forever it will stop.

—Herbert Stein

Every valley shall be filled, and every mountain and hill shall be brought low.

—Luke 3:5

A Family Affair

Beginning with gold and silver coins, to our recommendations in oil, agriculture, and other natural resources, everything recommended to this point has been something tangible or a means of investing in the producers and the prices of something tangible. Real things. Demand for resources. Hard assets.

But this is something different. This chapter is subtitled "A Crash Course" because that's exactly what will happen to U.S. Treasury bonds. Between interest rates climbing in response to inflation and the dollar falling as its reserve status deteriorates, U.S. debt—Treasury bonds—will be a place *not* to be. And you can make money by investing against them.

It starts with a story about a relative, say an uncle. Let's call him Sam. He's no longer young, but by no means old. He's a man of substantial accomplishment, independent and industrious from his youth. He has long been an object of admiration in town, not just for his affluence, but for his ingenuity and dynamism. Altogether an admirable sort, wouldn't you say?

Because he is family, you've had a closer look at his affairs. And there is something wrong. Maybe the success has gone to his head. Maybe he just wants to enjoy the fruits of his labor. Or maybe he has secretly developed some habits. Maybe he's drinking. An addiction? One can't be sure. What is clear is that his affairs are not as robust as they are believed to be. The town has grown and he has business competitors that he didn't have before. The new factories that have sprung up of late are bustling; your uncle's are—well, not quite bustling. Your uncle's retail locations aren't what they were either. There are new stores just outside town with better prices. Maybe they're hiring help from the rural areas at lower wages. Certainly their real estate costs are less.

None of this appears to bother your uncle. And it doesn't bother most of the town's men and women. But it is beginning to bother you because family is family. Not to mention that you work in your uncle's business, so your future well-being is involved. From your position you've had a peek at the books. You're not surprised that a businessman has to borrow money from time to time. So what? A gifted entrepreneur knows how to make money grow. But your uncle keeps borrowing more and more. And although business is down, he's spending more than ever. He has some bills that anybody can see, payroll, suppliers, things like that. But you've discovered that he has more than just those. Everything has been mortgaged. He owes people far and wide. In town and out. All those who have been happy to loan him money because of the reputation he built over the years are owed more than ever. But these days some of those creditors are beginning to whisper about your uncle.

They are beginning to suspect what is evident to you: your uncle can only pay his bills by borrowing. His income is down and there is no sign of the unshackled enterprise of days gone by. And it's clear that he'll have to borrow tomorrow—if he can—to pay the debts he takes on today.

Now, with that in mind, your uncle comes to you full of all the self-assurance of the past, even with the hint of a business-as-usual swagger, and utters the words you have begun to dread hearing:

"I need to borrow some money from you."

A Credit History

"Credit" means trust. How's my credit? Your credit is good. We give credit where credit is due. He's a credit to his family. Cash Only—No Credit. In God we trust. All others pay cash. A credit is an entry of payment or value on the right-hand side, the credit side of the ledger. I have to give you credit for a job well done. That's incredible! In Spanish one could say, *Yo creo,* "I believe." Same word.

That we have a credit crisis in the financial world is only a manifestation of a culture-wide crisis in trust. Predatory borrowers lie about their income to buy homes they can't begin to afford; lenders show them how to falsify the paperwork. Financial rating agencies give great ratings to bad paper to win additional rating business. Wall Street analysts give "Buy" ratings on what should be "Sell" stocks to win underwriting business.

State and local governments teeter on the edge of bankruptcy because they can't be trusted with their own fiscal affairs. The bankruptcy of the city of Vallejo, California, population 117,000, is instructive. Vallejo's solvency couldn't withstand both the cut in tax revenue from the economic downturn and its unsustainable spending. Columnist George F. Will has described the town's spiraling public employee spending. Huge union dues, $230 a month from each of the city's 100 firefighters and $254 each a month from its 140 police officers, produced enough, said Will, to "purchase a compliant city council."

> So a police captain receives $306,000 a year in pay and benefits, a lieutenant receives $247,644, and the average for firefighters—21 of them earn more than $200,000, including

overtime—is $171,000. Police and firefighters can store up unused vacation and leave time over their careers and walk away, as one of the more than 20 who recently retired did, with a $370,000 check. Last year, 292 city employees made more than $100,000. And after just five years, all police and firefighters are guaranteed lifetime health benefits.

Vallejo is the federal government in microcosm: "economic downturn, unsustainable spending"—a perfect description of Washington.

Bailouts are given in secret without accountability. The $50 billion Madoff Ponzi scandal went on right under the nose of the SEC, with its new budgets, bloated since the Enron scandal. The regulators' presence, if it did anything at all, only lulled investors into believing that somebody was looking out for their money for them. Are Senate seats for sale? You shouldn't need the Blagojevich bribery charges to make you suspect it. And look at the cost of the campaigns. Jon Corzine, another former Goldman Sachs chairman like treasury secretaries Robert Rubin and Henry Paulson, spent $63 million getting elected to the Senate in 2000. Look at the contributions and the porkfests that pass for legislation in Washington. There is no trust. Social Security Trust Fund, anybody?

"Bond" is something that binds. A man's word is his bond. Epoxy is a bonding agent. We speak of the bonds of matrimony, chemical bonds, a father-son bonding experience. A bond is a written and sealed instrument or certificate representing the promise of an issuer to pay a certain amount of money at a certain time. There are all kinds of bonds: bail bonds, performance bonds, bearer bonds, convertible bonds, revenue bonds, junk bonds. And U.S. Treasury bonds.

If the government's intent is to pay today's borrowers back with money of lesser value tomorrow, can it be said to be bound to its promise? If it does this year after year, does its credibility—its credit—rise or fall? Financial bubbles, like the dot-com bubble and the housing bubble, burst when credibility is destroyed.

At some point creditors, believers, begin to doubt. Apprehensive about what they already have at risk, doubters are unwilling to put more money at risk. In investment markets, not all believers become doubters at the same time. And not all doubters become disbelievers at once. They do not all begin to fear default at the same time, but the concern snowballs. At some point distrust reaches a critical mass and cannot be stopped.

What Comes Down Must Go Up

U.S. Treasury bonds had a special appeal for investors in the weeks and months surrounding the credit collapse. The market for U.S. Treasury debt instruments is the largest and most liquid debt market in the world. Bonds have a special appeal during deflationary periods when the purchasing power of the dollar can rise. So frightened were investors in hedge funds and other financial instruments as the stock market came tumbling down that they were willing to park their money, at least for the time being, in U.S. Treasuries at historically low interest rates—or even no interest rates!

In December 2008, the Treasury auctioned off $30 billion of four-week Treasury bills for a yield of zero percent. It was as if the buyers were saying, "Wrap this money in foil and put it in the freezer, bury it in the lawn behind the White House, but for goodness' sake don't put it in the stock market, don't give it to Bernie Madoff, and don't buy securitized mortgages. Just give it back intact in four weeks." In fact the panic was so great that the very appeal of U.S. Treasury debt was the printing press. Investors knew that they could get dollars back, even if the ink hadn't dried. The scramble for the printing press guarantee was so great that in the secondary market some were willing to park their money in bonds that yielded less than zero, that is, negative rates, returning slightly less than their cost on maturity.

Why so low? Taking a longer view, even before the four frenzied weeks of bailouts and takeovers in the fall, why had investors been settling for negative real rates of return, interest rates below the rate of inflation? More recently, but for the irresistible urge to get their money out of that hedge fund and park it anywhere for the time being while they scratch their heads and figure out what to do next, what explains the low rates? James Grant, the editor of *Grant's Interest Rate Observer*, offers this response:

> Creditors are settling for negative real yields because bond prices have, for the most part, been going up since 1982. It's not so much that creditors trust the Fed; rather, they believe in their hearts that past performance is indicative of future results. They are backward-looking investors. After a quarter of a century of mainly profitable experience, most people would be.

Sixty years ago long-term government bonds were only paying less than 2 percent annual interest. But in a move that took a generation to complete, bond yields climbed and bond prices fell until the early 1980s. In 1981, thirty-year U.S. Treasury bonds had yields as high as 15 percent; ten-year bonds saw yields between 15 and 16 percent. Since then yields have come down and bond prices have gone up for another entire generation. Today's investors haven't seen anything else.

But before becoming a captive of your generation, ask yourself a few questions. Suppose you invest $1,000 in a ten-year Treasury bond. With the government on a debt binge, what do you expect the purchasing power of $1,000 will be when you get it back ten years down the road? Or imagine you put your money in the long (thirty-year) bond. If you put $1,000 in, you'll get $1,000 out in thirty years. What do you suppose the purchasing power of that $1,000 will be in thirty years? Today, the dollar's position is much more precarious and the prospect of its returning to its intrinsic paper and ink value is nearer than ever, but let's look back. Imagine you had purchased a government bond thirty years ago that matures today. You will discover that 70 percent of its purchasing power has simply evaporated. A ten-year bond maturing today has lost almost 25 percent of its purchasing power in that time.

The bond bull market started in 1981. For an entire generation now bonds have gone up as interest rates have trended down. As 2009 got under way, ten-year government bonds returned only around 2.5 percent; thirty-year government bonds had yields in the neighborhood of a mere 3 percent. There is a lot more room for interest rates to rise than there is for them to move lower. This corresponds nicely with our out-look for U.S. debt and the dollar: interest rates will go up. The bond market will crash much as the dot-com market crashed, and just as the real estate market and the stock markets have crashed.

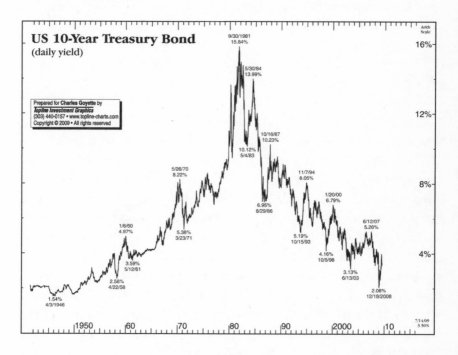

President Obama was being candid when he said shortly before his inauguration that the United States would run trillion-dollar deficits "for years to come." His economic stimulus program of tax cuts and federal jobs assures it. How does that square with the impact the global downturn is having on our creditors? Our primary creditor, China, selling less to the United States in these slow times, earns less. Chinese domestic spending rises, becoming a priority as China funds its own stimulus plans. China has less to invest in U.S. bonds at the same time the U.S. government insists on borrowing more.

We are at the intersection of reduced capacity of creditors to buy our debt, and a demand to borrow more than ever. It is at such crossroads that train wrecks take place. As more money is printed to cover the shortfall, expect inflation premiums to drive interest rates higher. When government debt grows faster than the nation's productivity, the risk premium rises as well. These higher interest rates will compound the debt and slow enterprise even more. Reduced tax revenue widens the deficits. A vicious cycle of interest rate increases and a bona fide bond market collapse results. In short, your Uncle Sam is not practicing sound economics. He is engaged in wreckonomics.

A Tip About TIPS

The late currency analyst and economist Dr. Franz Pick called government bonds "certificates of guaranteed confiscation." Any long-bond holder, having seen the purchasing power of the dollar sink by nearly 70 percent over the last thirty years, understands Dr. Pick's terse description. Some years ago, the U.S. Treasury, seeing inflation concerns as an impediment to the marketing of its bonds, created a new bond indexed to inflation to meet the objection. Treasury Inflation-Protected Securities (TIPS) promised to compensate for inflation by adjusting the bond's face value every six months based on increases in the Consumer Price Index. The interest rate the bond pays does not change throughout the life of the bond, but the principal amount of the bond is adjusted upward with increases in the CPI. The interest rate is paid on the new face value of the bond and the bond is redeemed at that new face value at maturity.

This begs the question why, if the government will adjust the payments of its obligations in constant value rather than nominal dollars; why, if there is no advantage to the government in inflation; why, then, not eliminate all the Rube Goldberg devices of a new series of debt instruments, the constant computations of adjusted interest payments, and the bother of changing principals? Why go to all the trouble?

It's time to become acquainted with John Williams and his Web site, Shadow Government Statistics. During his career as a consulting economist, Williams ran into problems his clients were having with business planning and sales forecasting because of reliance on faulty government statistics and worthless data. If you have ever wondered why the unemployment reports don't square with your experience in business and what you see and hear; if you've ever thought it curious that you couldn't reconcile your real-life experience paying more for clothes and health care, groceries and gas with the numbers reported in the CPI, Williams has an answer: "The problem lies in biased and often-manipulated government reporting."

The integrity of all the numbers has been compromised by political pressures, which Williams describes in detail. Gross domestic product, unemployment, money supply, reporting of the budget deficit—he scrutinizes the data and questions the changes in methodology that appear to make the numbers improve. These adjusted methodologies that Williams describes have been used to calculate much lower results for the CPI, the numbers used to index things like Social Security payments, and for our purposes, TIPS Treasury bonds.

I recommend visiting the Shadow Government Statistics Web page (shadowstats.com). A look at Williams's Annual Consumer Inflation chart, *which uses the same methodologies that were in place in 1980*, graphed along with the official CPI numbers, is an eye-opening experience indeed. The CPI understates actual price inflation, Williams says, "by roughly 7% per year." With a half trillion dollars in TIPS bonds outstanding and underpaying holders for the real rate of price increases, the question "why go to all the trouble?" is answered: Because Dr. Pick was right. Government bonds are certificates of guaranteed confiscation.

Investing for the Bond Market Crash

Huge fortunes are made (and lost) in big movements of the bond market. Remember that bonds trade inversely with interest rates. When interest rates, still at generational lows, turn sharply higher as they must, bonds will fall. Shorting bonds (selling bonds today to buy back later at lower prices) will be the source of great new fortunes in the future. It is the equivalent of betting on higher interest rates. This is because today's bonds, bearing current interest rates, become less valuable in the face of new bonds that pay more. While shorting bonds is a strategy that can pay off over the long term, to get there you have to live through the near term. And in the near term interest rates can do almost anything. Unless you are a fly on the wall in the Federal Reserve Open Market Committee meetings (yes, some people do know what will happen with interest rates in advance!), the chances of your being right about near-term moves in bonds are not much better than gambling. As sophisticated as the markets are today, there are not many good alternatives to avoid the leverage involved in shorting the bond market. One alternative is the Rydex Inverse Government Long Bond Strategy Fund (symbol: RYJUX).

This is a no-load mutual fund designed through the use of futures contracts and other instruments to perform inversely to the price movement of the current long-term (thirty-year) U.S. Treasury bond. As interest rates rise, the price of long-term government bonds will fall. As the price of Treasury bonds falls, the fund's share value increases. You will lose money if interest rates go down, and you will do well as interest rates rise. With the yield on thirty-year Treasuries recently between 3 and 4 percent, there are but a few points on the downside before rates hit zero, while there is nothing but open space overhead for rates to move up. It may be instructive to remember that because of the last big inflationary burst, in 1981 the yield was more than 10 points higher. When interest rates begin to move in response to deepening dollar depreciation, the reward for the prepared can be substantial.

The Rydex Inverse Government Long Bond Strategy Fund has an expense ratio of 1.40 percent. In mid-2009 it was a fund of more than $600 million. This is a no-load fund; there are no commission charges. You can buy it directly from Rydex Funds, which requires a $25,000 minimum to open an account in the Rydex Funds family, although it need not all be invested in one fund. You should also be able to buy RYJUX through most brokers and discount brokers. The discount brokers I checked with all allow you to buy the fund with an initial minimum of $2,500, and in minimum additions of $250 or $500 thereafter. With some brokerages the initial minimum is only $1,000 for an IRA. As always, you need to be aware of the risks of anything in which you invest. You should read the prospectus carefully, which you can access at the company's Web site, rydexinvestments.com. While you are there be sure to look at a long-term chart for the fund. At the time RYJUX was created in 1995, the yield on thirty-year bonds was about 7.5 percent. Since then yields have moved much lower, recently almost 5 percentage points lower. That means that bonds have risen and the shares have lost value as the Federal Reserve moved massively to drive interest rates lower. That is all right; in fact it is exactly the performance we want, just as we like to buy gold, oil, and natural resources at low prices, not at high prices. Remember we are not investing for what happened over the years gone by, but for the years ahead. This fund is recommended for a period of rising interest rates and falling bond prices.

Be aware that there are other investment vehicles such as ETFs designed to perform inversely with the price of U.S. Treasuries but that seek to do so with a higher return. One seeks to produce 200 percent of the performance of the inverse of a Treasury bond index. As described earlier, leverage is a wonderful thing when it is moving in your favor, not so great when it moves against you. A hypothetical example illustrates the point. Suppose you invested in a vehicle that provides double the moves of an index that is trading at 100. If the index falls 10 percent to 90, an investment that provides double the market result would have fallen to 80. If the index itself now rises 10 percent, it is close to the start at 99. But your result of twice the 10 percent move, 20 percent, only takes you back to 96. Given a little volatility, even within a typical trading range, and while the underlying index may remain close to where you started, your losses can grow. Such investment vehicles have appropriate uses, but are not suitable for the position trading strategy designed to help you survive a monetary breakdown and prosper.

Recommendation

Core Recommendation
Invest in the Rydex Inverse Government Long Bond Strategy Fund, symbol RYJUX, as a core investment for rising interest rates and a major bear market in U.S. Treasury bonds. Check with your broker or buy directly from Rydex at rydexinvestments.com.

CHAPTER SIXTEEN

Alternative Currencies

Worth Mentioning

The world is in permanent monetary crisis, but once in a while, the crisis flares up acutely, and we noisily shift gears from one flawed monetary system to another. We go back and forth from fixed paper rates to fluctuating rates, to some inchoate and aborted blend of the two. Each new system, each basic change, is hailed extravagantly by economists, bankers, the financial press, politicians, and central banks, as the final and permanent solution to our persistent monetary woes.

—Dr. Murray Rothbard

In contrast to political money, gold is honest money that survived the ages and will live on long after the political fiats of today have gone the way of all paper.

—Hans F. Sennholz

Foreign Currencies

This is one of the shortest chapters in this section of the book because no recommendation is being made in it. No recommendation is made to buy the paper money of some foreign country that holds its own currency reserves in U.S. dollars. There was a time when some foreign currencies could be called "hard currencies," which is to say that they had some redeemability in "hard money," gold and silver, or minimally had a statutory backing of some amount of gold in the reserves of the issuing government. This strictly limited their issuance and therefore limited the possibility of inflation. Ironically, even after the convertibility to gold ceased, the term "hard currencies" stuck to the dollar and some industrial-nation currencies, European and Japanese. Today there are no hard currencies. They are all squishy-soft. There may be gold in Switzerland's central bank, but the currency itself isn't redeemable. Apparently Swiss banking isn't the paragon of prudence and discretion that it was.

Up until 2000 the Swiss franc had a statutory backing of 40 percent gold, but it no longer has. At the same time that Swiss banks, under pressure from the United States, were agreeing to compromise customer confidentiality, there were also discussions in the European press of Switzerland's risking bankruptcy and a collapse of the franc. Billions in Swiss loans have been made to borrowers in places like Poland, Hungary, and Croatia. As the financial crisis ripped through Eastern Europe, where banks were even more leveraged than American banks, all of those local currencies fell substantially. This has made repayment of Swiss loans denominated in the costlier Swiss franc substantially more difficult for untold Eastern European borrowers, whose earnings are in their local currencies.

The suggestion that the Swiss franc could collapse is probably more cautionary than real, but any such prospect should be sobering to anybody who thinks that paper money anywhere in the world represents real refuge from a monetary breakdown. Solvency issues in Ireland and Iceland may be bellwethers of more to come.

To be prepared for a currency crisis, you must expect things to unfold in unforeseen ways. For example, in the case of severe restrictions or criminal sanctions on the ownership of, or investments in, gold and silver, investments in alternative currencies may be the only port in a dollar storm.

In such circumstances, exchange-traded funds in foreign currencies could prove to be very useful and are treated here for just such unforeseen circumstances. In the typical structure of a currency ETF, each share represents one hundred units of the underlying currency. The funds will commonly invest in foreign short-term investment-grade money market securities in the country concerned. In so doing, the currency shares earn interest at the prevailing overnight rates in the countries involved. That yield can be used to offset the funds' fees.

That interest rate differs from country to country. The yield is higher in currencies thought to represent less stability and more risk; the return is lower in currencies believed to be safer. Early in 2009, for example, the interest rate on the Mexican peso ETF was more than 7.5 percent; the Russian ruble ETF was over 3.5 percent. During the same period, in part because Japan had appeared to avoid much of the mortgage and credit meltdown, the Japanese yen was showing strong appreciation and, with investors scrambling to participate in the ride, the interest yield of the ETF was zero.

In the investments they make and their returns, foreign currency ETF trusts are very much like foreign money market accounts. Indeed, some U.S. investors use them in just that way. For example, some hold liquid assets in a Canadian dollar ETF. This proved to be a good practice while the dollar was falling relative to Canada's currency, not so good while the dollar was enjoying the bounce-back that started in the summer of 2008.

That highlights the speculative nature of the investment and the foreign-exchange risk involved. When you invest in a currency ETF as an alternative to the dollar, you are always assuming political and other risks of the specified country. It would be unfortunate indeed to seek to escape a period of rapid dollar depreciation by investing in a currency that depreciates even faster. The so-called hard-currency countries all have financial problems. The experience of the current economic calamity may be even more severe in Europe than in the United States, and even the political unity of the Eurozone nations may be at risk, while Japan has even more serious demographic challenges than Europe and substantial public debt as well. Some observers speculate that China could be moving in the direction of some linkage of its currency to gold. While possible, it does not appear to be imminent, although such a move would assure China's dominance in world commerce for many years to come.

Still, even before a redeemable state currency emerges, there may be a time when foreign currency ETFs are vital. Here, in no particular order, are some of the foreign currency ETFs and their market symbols that you may wish to consider:

Canadian Dollar ETF: **FXC**
Swiss Franc ETF: **FXF**
Euro ETF: **FXE**
British Pound ETF: **FXB**
Japanese Yen ETF: **FXY**
Australian Dollar: **FXA**
Swedish Krona: **FXS**
Russian Ruble: **XRU**
Mexican Peso: **FXM**

Each of the above funds is a Rydex CurrencyShares ETF. More information, including the prospectus which you should read before investing, is available at www.currencyshares.com.

Other currency ETFs include:

Brazilian Real: **BZF**
New Zealand Dollar: **BNZ**
Indian Rupee: **ICN**
Chinese Yuan: **CYB**

The foregoing are WisdomTree Dreyfus currency ETFs. Reading the prospectus of any fund is recommended before investing. These may be found at www.wisdomtree.com.

There are a couple of things to bear in mind about currency ETFs. Although the expense ratios are reasonably low, generally around 0.4 percent, you will pay a commission to buy and sell them just as you would any other ETF. This can make them an expensive substitute for a money market fund. The interest rate is not fixed but can change from day to day just as does a money market account. Remember that if you invest in a foreign currency ETF in an account here in the United States, you still have an investment in the United States and you should not mistakenly believe you have money out of the country. There are also leveraged and bundled currency ETFs, packaging different currencies together.

Digital Gold Currencies

On vacation last summer I walked into a bookstore in Vancouver and selected a book off the shelf that was priced in Canadian dollars. With a swipe of a credit card my purchase was effortlessly converted to U.S. dollars at the prevailing exchange rate and instantly charged to my account in Arizona. From handing my selection to the cashier to signing the charge slip, it was a thirty-second miracle that astonishes—precisely nobody!

In this digital age deducting even in the tiniest fraction of an ounce of gold from your account for purchases should be cyberspace child's play. Chapter 4 described the manner in which paper currency developed, first as a claim check for gold that was held in safekeeping elsewhere. The wide use of paper currency was originally a great convenience, resulting from the application of a new invention, the printing press. While there is nothing inherently crooked about the use of warehouse receipts and claim checks, the systemic corruption of money by government is now symbolized by references to the printing press as the enabler of all currency inflations.

Paper notes share one advantage with actual physical metals: anonymity in transactions. But even the confidentiality that paper currencies once provided is now under assault as detailed in chapter 9. Other than that, banknotes and paper currencies can seem downright archaic compared to the ease of digital transactions, many of which are taken for granted: imagine no one holding up the checkout line at the grocery store as they write out a check; no loose change to be counted back from each purchase, which in its diminished value just ends up in a jar on the dresser anyway; automatic records of the transaction provided for your convenience. Imagine then a dependable system of commercial transactions, not subject to governmental manipulation, incorporating the speed and global virtues of digital commerce along with the world's most long-lasting and universally valued monetary commodity. It turns out that systems with all of those advantages, allowing you to use gold as money on a digital platform, have been in place for several years. While perhaps not in their infancy, they are still quite young, and no recommendation is made for you to use them—yet. But the early signs are promising.

Among the more prominent digital gold currencies is GoldMoney. Founded in 2001, GoldMoney is the largest of the digital gold currencies, with some 400,000 ounces of gold and more than 15 million ounces of silver on deposit. Upon opening an account at GoldMoney—which requires you to establish your identity—you may wire funds in any of several major currencies, including U.S. and Canadian dollars, euros, Swiss francs, Japanese yen, and British pounds. Once the funds are in your account, you can log in to your account at any time to place an order for gold or silver that is then owned by you and held in an insured bullion vault in either Zurich or London. GoldMoney uses "goldgrams" as its basic unit of account for gold; even its processing and storage fees are charged in grams of gold.

GoldMoney also allows its members to make online payments in gold to one another for goods and services. The gold never leaves the vault, but when you authorize such a payment your account is debited and the recipient is credited the specified amount of gold.

Chief among the virtues of such a system is that the participant can elect for himself from among the two poles of a gold monetary system. He can choose to keep all or part of his gold (or silver) in his physical possession and conduct his business with it discreetly and anonymously for any reason, because of distrust of institutions or prevailing political conditions, or simply because of personal preferences. And he can choose to use a digital gold currency to the extent that the convenience and benefits of a digital exchange system prove attractive.

Inflation is only possible to the extent people continue to use the debauched currency. As alternative currencies challenge universal usage of dollars, you may expect legal tender laws to be put to work in a vain effort to arrest the abandonment of the dollar. Currently government courts refuse to enforce contracts denominated in gold in the same way they do dollar contracts. The use of gold as money is burdened by taxation as well. Congressman Ron Paul has attempted to have the legal tender laws repealed, since such laws are wholly unnecessary when the currency is sound, and victimize the people when it is not sound. His attempts have been futile. But having destroyed the integrity of the U.S. dollar, desperate politicians will not be able to stop the people from finding alternatives like digital gold money.

In the earliest days of charge cards or credit cards, most businesses did not accept them. The first Diners Club cardholders had to check with an establishment before ordering a meal or be prepared to pay cash—or wash dishes! But the year after Diners Club began there were already twenty thousand cardholders and a growing number of businesses eager to have their patronage. Digital gold currencies are at a stage like the very earliest charge cards. You cannot use them at the pizza restaurant, the gas station, or grocery store. Except for businesses that have some connection to the precious metals industry such as some investment advisory newsletters, digital gold currencies are accepted by few businesses. That will change in a monetary crisis, and can change quite quickly as merchants seek out ways of being paid in a dependable currency. Today's digital gold currencies are pioneering new ways of conducting commerce that will rise just as fast as the dollar falls. In their mature form they promise to be as big as MasterCard, Visa, and American Express.

Recommendation

Deserving Mention
Exchange-traded funds of select foreign currencies may be useful in a monetary breakdown. Rydex CurrencyShares has ETFs for many of the major foreign currencies. Learn more about them at www.currency shares.com.

WisdomTree Dreyfus has other currency ETFs, including several from emerging countries. These may be found at www.wisdomtree.com.

Deserving Mention

Digital gold currencies may be useful to you now. They certainly bear watching and can end up being an indispensable component of a new, sound monetary system. GoldMoney is the most successful of such innovations. Its Web site is www.goldmoney.com.

CHAPTER SEVENTEEN

Last Thoughts

It is impossible to grasp the meaning of the idea of sound money if one does not realize that it was devised as an instrument for the protection of civil liberties against despotic inroads on the part of governments. Ideologically it belongs in the same class with political constitutions and bills of rights.

—Ludwig von Mises

Those palates who, not yet two summers younger,
Must have inventions to delight the taste,
Would now be glad of bread, and beg for it.

—Shakespeare, *Pericles*

The quote above from Shakespeare richly evokes the sudden change of circumstances in an economic crisis. It comes from the scene in the play when the young prince Pericles has discovered famine in the port city of Tarsus, once renowned for its prosperity, on the Mediterranean coast of Anatolia (Turkey). In the century of Shakespeare's death Anatolia did experience an inflation and accompanying famine. It is a story that should be familiar at this point: an overextended military empire, the coinage repeatedly debased, runaway prices, and laws enacted forcing the acceptance of the new currency at the old values. Thousands died of starvation, thousands more sought to survive subsisting on grass and walnut shells. Such episodes are so frequent in the records of history, they should not need retelling and the economics of unsound money should not need to be repeatedly reexperienced. But such lessons are seemingly never learned and so are replayed again and again. Sometimes the consequences are experienced in a more or a less severe manner, but it is the same notes, only played in a different octave.

The Dollar Meltdown was written to help you foresee an unavoidable currency calamity and to profit as unfortunate events unfold. And while hard conditions will mean sorrow for many, the more people prepare for the future, the less destructive it will be. Still, we are all in this together. If the people's freedom slips away, ours goes with it. If the nation's prosperity is diminished, all of us will experience diminished circumstances and opportunities.

American ideals have changed, so it should be no surprise that America's economy is in transition. Present trends suggest that America's near-term future lies somewhere between the prosperity of a free economy based on sound money, and a command economy's colorless world of shortages and poverty. The change in ideals that foretells this change in our circumstances can be detected in our symbols.

America's earliest coins portrayed Liberty. Not rulers and politicians. Just Liberty. A symbolic representation of the country's highest ideal. In the beginning Americans had an affair of the heart with Liberty. She was their muse and they were aflame in their love for her. They talked about her everywhere, in their churches and taverns and town squares. But she hasn't appeared on our circulation coinage for more than sixty years, not since the beautiful "Walking Liberty" half-dollar. It represented Liberty striding gracefully into the rising sun of the future, arm extended in peace and carrying a bounty of riches. It was a beautiful representation, well chosen, because abundance accompanies Liberty wherever she goes. Our devotion to her would be no less if it were not true, but it is one of her secrets: Liberty creates prosperity.

Today's coinage, looking each year more like subway tokens, celebrates the state. Just as words replace deeds and paper substitutes for gold, politicians have displaced ideals. The American state, which was created to serve Liberty, is now commemorated instead.

Sometimes another is mistaken for Liberty. In 1989 a spark of ardor ignited among the students and people of China. They even crafted a copy of our muse for their demonstrations in Tiananmen Square—their own statue of Liberty. Unfortunately somebody, probably a confused journalist, thought to call it the goddess of democracy. But democracy is just a method, a mechanical process. Perhaps it can serve as a handmaiden to Liberty, but it should never be confused with her.

We are much too intellectual and sophisticated to anthropomorphize concepts like truth and beauty and liberty, to envision them as living ideals. But in not doing so, we lose something of the feeling tone, the color and richness of these ideals. So I invite you to try focusing on Liberty in that way: enter into the spirit of the exercise as though it were a real encounter. The Walking Liberty image is a beautiful one to use. You can find it on one-ounce U.S. Silver Eagle bullion coins. Look at it and meditate on the living ideal of Liberty for a few minutes and see if it puts you in touch with the archetypes of myths and poets and visionaries.

A moment or two of such reflection awakens a new appreciation of Liberty and her transpersonal significance as an enduring ideal. Her blessings, among them abundance and opportunity, become visible in a moment of stillness. See if your regard for Liberty doesn't deepen as it becomes fixed in your consciousness. The contemplation can be rewarded with a sense of responsibility to be more than a consumer of Liberty's blessings, but also a custodian of them.

If Americans, born in Liberty, don't seek to protect her and put her on a pedestal, who will? If Americans, blessed by Liberty, believe her to be the daughter of coercion, who will correct us? If Americans, enriched by Liberty, lose our memory of her ideal, what is to become of us?

And what will become of our prosperity?

Information and Resources for Investors

Newsletters

The Daily Reckoning

Bill Bonner writes on markets and the economy with a detached bemusement and irony, not to mention a keen understanding of today's challenges and the historical precedents that illuminate them. He's joined by contributions from Addison Wiggin, the Mogambo Guru, and others. Delivered free daily by e-mail. Subscribe at www .dailyreckoning.com. Subscribers also get Dr. Gary North's twice-weekly e-mail news letter, *Gary North's Reality Check*. Not to be missed.

Grant's Interest Rate Observer

A "contrary-minded journal of the financial markets," this newsletter's Web site says. "Without bragging, we like to think that we are the financial-information medium that least resembles CNBC." *Grant's* identifies issues in finance and business and investment opportunities from a thoughtful and well-grounded economic perspective. As a bonus, editor James Grant is an exceptionally good writer. Published twenty-four times a year; annual subscription $850. www.grantspub.com. *Grant's Interest Rate Observer*, Two Wall Street, New York, NY 10005.

U.S. & World Early Warning Report

I consider *Early Warning Report* to be one of the best. Newsletter writer Richard Maybury is an original thinker steeped in history and with keen geopolitical insights. For years before 9/11/2001, Maybury presciently warned of the consequences of U.S. meddling in an area of the world he calls Chaostan, the land of the Great Chaos. You can learn more about this concept and *Early Warning Report* at www.Chaostan.com. Maybury shares his thoughts on politics, economics, and investments ten times a year. $300 per year. Published by Henry Madison Research, P.O. Box 84908, Phoenix, AZ 85071.

Shadow Government Statistics

John Williams's *Shadow Government Statistics: Analysis Behind and Beyond Government Economic Reporting* was described in chapter 15. The electronic newsletter is published eight or more times per year supplemented by frequent "Flash Updates" and

"Alerts" on financial and economic conditions. $175 per year. Williams also makes a good deal of his background material and reporting on flawed economic data available in open material for nonsubscribers on his Web site. Highly informative, highly recommended. Information at www.shadowstats.com.

The Elliot Wave Theorist

Robert R. Prechter, Jr., is president of Elliott Wave International, which publishes analysis of global stock, bond, currency, metals, and energy markets based on swings in market psychology from extremes of pessimism to optimism. He has been publishing *The Elliott Wave Theorist* since 1979. I consider his descriptions of the long-term trends in public and investor moods to be superior. Published twelve times a year; $20 per month. www.elliottwave.com.

The High-Tech Strategist

Fred Hickey edits this monthly newsletter. As the name implies, he covers the high-tech industry and its stocks, but he has a good understanding of the fundamental economic issues and has been heavily positioned in gold, and shorts the tech market when necessary. $140 per year; $60 for a three-month trial subscription. *The High-Tech Strategist*, P.O. Box 3133, Nashua, NH 03061-3133.

Trends Journal

I have often called on Gerald Celente at the beginning of a new year to identify likely social, business, consumer, economic, political, and technology trends that will become visible in the year ahead. Celente is a trend strategist and founder of the Trends Research Institute. Businesses, investors, governments, and others rely on his forecasts in the *Trends Journal*. Published quarterly. Online edition $99 per year; print and online $185. www.trendsresearch.com.

Web Sites

The Ludwig von Mises Institute

Wouldn't it be helpful to encounter a school of economics that had foreseen and forewarned about the financial calamity visited upon us; one that champions sound money, not money created out of thin air; one that is not on the payroll of and subservient to the state, but that champions free markets and free individuals? The Ludwig von Mises Institute is the research and educational center of classical liberalism, libertarian political theory, and the Austrian School of economics. New articles daily, with useful insights about markets and economics. You'll find a visit to the Web site informative and intellectually rewarding. www.mises.org.

Lewrockwell.com

This page is among the top political sites, and certainly the number one libertarian site on the Internet. Lew Rockwell is the former congressional chief of staff to Ron Paul and founder and president of the Ludwig von Mises Institute. The site provides informed commentary and analysis of political and economic issues from an "anti-state, anti-war, and pro-market perspective." An indispensable tool for those willing to confront economic and monetary reality. Highly recommended: www.lewrockwell.com. The Web site's companion blog is equally valuable: www.lewrockwell.com/blog.

Antiwar.com

For those interested in assessing the crippling costs of empire, the prospects for future wars, and what is really going on in geopolitics, www.antiwar.com is a resource without peer. The Web site identifies its principles as libertarian and says, "The editors take seriously our purely journalistic mission, which is to get past the media filters and reveal the truth about America's foreign policy." It is a complete daily collection of news accounts and commentary from around the world. It would be hard to be fully informed about global economic conditions, much less the prospects for war and peace, without reviewing the material that antiwar.com provides daily. Highly recommended.

Mish's Global Economic Trend Analysis

Time magazine got it right when it led its 2009 report on the "25 Best Financial Blogs" with Mish's Global Economic Analysis. Michael Shedlock, "Mish," noted *Time*, "adroitly gets into the thick of economic data," and "is not afraid to attack conventional wisdom." Mish saw the destruction of the credit collapse and the reverberation of its effects well in advance of the purveyors of conventional wisdom. He also latches on to and analyzes significant financial news that goes unnoticed by others. www.globaleconomicanalysis.blogspot.com.

Bloomberg.com

The most useful investor tool on the Internet, Bloomberg.com is a source for news and information on the global markets, featuring price quotes and excellent interactive charts with convenient historical daily price details and tools for the technical trader. It also makes available useful calculators for loans, mortgages, currencies, and more, as well as market and portfolio tracking tools. www.bloomberg.com.

Dollarcollapse.com

This is a very useful site, providing a daily compendium of links to commentary and breaking news about the economy, the dollar, precious metals, the real estate market, and more. www.dollarcollapse.com.

Clusterstock.com

Business and financial news and commentary, gossipy at times, but willing to take a close-up look at the dark side of Wall Street. No other source provided as much information about the Bernie Madoff scandal as www.clusterstock.com.

Credit Writedowns

Featuring news and opinion on finance, economics, and markets, the site seeks to provide early warning signals for what to expect in the global economy. Especially good at spotting European economic news that is missed elsewhere. The site's "Credit Crisis Timeline" is a comprehensive collection of accounts of the unfolding credit crisis, while it also provides an overview called "The Dummy's Guide to the U.S. Banking Crisis." www.creditwritedown.com.

World Gold Council

The marketing body of the world's leading gold mining companies, this site provides interesting news about the use of gold in biomedical, nanotechnology, and other scientific endeavors and industrial applications, as well as key information and research reports on gold fundamentals including price, supply and demand, and other investment statistics. www.gold.org.

The Silver Institute

The Silver Institute is an international association of miners, refiners, fabricators, and wholesalers of silver and silver products. Its Web site provides rich material on the history and uses of silver, from its traditional usage in coinage, jewelry, and tableware to its uses in photography and electronics as well as in emerging technologies. It provides fundamental information on supply and demand and price history as well. www.silverinstitute.org.

Kitco.com

Helpful site providing precious metals price quotes not only in U.S. dollars, but in other major currencies, along with price charts, news, and commentary. www.kitco.com.

321gold.com

Up-to-date precious metals and precious metals shares news and commentary. www.321gold.com.

Silverstrategies.com

News, analysis, reports, and general information about silver companies, silver stocks, and silver bullion as investments. www.silverstrategies.com.

International Energy Agency

The IEA is a multinational energy adviser to twenty-eight member countries. Serious investors will find this site useful, especially the Oil Market Report, which is linked on the IEA site. Although the monthly Oil Market Report is a subscription service, a free public access page contains highlights of its supply, demand, and price information. www.iea.org.

Energy Information Administration

The EIA provides a helpful source for current and historical official energy statistics from the U.S. Department of Energy. Included among the reports to be found here is the Annual Energy Outlook reports with analysis of U.S. energy supply and demand. This site reports on petroleum, natural gas, electricity, coal, nuclear, and renewable energy. www.eia.doe.gov.

321energy.com

Up-to-date news and commentary on petroleum and other energy markets. www.321energy.com.

Energy Bulletin

A clearinghouse for news, research, and analysis about global energy supplies. www.energybulletin.net.

ResourceInvestor.com

News and information source for base metals, agricultural commodities, and more. www.resourceinvestor.com.

CommodityOnline.com

Based in India, this portal provides news, information, and reports on a broad spectrum of commodities: precious and base metals, oil, and agricultural. The site's great virtue is its thoroughness. It so overwhelms with news that you can even find information on exotic products from mustard seed and coconut oil to pepper and chili. www.commodityonline.com.

Acknowledgments

A moment spent contemplating how indebted we are to others, not only for our material blessings, but also for the quality of ideas available to us, should spur us to redouble our efforts to reassert a free economy and open society.

In my own case, because I have chosen a career in the public debate, I have been fortunate to speak on an almost daily basis with exceptionally distinguished and thoughtful people about important ideas. I have referred already to some of those in this realm of economics and investments who have been generous with their time in making themselves available to my radio shows over the years and am so indebted to them that I don't mind repeating their names, including Jim Rogers, Addison Wiggin, and Michael Shedlock, all of whom have had regular weekly segments on the *The Charles Goyette Show*. Others I have called on repeatedly for stimulating discussions about the economy include Peter Schiff, Lew Rockwell, Robert Prechter, Robert Kiyosaki, the late Jude Wanniski, and many others. More than twenty-five years ago I was able to arrange for Ron Paul and the late Dr. Murray Rothbard, both of whom have also been welcome radio guests, to share dinner-speaking duties at events I hosted. Had Dr. Rothbard been heeded, we wouldn't have experienced this financial collapse; had Dr. Paul been elected, we would have been climbing out by now and growing robustly instead of digging ourselves in deeper. Their principles are vindicated by developing events and both deserve to be honored for their great insight and equally great courage. A few years before his death I had the opportunity to fly to San Francisco to take Dr. Milton Friedman to dinner at one of his favorite Italian restaurants in honor of his birthday. He has informed my views in some respects. My advice is if you have a chance to dine with a Nobel Prize winner, take it. I have learned from all of these people and am indebted to them.

Since the early 1980s I have been a member of a monthly dinner group of people devoted to liberty and its economic manifestations, organized by my old friends Roy Miller and the late Chet Anderson, former chairman of the Institute of Humane Studies. The group is explicitly faithful to the spirit of Leonard Read, founder of the Foundation for Economic Education. Read understood that thoughts rule the world (the title of one of his books) and that rather than the achievement of political ends, the freedom philosophy is best spread as each devotee of liberty seeks to improve his own knowledge and understanding. The group's vigorous discussions and its members have been indispensable in the development of my own thought and I recommend the approach as a model to others who would like to preserve our prosperity and freedom.

Others with whom I have discussed the ideas in this book to my advantage during the writing process include John Wares, Todd Hartley, Tony Tardino, as well as several who prefer their anonymity. My old friend Neland Nobel, first vice president of UBS, Phoenix, has made important suggestions.

Bestselling author Paul Perry, a great friend of long standing, has been a source of important advice throughout the writing process. It is Paul who suggested his agent, Nat Sobel, to represent the book and I am grateful to them both for their wisdom and guidance. Jeffrey Krames, of Portfolio, brought his years of experience to the project and made this a better book from our very first phone conversation. Courtney Young edited the manuscript with great skill and I am fortunate to have had her insight. Jillian Gray and the other people at Portfolio have been professional and attentive and I am grateful to them all.

Visit:
www.charlesgoyette.com
www.thedollarmeltdown.com

Bibliography

Bastiat, Frederic. *Economic Sophisms*. Irvington on Hudson, NY: Foundation for Economic Education, 1964.

———. *The Law*. Irvington on Hudson, NY: Foundation for Economic Education, 1979.

Bittle, Scott, and Jean Johnson. *Where Does the Money Go? Your Guided Tour to the Federal Budget Crisis*. New York: Collins, 2008.

Browne, Harry. *You Can Profit from a Monetary Crisis*. New York: Macmillan, 1974.

Bryce, Robert. *Gusher of Lies: The Dangerous Delusions of "Energy Independence."* New York: PublicAffairs, 2008.

Fleckenstein, William A., with Frederick Sheehan. *Greenspan's Bubbles: The Age of Ignorance at the Federal Reserve*. New York: McGraw Hill, 2008.

Grant, James. *Mr. Market Miscalculates: The Bubble Years and Beyond*. Mount Jackson, VA: Axios Press, 2008.

Hayek, Friedrich A. *The Road to Serfdom*. Chicago: University of Chicago Press, 1944.

Hazlitt, Henry. *The Inflation Crisis, and How to Resolve It*. New Rochelle, NY: Arlington House, 1978.

Jastrom, Roy W. *The Golden Constant*. New York: John Wiley and Sons, 1977.

Johnson, Chalmers. *Nemesis: The Last Days of the American Republic*. New York: Metropolitan Books, 2006.

———. *The Sorrows of Empire: Militarism, Secrecy, and the End of the Republic*. New York: Metropolitan Books, 2004.

Johnson, Paul. *Modern Times: The World from the Twenties to the Eighties*. New York: Harper & Row, 1983.

Karmin, Craig. *Biography of the Dollar: How the Mighty Buck Conquered the World and Why It's Under Siege*. New York: Crown Business, 2008.

Mises, Ludwig von. *Human Action*. Chicago: Contemporary Books, 1963.

———. *Socialism*. Trans. J. Kahane. Indianapolis, IN: LibertyClassics, 1981.

———. *The Theory of Money and Credit*. Indianapolis, IN: LibertyClassics, 1980.

Morris, Charles R. *The Trillion Dollar Meltdown: Easy Money, High Rollers, and the Great Credit Crash*. New York: PublicAffairs, 2008.

Paul, Ron, and Lewis Lehrman. *The Case for Gold*. Washington, DC: Cato Institute, 1982.

Phillips, Kevin. *Bad Money: Reckless Finance, Failed Politics, and the Global Crisis of American Capitalism*. New York: Viking, 2008.

Rogers, Jim. *Hot Commodities: How Anyone Can Invest Profitably in the World's Best Market*. New York: Random House, 2004.

Rothbard, Murray N. *America's Great Depression*. Kansas City: Sheed and Ward, 1972.

——. *The Case Against the Fed*. Auburn, AL: Mises Institute, 1994.

——. *A History of Money and Banking in the United States: The Colonial Era to World War II*. Auburn, AL: Mises Institute, 2002.

——. *What Has Government Done to Our Money?* Auburn, AL: Mises Institute, 2008.

Sarnoff, Paul. *Silver Bulls: The Great Silver Boom and Bust*. Westport, CT: Arlington House, 1980.

Schiff, Peter D., with John Downes. *Crash Proof: How to Profit from the Coming Economic Collapse*. Hoboken, NJ: John Wiley, 2007.

Stiglitz, Joseph E., and Linda J. Bilmes. *The Three Trillion Dollar War: The True Costs of the Iraq Conflict*. New York: W. W. Norton, 2008.

Sutton, Antony C. *The War on Gold*. Seal Beach, CA: '76 Press, 1977.

Wanniski, Jude. *The Way the World Works*. Washington, DC: Regnery, 1998.

White, Andrew Dickson. *Fiat Money Inflation in France*. New York: Appleton-Century, 1896.

Yule, Henry. *The Book of Ser Marco Polo the Venetian Concerning the Kingdoms and Marvels of the East*. Translated and edited by Henry Yule. New York: Charles Scribner's Sons, 1903.

Index

Adams, John, 49
Agriculture
    exchange-traded funds (ETFs), 200, 202, 208
    exchange-traded notes (ETNs), 205
Alexis Comnenus, Byzantine emperor, 61–62
Ancient Greece, coinage of, 46–47
Ancient Rome
    coinage debasement, impact of, 61
    price controls, 128
Assignats, 64–65
Australian dollar ETF (FXA), 225
Australian kangaroo, 150
Austrian economics, 142, 234

El-Badri, Abdalla, 118, 188
Bailouts, 6–7, 11–20
    under Bush, 11–16
    combined with stagflation, impact of, 99
    negative view of, 16–17, 19–20
Bank of America, 12–13
Banks
    bank failures, 12, 15
    deposits, structuring crime, 133–34
    nationalization, 122–23
Base metals, 201–4
    exchange-traded funds (ETFs), 200–202, 210
    exchange-traded notes (ETNs), 206
Baytex Energy Trust (BTE), 194–95
Bear Stearns, 12, 14
Bernanke, Ben
    and bailout, 13–14, 18, 20, 24, 94–95

on Chinese and saving, 4
on deflation, 92–93
on housing bubble, 80
on inflation, 57
and interest rate cuts, 21
on wage-price spiral, 101
Bezant, 47
Bid-ask spread, precious metals, 152
Bilmes, Linda, 115
Bonds as investment, 219–21
    and interest rates, 219–20
    mutual funds, 220–21
    shorting bonds, 219–20
Bonner, Bill, 233
Brazilian Real ETF (BZF), 225
Bretton Woods agreement, 107, 114, 118, 146, 180
British pound ETF (FXB), 225
Brown, Gordon, 57
Browne, Harry, 146
Bryce, Robert, 179
Bündchen, Gisele, 117, 118
Burns, Arthur, 98
Bush, George H. W., 98
Bush, George W.
    bailouts under, 11–16
    debt ceiling increase, 5
    on inflation, 56
    Iraq war, 54, 114–16
    Medicare prescription drug bill, 36–38
Byzantine Empire
    coinage debasement, impact of, 61–62
    gold bezant, 47

Canada, energy trusts, recommendations, 193–95
Canadian dollar ETF (FXC), 225
Canadian Gold Maple Leaf, 150, 154, 161, 164
Canadian Royalty Trusts, 193–95
Canadian Silver Maple Leaf, 175, 176
Carter, Jimmy
  and energy independence, 177–78
  and inflation, 57–58, 102, 142–43
Celente, Gerald, 234
Cheney, Dick, 125
Chiang Kai-shek, 128
China
  American dollars, flow to, 108–10
  caloric intake, increase in, 197–98
  disinvestment in U.S., threat of, 112–14
  economy, growth of, 109–10, 122
  energy interdependence, 179–80
  exchange rate, U.S. conflict, 110–14
  gold, increasing reserves, 119, 224
  price controls, 128
  -Russia alliance, 116, 118
  stimulus package, 110
  trade surplus, 109
  U.S. debt instruments held by, 109, 112–14
Chinese yuan ETF (CYB), 225
Chirac, Jacques, 54
Clay, Lucius, General, 127
Coinage
  devaluation and inflation, 61–62
  gold or silver. See Gold coinage; Silver coinage
Collectibles, precious metals as, 161–62
Command economy, 121–35
  as anti-American, 123, 126–27
  bank nationalization, 122–23
  currency controls, 134–35
  features of, 121–22
  financial behavior, reporting, 132–34
  and poverty, 122, 123
  shortages and rationing, 130–32
  wage and price controls, 124–28
Commodities as investment, 200–210
  exchange-traded funds (ETFs), 200–202, 207–10
  exchange-traded notes (ETNs), 205–6, 210

Rogers International Commodity Index (RICI), 203–4
Consumer Price Index (CPI), core inflation rate as alternative, 199
Consumption, decline and deflation, 92
Core inflation rate, 199
Corzine, Jon, 214
Cost-push inflation, 101
Counterfeit, gold coins, 164
Countrywide Financial, 12
"Crack-up boom," 103–6, 149
Credit, artificial and malinvestment, 82–83
Credit crisis, 213
Credit Suisse, 151
Currency
  controls, and monetary breakdown, 134–35
  foreign. See Foreign currency as investment
  hard currencies, 222–23

DB Commodity Services LLC, 200
Debt, federal. See Federal debt
Debt securities
  exchange-traded notes (ETNs), 205–6
  U.S. government. See Treasury bonds
Deflation, 90–95
  bailout, effects on, 94–95
  economic impact of, 90–91
  myths about, 91–92
  "pushing on a string" argument, 92–94
De Gaulle, Charles, 54–55
Deng Xiaoping, 198–99
Digital gold currencies, 226–29
  GoldMoney, 227, 229
Dollar
  as currency reserves, 120
  deterioration, and oil-pricing alternatives, 118, 188–90
  devaluation and Fed, 81
  overseas holdings, 119–20
Dollar standard
  benefits to U.S., 107–8
  global dumping of, 117–19

Economic collapse, signs of, 134–35, 163
Economic crisis (2008–)
  bailouts, 11–20
  command economy threat, 121–35

credit crisis, 213
and dollar standard, 117–20
federal debt, 29–40
government actions. *See* Federal Reserve
housing crisis, 7, 21, 94
impact of, 6–7, 90
and interest rate cuts, 76
Iraq war, cost of, 115
and job losses, 6
See also specific topics
e-gold, 227, 229
Elements ETNs, 205–6, 210
Emergency Economic Stabilization Act
    (2008), operation of, 16–20
Energy independence, myth of, 177–82
Energy trusts, recommendations, 193–95
Enerplus Resources Fund Trust (ERF),
    194–95
Engelhard, 175, 176
England
    coinage debasement, impact of, 62
    goldsmith as banker, 62–63
    inflation and paper money, 63
    See also Great Britain
Erhard, Ludwig, 127
Ethanol, 129, 181
Euros
    euro ETF (FXE), 225
    replace dollar, 117–18, 189
Exchange-traded funds (ETFs)
    bond, 221
    cautions about, 157–58
    commodities-based, 200–202, 207–10
    foreign currency-based, 223–26, 227–29
    gold-based, 158–60, 165
    nationalization risk, 162–63
    oil-based, 192–93
    silver-based, 175–76
    trading/operation of, 157, 208–9
Exchange-traded notes (ETNs)
    commodities-based, 205–6
    Elements ETNs, 205–6

Fannie Mae, 12, 18, 19, 23, 25, 80, 105
    China/Japan holdings, 114
Federal debt, 29–40
    amount of (2009), 31–32, 149
    debt ceiling, increase, 5, 14, 32, 149, 217
    foreign holders of, 31, 109, 112–13

hidden debt, 33–36
infinite horizon discounted value
    concept, 34–35
inflation as remedy, 88–90
interest expense on, 39
Medicare Part D, unfunded liability
    example, 36–38
monetizing debt, 72–75
percentage of GDP, 31
in trillions, 14, 32, 149, 217
Federal deposit insurance, 24–27
Federal Reserve
    auditing of, 77–78
    bailout funds, 14
    cooling economy, actions for, 74
    criticisms of system, 75–84
    and debt monetization, 72–75
    and devaluation of dollar, 81
    federal funds rate, 73
    fractional reserve banks, 72–73
    inflation, creating by, 74–75
    interest rate cuts, 21–22, 74, 76, 94
    and monetary policy, 87–88
    and mortgage meltdown, 21
    open market operations, 95
    and Plunge Protection Team, 78–79
    and politicized money, 76
    public/private nature of, 77
    secrecy related to, 76–79
    stimulating economy, actions for,
        73–74
    as unconstitutional, 75
Federal Reserve Act (1913), 77
Federal Reserve Notes, 75
Fiscal policy, defined, 87
Fisher, Richard, 34–36, 38, 104–6
Florin, 48
Food production
    demand, future view, 197–98
    See also Commodities as investment
Ford, Gerald, 57
Foreign currency, hard currencies, 222–23
Foreign currency as investment, 222–29
    digital gold currencies, 226–29
    exchange-traded funds (ETFs), 223–26,
        228–29
    speculative nature of, 224
Foster, Richard S., 37
Fractional reserve banking, 63, 72–73

France
  dollar to gold conversion request, 54–55
  Reign of Terror, economic conditions,
    64–65, 128
Franklin, Benjamin, 4, 83, 117
Freddie Mac, 12, 18, 19, 23, 25, 80, 105
  China/Japan holdings, 114
Free market economy, versus command
    economy, 122–23
Friedman, Milton, 99, 143

Geithner, Timothy, on Bush bailout, 14
General Accounting Office (GAO), Federal
    Reserve, auditing by, 77–78
Germany
  postwar recovery, 127
  war reparations, inflation as impact of,
    67–69
Gold
  and economic crisis (2008), 92
  and hard currencies, 222–23
  increasing reserves, global view, 119
  as money, benefits of, 44–50. See also
    Gold coinage
  rise in price (2002–2008), 5, 8, 13, 171
Gold as investment, 148–65
  broker, finding, 153–55
  bullion bars, 151, 152
  coins, 150, 154, 164
  commissions to seller, 152–53
  digital gold currencies, 226–29
  exchange-traded funds (ETFs), 157–60,
    162–63
  gold/silver ratio, 171–73
  gold stocks, 159–61
  index-type fund, 160–61, 165
  percentage of portfolio, 150
  premium, 152
  price forecasts, 148
  pricing, 151–152
  rare coins, avoiding, 154–55, 163–64
  sale, IRS reporting requirements, 161–62
  storage, physical, 162
Gold coinage
  authentic, identifying, 164
  to buy, recommendations, 150, 154, 164
  and development of civilizations, 46–50
  rare coins, 154–55, 163–64
  U.S., historical view, 48–53, 135

Goldman Sachs, 20
GoldMoney, 227, 229
Gold Reserve Act (1934), 50–52
Goldsmiths, as bankers, 62–63
Gold standard
  abandoned, United States, 50
  Bretton Woods agreement, 107, 114, 118,
    180
Grant, James, 108, 216, 233
Great Britain
  gold standard, 48
  nationalization, 122
  oil reserves of, 178, 187
Great Depression, 24, 84, 92, 96
Greenbacks, 50
Greenspan, Alan
  on dollars held abroad, 119
  on housing bubble, 80, 97
  interest rate cuts, 21–22, 76
  on WIN program, 57
Gresham's law, 53, 141
Gross domestic product (GDP), federal
    debt in, 31
Gulf War, 66

Hard Assets Producer (HAP) fund, 201–2,
    207
Hard currencies, 222–23
Hayek, F.A., 81, 127–28, 142
He Fan, 112
Hickey, Fred, 234
Hitler, Adolf, 67
Housing crisis
  and Fed, 94
  and interest rate cuts, 21–24
  jingle mail, 89
Hunt, Bunker, 166, 169, 172
Hunt, Herbert, 169, 172
al-Husseini, Sadad, 183
Hyperinflation, 100–106
  and "crack-up boom," 103–6, 149
  features of, 102–5
  Israel, 100
  past periods of, 100, 103
  political implication of, 101–2

Index-type fund, gold-based, 160–61, 165
India, poverty, decline of, 199
Indian rupee ETF (ICN), 225

Infinite horizon discounted value, 34–35
Inflation, 56–75
    as alternative to taxation, 88
    and coinage debasement, 61–62
    core inflation rate, 199
    and distortion of market, 83–84
    double-digit. *See* Hyperinflation
    Federal Reserve, creation of, 74–75
    historical view, 60–70
    inflationary recession, 96, 99
    and malinvestment, 82–83
    as monetary phenomenon, 58–61
    official explanations of, 57–58
    persistence of, 56–57, 88, 100
    and price ceilings, 130
    and price increases, 59, 74
    as remedy to debt, 89–90
    as remedy to inflation, 96
    and stagflation, 95–96
    as theft, 101
Interest rate cuts
    economic impact of, 21–22, 76, 94
    and housing crisis, 21–24
    to stimulate economy, 74
Interest rates
    and bond prices, 219–20
    raising, to cool economy, 74
    and stagflation, 96–97
Investment recommendations
    bonds, 219–21
    commodities, 200–210
    foreign currencies, 222–29
    gold, 148–65
    gold/silver ratio, 171–73
    information/resources for investors,
        233–36
    oil, 190–95
    silver, 166–76
Iran, oil, pricing in euros, 118
Iraq war
    cost of, 115
    and global rejection of America, 115–16
    nonsupporting countries, 54
IRS
    bank transactions, reporting to,
        133–34
    financial behavior, reporting to, 132–34
    See also Taxation
Isaac, William, 26–27

iShares COMEX Gold Trust (IAU),
    159, 165
iShares Silver Trust (SLV), 175, 176
Israel, hyperinflation, 100

James II, King of England, 62
Japan
    Fannie and Freddie holdings, 114
    yen payable Treasuries, call for, 117
Japanese yen ETF (FXY), 225
Johnson, Chalmers, 115–16
Johnson, Lyndon B., 52–53, 135
Johnson Matthey, 151, 175, 176
Johnson, Paul, 68
JPMorgan Chase, 12

Kahn, Alfred, 58
Keynesian economics, 96, 101
Khrushchev, Nikita, 116
Kiyosaki, Robert, 143
Kublai Khan, 60
Kyl, Jon, 7–8

Legal tender, meaning of, 63
Lehman Brothers, 13, 105
Leveraged funds, ETFs, 157–58
Levine, Irving R., 58
Liquidation only trading, silver, 134,
    170–71

McCain, John, 79
Madoff, Bernard, 214
Malinvestment, causes of, 82–83
Mao Zedong, 116
Martin, William McChesney, 98
Marx, Karl, 76, 142
Maybury, Richard, 233
Al Mazroui, Mohammed, 190
Medicare, 11–12
    Part D, negative view of, 36–38
    as unfunded liability, 35
Merrill Lynch, Elements ETNs, 205–6
Metals
    base. *See* Base metals
    precious. *See entries under* Gold; Silver
Mexican Onza, 161
Mexican peso ETF (FXM), 225
Midler, Bette, 118
Monetary policy, defined, 87–88

Monetizing debt, 72–75
Money
  currency controls, 134–35
  functions of, historical view, 43–44
  gold, benefits of, 44–50
  Gresham's law, 53, 141
  politicization of, 76
Money supply
  decrease, and deflation, 90
  increase, and inflation, 58–59
Mortgage-backed securities, 145
Mortgages, adjustable, 21–22
Mugabe, Robert, 70
Mundell, Robert, 111
Munger, Charlie, 181
Mutual funds, bond-based, 220–21

Al-Naimi, Ali, 182–83
Nationalization
  banks, 122–23
  gold ETFs, 162–63
  oil resources, 187
  See also Command economy
Nero, emperor of Rome, 61
New Zealand dollar ETF (BNZ), 225
Nixon, Richard, 55, 96, 98, 116
  and energy independence, 177
  wage and price controls, 124–26, 140–41
North, Gary, 233
Numismatic coins, avoiding, 154–55, 163–64

Obama, Barack
  and economic crisis (2008–), 6–7, 32
  and energy independence, 177, 182
Oil
  China imports, 179–80
  demand, future growth, 186–87
  domestic production, 178
  and economic crisis (2008), 92
  embargo (1973), 180
  energy independence, myth of, 177–82
  Middle East imports, 179
  prices. See Oil prices
  proved reserves, 182–84
  U.S. imports, annual, 178
Oil as investment, 190–95
  Canadian energy trusts, 193–95
  exchange-traded funds (ETFs), 192–93
  rationale for, 190–92

Oil prices
  dollar, pricing alternatives to, 188–90
  pricing in euros, 118
  production cuts, 185
  and recession, 184–85
  rise in price (2001–2008), 184
  and stagflation, 96
O'Neill, Paul, 17
OPEC
  dollar dumping, 118, 188–90
  See also entries under Oil
Open Market Committee, 77–78
Open market operations, Fed, 95

Paper money
  as archaic, 226
  supply, and inflation, 59–60
  United States, historical view, 50–53
Paul, Ron, 19, 77–79, 143, 228
Paulson, Henry
  and bailout, 13–14, 17, 18, 20, 24, 27, 97
  and bank nationalization, 123
  campaign spending of, 214
  China mission, 111–12
Penn West Energy Trust (PWE), 194–95
Persian Gulf nations, gold, increasing
    reserves, 119
Pick, Franz, 218, 219
Plunge Protection Team, 78–79
Polo, Marco, 60
Population, projections (1979–2050), 197
Position trading, commodities, 208
Poverty, and command economy, 122, 123
PowerShares DB Agricultural Fund (DBA),
    200, 209
PowerShares DB Base Metals Fund (DBB),
    200–201, 209
PowerShares DB Commodity Index
    Tracking Fund (DBC), 202, 209
Prechter, Robert, 143, 234
Precious metals. See entries under Gold;
    Silver
President's Working Group on Financial
    Markets, 78–79
Price elasticity, defined, 168
Prices
  controls, in command economy, 129–30
  government control, negative impact of,
    131–32

high, as antidote to high, 129–30,
   185–86
and inflation, 59, 74
oil. *See* Oil prices
price ceilings, 129
price floors, examples of, 129
and shortages, 130–32
"Pushing on a string" argument, on
   deflation, 92–94
Putin, Vladimir, 118

Rare coins, avoiding, 154–55
Rationing, and shortages, 130–32
Reagan, Ronald, 124
Recession
   inflationary, 96, 99
   inflation as remedy, 96
   and oil prices, 184–85
Regan, Donald, 26–27
Reid, Harry, 6
Reign of Terror, 64–65, 128
Renaissance, 48
Retirement plans
   and economic crisis (2008–), 6
   gold, holding in, 156
Roberts, Paul Craig, 112–13
Roberts, Dr. Russell, 23
Rockwell, Lew, 234
Rogers, Jim, 87, 114, 143, 196
   commodity index, 203–6
Rogers International Commodity Index
   (RICI), 203–6
   Elements ETNs linked to, 205–6, 210
   features of, 203–4, 206
Rogers-Van Eck Hard Assets Producer
   (HAP) fund, 201–2, 209
Roosevelt, Franklin D., 51
Rothbard, Murray, 77, 128, 143
Royalty trusts, Canadian, 193–95
Rubin, Robert, 214
Rumsfeld, Donald, 125
Russia
   -China alliance, 116, 118
   resource nationalism, 187
   trade currency, proposal for, 118
Russian ruble ETF (XRU), 225
Rydex CurrencyShares, 228
Rydex Inverse Government Long Bond
   Strategy Fund (RYJUX), 220–21

Savings
   Chinese versus Americans, 4
   negative rate (2005), 83–84
Schiff, Peter, 143
Scully, Thomas A., 37–38
Shadow Government Statistics Web site,
   218–19, 233–34
Shedlock, Michael, 143, 235
Sherman, Brad, 17
Shi Jianxun, 117–18
Shortages
   and prices, 130–32
   and rationing, 130–32
Short sales, ban on, 134–35
Silver certificates, 52–53
Silver coinage
   abandoned, in U.S., 50–54, 140–41
   to buy, recommendations, 174, 176
   U.S., historical view, 50–53, 172
Silver as investment, 166–76
   bags and bars, 174–76
   bull market, end of, 170–71
   coins, 174, 176
   demand-supply for silver, 167–69, 171
   exchange-traded funds (ETFs), 175–76
   gold/silver ratio, 171–73
   Hunt brothers purchases, 166–67, 169
   liquidation-only trading, 134, 170–71
   percentage of portfolio, 150
   volatility of, 173
Silver as money. *See* Silver coinage
Snow, John W., advice to Chinese, 4–5
Social Security, 11–12
   shortfall, dealing with, 35
   Trust Fund, as fraud, 26, 84
South African Krugerrand, 150, 154, 161,
   164
Spain, age of exploration, inflation in, 60
Sparta, 46–47
SPDR Gold Trust (GLD), 158–59, 165
SPDR S&P Metals and Mining ETF
   (XME), 202, 209
Spitzer, Eliot, 133–34
Spot price, precious metals, 151
Stagflation, 95–99
   combined with bailout, impact of, 99
   defined, 95–96
   and interest rate volatility, 96–97
   past periods of, 96–97

Stahl, Leslie, 183
Stark, Pete, 29
Steel, exchange-traded funds (ETFs), 207
Stiglitz, Joseph, 115
Stimulus
  amount spent per person, 139
  China, 110
Stock market, and economic crisis
    (2008–), 7
Subprime mortgages, 24
Swedish krona ETF (FXS), 225
Swiss franc, collapse, threat of, 223
Swiss franc ETF (FXF), 225

Tanaka, Nobuo, 186–87
Tauzin, Billy, 38
Taxation
  versus inflation, 88
  sale of gold, reporting requirements,
    161–62
Timber, exchange-traded funds (ETFs),
    208
Treasury bonds
  inverse performance investments,
    220–21
  mutual fund investment, 220–21
  prepurchase questions, 216–17
  TIPS, 218–19
  yen payable, call for, 117
  zero percent (2008), 215
Treasury Inflation-Protected Securities
    (TIPS), 218–19
Treaty of Versailles, 66–67
Troubled Assets Relief Program (TARP),
    16, 18

United States
  command economy scenario, 121–35
  gold and silver coinage, 48–49
  gold and silver coinage abandoned, 50–54
  gold certificates, redeeming, 51–52
  gold holdings, decrease in, 50, 55
  gold-inflation connection, 55
  off-gold standard, 50

United States Oil Fund (USO), 192, 194
United States 12 Month Oil Fund (USL),
    192–93, 194–95
U.S. Buffalo, 150
U.S. Gold Eagle, 150, 154, 164
U.S. Silver Eagles, 175, 176
U.S. Treasury bonds, 215–18

Van Eck's Market Vectors Gold Miners ETF
    (GDX), 160–61, 165
Venezuela
  euro versus dollar, 118
  gold mines, seizure of, 160
  resource nationalism, 187
Volcker, Paul, 170
von Mises, Ludwig, 71, 103, 105, 142, 149,
    230, 234

Wachovia Bank, 15
Wage and price controls, 124–28
  lifting, impact of, 127
  Nixon era, 124–26, 140–41
Wage-price spiral, 101
Walker, David, 33–34, 40
Walking Liberty half-dollar, 231–32
Washington Mutual, 15
Water
  exchange-traded funds (ETFs), 207
Wells Fargo, 15, 123
Wen Jiabao, 117
White, Andrew Dickson, 64–65
Wiggin, Addison, 143, 233
Will, George F., 213–14
Williams, John, 218–19, 233–34
Wilson, Woodrow, 66
WIN (Whip Inflation Now), 57
WisdomTree Dreyfus, 228
Wolfowitz, Paul, 115
World War I, Germany, war reparations,
    69

Xia Bin, 111

Zimbabwe, inflation crisis, 69–70